No Road Home: Fighting for Land and Faith in Gaza

James Rodgers

Published 2013 by Abramis academic publishing

www.abramis.co.uk

ISBN 978 1 84549 580 0

Printed and bound in the United Kingdom

Typeset in Garamond 11pt

Abramis is an imprint of arima publishing.

arima publishing
ASK House, Northgate Avenue
Bury St Edmunds, Suffolk IP32 6BB
t: (+44) 01284 700321

www.arimapublishing.com

For my mother and father

Acknowledgments

I would like to express my great gratitude to my BBC colleagues in Gaza from 2002-2004: Fayed Abushammala; Rushdi Abu Alouf; Hamada Abu Qammar; Ibrahim Adwan; and Tamer Almisshal. Everything I achieved then as a reporter was in large part due to them; any faults then, as in the present book, are mine. I would also like to thank the BBC team in Jerusalem during those years, and make special mention of Ian Druce, who filmed and edited most of the TV reports for which I was correspondent. I would like to thank my wife, Mette Jørgensen Rodgers. It was in Gaza that we met. Over the years we have spoken of our time there on countless occasions, and those conversations have inspired me to give here the best account that I can.

I would like to thank David Higham Associates, the Hakluyt Society, and Picador, for permission to reproduce an extract from *The Travels of Ibn Battutah* Tim Mackintosh-Smith (editor) London, Picador (2003).

My thanks go too to Richard Franklin, of Abramis, for his enthusiasm for the book, and to Patrick Garrett for his assistance with the index. If Arabic speakers discover some inconsistencies of transliteration, I can only apologize. As in the main text, the errors are mine.

Foreword

by Jeremy Bowen

Just like James Rodgers when he started his time in Gaza, the first chance most foreign visitors get to taste its unique atmosphere is at the Erez checkpoint, the main crossing from Israel. It makes sense, as so much of life in Gaza is conditioned and shaped by the conflict with Israel. The first time I went to Gaza in 1991 the checkpoint was a wooden shed in the middle of fields of razor wire, where visitors showed their documents before driving through the wire into a place that directed heat and hatred at the Israeli military patrols that still cruised the streets. Around a decade and a half later, the shed had become a gleaming terminal, the kind of building that would not have disgraced an airport. Getting permission from the Israelis to cross Erez is not easy, even at times for journalists. For weeks on end in recent years so few visitors made the journey that footsteps echoed through the terminal's vaulted halls, and the security guards with their powerful looking rifles and soldier girls texting their friends in the passport window looked ready to expire from boredom.

Once the Israelis had pulled its troops and settlers out of Gaza in 2005 it felt more than ever like a journey between two parallel, warring universes. The neat fields around kibbutz Yad Mordechai on the Israeli side stopped abruptly at the approach to the high concrete wall, studded with watch towers, that the Israelis had built to keep the Palestinians of Gaza where they were. After the pullout Israel continued and deepened the operation that James had witnessed while he was in Gaza, clearing a broad swathe of farmland and factories along the Gaza side of the divide, creating a wasteland to deny any attackers cover, and to remind Palestinians who was boss. It was a lesson that Gaza's residents never wanted to learn. Boys and men with donkey carts poked around in the rubble. Warning shots over their heads would crackle around the dust and smashed concrete if their pursuit of anything that could be sold took then too close to the watchtowers.

Israel responded to the take over of Gaza by Hamas in 2007 by imposing tough sanctions. Isolation had strange effects. Gaza uses Israeli money, and for a while the 10-agorot coin, one tenth of a shekel, scarcely worth picking up from the gutter on the Israeli side, was worth more than its face value in Gaza. The coins were prized because they were melted down to make electrical fittings that were banned under the sanctions regime. Dozens of tunnels were dug over the other border with Egypt, to bring in everything Israel did not want to see in Gaza. Some were even big enough to smuggle Mercedes and live animals.

Israel likes using technological solutions. Visitors walk through a series of remotely-operated electric steel doors and fences once their passports have been stamped at Erez. When the last one slides open, if they are lucky, they are greeted by Palestinians who are like trusties in a jail, allowed to approach Israel's fortifications to wait with carts to carry bags. Sometimes they are not there, which means it is always advisable to travel light, not easy if it is a time of trouble and you're with a TV crew with flak jackets, helmets and half a dozen heavy cases of equipment.

At the height of the Israeli blockade after 2007, it was possible to judge the state of the tunnel economy from the garbage that would blow across the dusty, blasted road. Imports from Israel with Hebrew packaging became rarities, replaced with crushed cigarette packets and dented soft drinks cans with Arabic writing. In the shops, goods in shops could be a little sandy after their journey under the border from Egypt.

The prospect of a visit to Gaza can be daunting, because of the performance involved in getting in and the thought of the stress and tension that probably lie ahead. Any place with so many guns, that is sometimes bombed, and where a minority of the people are not welcoming is never going to be a soft touch. They can be full of rage too. The built up parts of the Gaza Strip include some of the most densely populated streets in the world. Different factions compete fiercely, sometimes violently. Families live on top of each other and the conflict with Israel is never less than a looming, dominating black cloud of trouble. Until the very end of the war between Israel and Hamas over the New Year of 2009, the Israeli government stopped journalists crossing Erez. A few happened to be there when Israel's bombing offensive started, but hundreds of later-arriving foreign news teams spent days on a lump in the landscape that they dubbed the hill of shame, where they could watch the explosions through long lenses. Just behind was Sderot, the Israeli border town that was often targeted by rocket crews in Gaza. In another, less bloody, bombing campaign at the end of 2012, journalists were allowed into Gaza by Israel, and had a chance to share the feeling of being under fire. In the early hours of one morning, after another long day, I had just got out of the shower when an enormous explosion about 200 yards away smashed the windows in my hotel room. It was a small slice of Gaza life.

But I have almost always enjoyed my time in Gaza, even though it is not easy and sometimes not all that safe. The reason is that for all its problems the human spirit burns very brightly among the Palestinians of Gaza. For people who have hard lives, they laugh a lot. Pockets of peace exist in the Gaza Strip. Children fly home made kites, expertly made out of pieces of wood and plastic and newspaper that rich kids in Europe would not give a second glance. Gaza has beaches and open fields. Its people can extract pleasure out of very little.

James Rodgers is a brilliant and thoughtful guide to Gaza. He saw today's Gaza being created. This book is a great introduction for beginners, and full of insight and analysis for veterans.

Introduction

The spring sun sank into the sea like the head of a dying casualty. I had watched this rapid sunset so many times that I could not believe I would not see it again the next day, or the day after that. I turned away from the window, and looked back into the room behind me. It was emptying. I looked down at the floor. My boots – battered from months of scuffing against rubble, their soles studded with broken glass – did not go well with my suit. I wore the suit because I wanted to look smart out of respect for the Palestinian colleagues who had been so good to me for the last couple of years, but, for footwear, it was either the boots, or flip-flops. In Gaza I had never needed anything else, until today. It was March 2004, and my farewell party was ending. The next morning, I left the uniquely troubled territory where, during my posting as the BBC's correspondent, I had been the only resident foreign journalist.

I tried, during that period from August 2002, to tell the story of what was happening in the Gaza Strip as completely as I could: I spoke to hundreds of people – some in positions of power, others crushed by poverty, many traumatised – and, in order to do so, made journeys which few then could. As a reporter, I was able to go both into the sunless alleys of the shanty towns which were the Palestinian refugee camps, and to the neat white streets of the Jewish settlements which stood there then. Yet I felt that daily journalism was not always enough. There was a lack of time to talk of history, and how it overshadowed the present. There was not enough space to discuss the apparent power of faith, the sense of divinely-granted ownership of land, and religious duty to defend it. Too much emphasis was placed upon the words of Presidents and Prime Ministers; not always enough on those whose words were wiser with the weight of experience, and a sense of destiny: shopkeepers, students, soldiers and countless others caught up in the conflict over a tiny slice of land sacred to millions across the world.

That is why I have written *No Road Home*. It is the story not of my time in Gaza, but of the people whom I met during that time. It is a story which no one else can tell now, for the Gaza which I knew – run by people loyal to Yasser Arafat, and partly occupied by Jewish settlements – is gone. Yet it is a story which I am convinced contains important lessons about the Israeli-Palestinian conflict at a time when, after the 'Arab Spring' more attention is focused on the wider region than has been the case for decades. These are lessons which have not been learnt by those who make policy – at least, not while they do so. This book aims to fill a gap in the understanding of a conflict which has consumed so much diplomatic time and energy, and still defied a solution. At the time of writing, in January 2013, the peace process is at a standstill – yet the status quo seems quite untenable in the longer term. A United Nations Report[1] published in August 2012 asked whether, given expected population increase, and the consequent strain on already scarce resources, Gaza would even be 'liveable' in 2020. Since my time in Gaza, Israel has walled off much of the West Bank, and Gaza has endured long periods under siege. Ordinary people on both sides know less and less of each other, the dehumanizing process serving only to increase anger and hatred. It is a process which has been underway for years. The final form of that process, and its consequences, can only be guessed at – but they are like a cancer eating away at the few prospects which remain for longer term peace in the region. 'Did you know the soldiers are the same age as us?' a young Gazan asked me in 2003. He was aged around twenty. He had been allowed to leave Gaza to go to a conference for young Palestinians and Israelis in Jericho. Because of the reason for his journey, he had been given rare permission to go out through the crossing usually reserved for foreigners and VIPs. His route meant that he came into contact with Israelis face to face – a rare event then for a Gazan. He had been permitted to pass through the Palestinian police post, and head into the no man's land that ended with the concrete cylinder of an Israeli sentry box. A window at about the height of a check-in counter framed a soldier's face; 'I am a c***', written in English, with an arrow pointing upward, was scratched in the paint below, completing the picture like the on-screen caption identifying a television interviewee. Another short walk brought the traveller to the air-conditioned office where documents were checked; a delay here was the occasion for my assistant to learn that the Israeli army was not only made up of combat-hardened thirty year olds. From the soldier who stood guard, and to whom he had talked, he learned that not all Israelis thought that the Jewish settlers (whose presence in Gaza was seen by almost all the world as illegal occupation – the dissenters were the Israeli government and some neoconservative Americans) should be there. This soldier was among those who wanted his colonizing compatriots out of Gaza, especially as a friend of his had been shot while protecting the nearby settlement of Dugit. The young Gazan was astonished but never, I think, able to continue the conversation and learn something more of the enemy he had previously come to see as a two-dimensional, faceless, monster.

His astonishment would not have surprised an older Palestinian, a cafe owner in the Old City of Jerusalem, whom I interviewed in the summer of 2003 while a

---

[1] Gaza in 2020: A liveable place? Available at
http://www.unrwa.org/userfiles/file/publications/gaza/Gaza%20in%202020.pdf,
accessed 9 January 2013.

temporary cease-fire allowed everyone living between the river and the sea to breathe just a little more easily for a few weeks. He articulated the process of separation, remembering a time when he would do business with Israelis. They were perhaps not friends, but, as business contacts, they did at least have a mutually beneficial relationship. That time had gone. The cafe owner described a world then where the young people had been children during the first *intifada* (Palestinian uprising against Israel) of the 1980s, and now reached adulthood in the second, which had begun in the late summer of 2000. That generation, of which my assistant was a typical member, knew no Israelis. The only ones they ever encountered were settlers or soldiers, and they were behind barriers, armour, or gun barrels. Israelis were not only different in the eyes of Palestinians of that age, they were losing human characteristics. The same was true the other way round, of course. Israelis who had welcomed the Palestinians into their businesses and onto their farms as workers and agricultural labourers could no longer keep those jobs open. Uncertainty over whether or not they would be permitted to leave Gaza – and thus turn up to work – meant that more reliable solutions had to be found. That contact too was gone. Those Palestinians whom I knew over the age of 25 or so had mostly had jobs in Israel at one time or another. The experience was not sufficient to make them necessarily like Israelis – plenty, too, had had contact with Israelis after spending time in Israeli prisons – but it did give them the basis for some simple form of understanding, and cooperation. With the Palestinians almost completely kept from leaving Gaza, shut up, in effect, in a kind of huge open prison, they too became distant, faceless, and somehow less human. They were distant, different, and dangerous – and that was just the way it was.

My purpose in writing the book is not to propose a way of ending the conflict. Finer minds than mine have attempted that, and failed. Instead I want to offer another means of understanding it, in the hope that understanding may be the departure point for a move away from journalistic and diplomatic discourses which have led nowhere. My title questions the principles of the *Road Map*, launched in 2003 as the international plan for ending the fighting between Israelis and Palestinians. For I left Gaza after two years convinced that the two-state solution could not work, at least not in the longer term. In May 2012, The European Council (i.e. European Union Foreign Ministers) conceded that it was looking less of a realistic option, saying in a statement that while, 'Reiterating its fundamental commitment to the security of Israel, it expressed at the same time deep concern about developments on the ground which threaten to make a two-state solution impossible.'[2] The 'developments on the ground', also discussed at

---

[2] Press release from The Council of the European Union. Brussels, May 14 2012. Available at http://www.consilium.europa.eu/uedocs/cms_data/docs/pressdata/EN/foraff/13024 8.pdf, accessed 9 January 2013.

greater length in documents leaked to news media, were increased settlement activity. In other words, since I left Gaza, the prospects for such an end to the conflict seem only to have become more remote, and the moment when they could be envisaged may even have passed. Then, in 2004, I already felt that conventional diplomatic initiatives, of the type contained in the *Road Map* concentrated too closely on ideas of economic factors, and resources – while shying away from addressing the strength of religion, and a more spiritual idea of home, as reasons for taking up arms to kill, and to die. This idea of home lies at the heart of the book: the idea of home not just as bricks and mortar or even land and water, but home as a concept which includes ideas of faith, statehood, and patriotism. So my hope is that *No Road Home*, through the stories which people tell there, will enable readers to look at the Israeli-Palestinian conflict as one which defies solution purely in terms of economics, and territory. I do not deny that addressing these issues could bring a degree of stability, and perhaps even peace, in the short term, at least. But addressing them successfully, and creating a Palestinian state, cannot, in the longer term, end a war which has land and faith at its core: doing that will involve answering questions which the conventional diplomatic approach does not even ask. The stories told by the people in *No Road Home* explain why these are issues which must be addressed.

My strong feeling on my departure from the region was either that the two peoples would have to learn to live together (increasingly unlikely given the way they continue to dehumanize each other), or one of them would have to leave (presumably a solution acceptable in principle to both parties, provided they were not the ones to go). A visit to Jerusalem, and to the West Bank, in September 2011, reinforced a conviction which I have continued to hold since I watched the sun sink into the Mediterranean on that evening in March 2004. Since I left Gaza, the Islamists of Hamas have taken over control of the territory. A society which was already conservatively devout has become more so. The reported moves by ultra-Orthodox Jews in Beit Shemesh in December 2011 to introduce segregation in public between the sexes provoked protest demonstrations, and also raised issues for which the traditionally more secular political establishment has no obvious response. The same is true of the debate in Israeli society over whether the ultra-Orthodox should still be exempt from the compulsory military service which is the obligation of most Israelis. Faith, always underlying enmity between Israelis and Palestinians, is coming more and more to the surface.

A few days before I left for that 2011 trip, I heard Daniel Levy, a former Israeli government advisor, speak at the European Council on Foreign Relations in London. He described then an Israeli government seemingly more focused on conflict management, than conflict resolution – the latter apparently a goal which was unachievable either because it was unrealistic, or undesirable. In a paper published by the ECFR during Israel's military operation 'Pillar of

Defense' in Gaza in November 2012, Mr Levy, looking at that operation in the context of the forthcoming Israeli election, wrote of an 'internal logic', in Israel which

has Israel as a permanent occupier of the Palestinians, therefore placing acceptance and normalisation with its surrounding region off the agenda and in turn determining that Israel will live indefinitely by the sword, including unleashing occasional violent outbursts such as this one. It is a conflict management strategy that relies on Western and notably US support (and that of enough of the Jewish diaspora), Arab weakness and internal strife, and an Israeli military edge and ability to insulate its economy.[3]

Simply trying to preserve the status quo is immoral while living conditions in Gaza continue to deteriorate, and the people who are trapped there continue to be brutalized, and denied many of the things which might help them to live with dignity. It may also be strategically unwise from Israel's point of view. Apart from the challenges, mentioned in the United Nations report referred to above, of an expanding population in Gaza, and resources which will no longer suffice, there is no guarantee that those factors upon which Mr Levy says Israel currently relies will last. They are, as he went on to write in the same paper, 'brittle and fraying to various degrees, especially in the face of developments in the Arab world in the past two years.' In a world which has yet to absorb fully the shocks of the collapse of the Soviet bloc, the attacks of September 11th, and the financial crisis, it seems imprudent to count on anything being there in the longer term – especially when those things may already be 'brittle and fraying'.

These more pressing economic, political, and military factors, I would argue, serve only to reinforce the need to look at the Israeli-Palestinian conflict again, and, in doing so, include other viewpoints, however challenging they may be. Reflecting my belief that the idea of a homeland lies at the centre of the conflict, I have divided *No Road Home* into chapters defined not by time, but by place. The book takes the form of a journey from the north to the south of Gaza, letting the people who lived there then tell their stories: stories which invite us to see their lives from their point of view, not from the point of view of policy experts who have tried, and failed, to solve what perhaps they did not fully understand, or did not wish to admit. My time in the territory gave me a unique perspective on the Israeli-Palestinian conflict, one which I now seek to share.

---

[3] Levy, Daniel (2012) Israel: Living by the sword. European Council on Foreign Relations paper published 16 November 2012. Available at http://ecfr.eu/content/entry/commentary_Israel_Living_by_the_sword. Accessed 9 January 2013.

CHAPTER 1
SAFE PASSAGE

'Be careful. The Arabs in there are animals,' warned the soldier.

He was speaking Russian. He had noticed a Russian visa in my passport, and had started to chat. Our conversation was short. Night had fallen so I wanted to cross the border area quickly. I wondered what had brought the soldier there. Perhaps he had decided that he would be more at home in the Israeli Army than fighting Chechens in the numbing cold of a north Caucasus winter. Now he stood guard at the entrance to the Gaza Strip. It was as if his ham fist gripped a huge net in which more than a million Palestinians flapped, gasped, or just lay still, exhausted from lack of air. He controlled their entry and exit to a land which he now called home, but which most of them still thought of as theirs. Now if they ever went back, it was for miserable jobs as casual labourers. It was autumn. In the darkness, nothing was visible beyond the pools of stark white light falling from the lamp posts along the road ahead, which led from Israel into the Gaza Strip. I had been crossing the checkpoint regularly for the preceding five months, so I was easily able to picture what lay in the murk beyond the street lamps. What I could not see, I could fill in from memory. I had come in May, when it was still, and hot. The intermittent breeze then brought little relief, and a strong smell of sewage. Each time I came or went, I noticed new details: rules and regulations were tightened; more barbed wire was rolled out; buildings were strengthened, or blown up. The Erez crossing point into the Gaza Strip was the end of the road; the end of Israel. Beyond it, more than a million people were crammed into an area of land shaped like a crude meat cleaver. It measured 45km from north to south, and just 10km across at its widest. In the Israeli imagination, it was a place of indescribable horror. The Hebrew phrase, 'Go to Gaza', means 'go to hell'. The sign before the crossing pointed towards "Safe Passage' to the Gaza Strip': the inverted commas unusual punctuation, or questionable joke.

The soldier who checked my documents on the first crossing looked a little like Naomi Campbell. I supposed she was Ethiopian, an apparent descendant of one of Israel's ancient tribes, lost for centuries in Africa, and now become a supermodel squaddie. She was in the place later occupied by the brutish Russian.

She waved me through and I went on to the next post, an air-conditioned one storey building grandly marked for VIP's. It was divided into two sections: one for people going into Gaza, and one for people coming out. In front of it, there was an open stretch of tarmac. To the right, there was the post guarded by the Russian or the Ethiopian. To the left, a colossal hangar, open at both ends, covering inspection pits and a huge x-ray machine, which were used to examine cars and luggage on their way out of Gaza. This was the passenger crossing. The cargo terminal, at Karni, a few kilometres south, was the entry and exit point for all goods going in and out of Gaza. Everything from humanitarian aid to cigarettes passed through it. Fruit and vegetables, grown in the sandy soil of this parched corner of the Mediterranean, went out. The Israelis were so wary of what came forth from 'hell' that even boxes of tomatoes went through a massive x-ray machine to check that they didn't contain bombs.

Inside the 'VIP section', there was another document check, this one a little more thorough. When I first arrived in Gaza, having a foreign passport was enough to allow you to cross. That is, unless the Israelis suspected the holder of being a Palestinian who also had foreign citizenship. Then the luckless traveller might sit for hours while the Israelis made up their mind. For others, it was usually a formality: passport check, stamp, stumble on. It was bright, too bright for eyes used to the gloomy skies of Europe. The light in the Middle East was blindingly clear. It bore down on uncovered heads, and bounced up to burn beneath chins. I shouldered my bags and began to walk across. I passed the last Israeli flag. It flew above a concrete cylinder with a slit through which you could just see a helmet, eyes, and the barrel of a gun. I had about 100 metres to walk before I was able to call over a taxi to come to pick me up and drive the short distance to the Palestinian side. All around was silent, and the walls which flanked the road on both sides ensured that this was a real no man's land; a no-life land.

If the Israeli guard post had the air of menacing efficiency, then the Palestinian side had the air of demoralized squalor. The guards didn't stand in the middle of the road, but sat in a shabby hut or under a sparse sunshade off to the side. Rubble and rubbish lay along the walls of the hut. A few metres away – on the road itself – the 'Palestinian Authority tourist bureau' was deserted. No amount of Mediterranean coastline or sunshine would tempt holidaymakers now. Bits of paper and plastic had caught on a coil of razor wire, and now flapped in the breeze like fish caught in a net meant for some larger prey. The taxi sent to take me to town soon arrived. Brief greetings were exchanged and luggage loaded up. Hamada, the BBC colleague who had come to take me to the hotel, repeated words of welcome. I sat mostly in silence – smiling or nodding politely when spoken to. I just wanted to look.

The roads were lined with rubbish. Here and there plumes of stinking smoke rose from the refuse. Donkeys wearily pulled carts. We passed a sign 'Gaza international airport, 40 km'. No flights now, nor was there a runway. The sign did not mention that. It wanted to pretend that there really was an airport, or perhaps just hoped that one day there would be. Every so often we had to slow down to move through a chicane caused by piles of earth and rocks in the road. These were defences against an expected advance by the Israeli army. The contrast with this grim war zone, and the fields of southern Israel which line the last stretch of road from Jerusalem to Gaza could not have been greater. The farmland there could have been a poor part of southern Europe. The Gaza Strip, even just a few hundred metres beyond the fence, could not. It might as well have been on the other side of the world. Why had I come? Why was I going to live in Gaza? There were the professional reasons, of course, it was going to be a good story and I wanted the challenge. But I also wanted the personal challenge. I wanted to see if I could cope. I had spent two years living in the comfort of western Europe and I wanted to live once again in a country where you could never be quite sure what was going to happen. Russia and my travels in the wars of the Caucasus seemed a distant memory. I wanted to live in the Middle East. I had always been fascinated by the Holy Land – this barren strip which meant so much to billions of believers across the world. I wanted to live amongst Muslims, to meet the people who, after the attacks of September 11th, were increasingly feared and demonized in my homeland.

The Al-Deira hotel, on the seafront, was magnificent, but empty. Its exterior wall was terracotta-coloured, a blast of colour brightening the dusty street. A corridor, open to the sky, led all the way through to a terrace at the back. The terrace reached right to the edge of the Mediterranean. High walls on either side ensured that the distinguished guests saw no squalor while they ate their breakfast or sipped their tea. The rooms were light and airy, with high, domed ceilings. For all it looked like a centuries-old resting place for caravans of traders, the Al-Deira had been built less than a decade before. It, and the other hotels which lay along the seafront, had grown up in the mid 1990s. Millions of dollars had been spent in the optimistic times which followed Yasser Arafat's return from exile, and the declaration of Palestinian autonomy. Now Yasser Arafat was held under siege in Ramallah, unable to visit Gaza or anywhere else and be sure he could return. A little further along the coast from where the hotels lined the beachfront, his compound lay in ruins, bombed by the Israeli Air Force as the conflict which flared up in September 2000 continued to burn.

I went to the office where to meet the other people I would be working with. Fayed Abushammala was the correspondent for the BBC Arabic service. He had greying hair and a neatly trimmed beard. We shook hands and said how pleased we were to meet. I tried to disguise the fact that I was looking at the strips of tape which criss-crossed the window panes to prevent their shattering in an air raid. I was an object of curiosity, and I was curious. We spent a couple of hours in the office chatting – I did more listening than talking, wary of saying the wrong thing. When Fayed and the others were distracted by work, I looked out of the window. Ten floors up, you could see across Gaza City and into Israel beyond. There was no green until your eye settled onto the agricultural land past the fence which surrounded the Gaza Strip. Below, everything was grey or sand coloured. At that time of day, noon in early summer, contrast was flattened by the sunlight from directly above.

Fayed had arranged a welcome lunch. We drove to a restaurant on the seafront where the waiters made a great fuss of us. They appeared to have been well briefed. Plate after plate of starters slowly covered the white tablecloth before us. The sun shone on the sea below, and a faint scent of salt air and sewage came through the window. Platters of fried and grilled fish followed the meze. The conversation was stilted but friendly. I remained nervous of offending my hosts. The ice was broken when we moved to another table for dessert. Sweets, fruit, and coffee then water pipes. With the mild, cool, fruit-flavoured tobacco, the jokes began. It seems the Gazans told gags about the people of Hebron, such as 'Why did the man from Hebron buy two television sets?' Answer: 'Because he wanted to put one on top of the other and see the legs of the man reading the news.' This got a huge laugh. Hamada brought the house down with an account of his travels to Paris. He seemed to have been to some kind of dance club which stayed open all night. For his fellow Gazans, it was wild exotica. They heard and discussed reports of suicide bombs in Israeli discotheques. They themselves had never been to such a place. After lunch, we strolled on the beach below. It was a thin strip of sand, heavily built up right down to within a few metres of the sea. I told Fayed it was beautiful. He looked at me: 'When it gets hard here, I come down to the sea for half an hour a day. It's good for the mental health.' I pictured myself doing the same.

That evening, Fayed took me to meet an official in the Palestinian Security forces. The conversation took place in a spacious office, richly decorated and expensively furnished. Palestinian flags hung from the walls. It was depressing to see how bereft of real ideas for a solution to the conflict was one at its centre. The authority had to reform for there to be peace, but they needed the stability of peace to carry out the reforms. When we left, night had fallen. Lights winked off shore: Israeli navy patrol boats watching the one border of the Gaza Strip which the army could not.

The next morning, after a breakfast of hummus and fresh flat bread on the terrace, I went back to the office. A group of Palestinian policemen, kalashnikovs across their knees, sat in the garden across the road. Several media organizations had their bureaux in the building. The police were there to ensure that no representative of Hamas or Islamic Jihad found their way in to give an interview. Fayed took me to see the flat where I would be living. It was the biggest place that had ever been my home, for the lowest rent I had ever paid. There were three bedrooms, three bathrooms, a huge dining and living area, and four balconies. Although the building was modern, built, like the Al-Deira hotel during the mid-1990s, it too had some Arab features which seemed attractively exotic. The window frames were curved, not rectangular, as might have been expected in a new block of flats. The curtains were a rich gold colour: not what I would have chosen in Europe, but perfectly apt here. The balconies at the front of the house looked onto open land, part of which was covered by a playground. Beyond there was a school, to the left, a football stadium. The Egyptian consulate was across the road. In other words, there was nothing near the flat which the Israeli Air Force might consider a target. I decided to take it immediately. The rent was $500 a month: barely enough for a room in many parts of London. We had a brief chat with the landlord, a Palestinian Christian. He had once lived in Sussex. He told me how he had enjoyed walking his dog on the downs, and of his memories of bonfire night in Lewes. Then he spoke of how hard it had become to run the import-export business his family had had in Gaza since the 1950s. His elderly father looked straight ahead and said nothing.

I liked the landlord, and he seemed keen to have me as a tenant. There were two other flats in the building – both lived in by members of his family. This was a relief. One foreign journalist had once met a Hamas activist in the lift of the block she was staying in. She immediately feared that the house might one day be attacked and moved out. No such dramas here, I hoped. The landlord did tell me that the cellar of this block was full of the possessions of a Scot contracted to work on Gaza International Seaport (as much of a reality as the airport). He had fled without his belongings after the *intifada* – the Palestinian uprising against Israel – began in the autumn of 2000.

In the afternoon, Fayed took me for a brief tour of the area around Gaza city. The route was dictated by road closures – a consequence of the conflict. We were able to cover little of the area. We stopped at a housing estate where tower blocks of the kind you see now in any city in the world rose above an open central area. Children played football, as they might anywhere in the world. Beyond the place where they played, there was a huge mound of earth. Its purpose soon became clear. The housing estate was just a few hundred metres from the Jewish settlement of Netzarim. Suddenly the sound of gunfire came from that direction – a few short bursts. It was impossible for my untrained ear to tell if the fire was incoming or outgoing. We decided to leave anyway. The football match continued. The players seemed oblivious to the shooting. They ignored it as kids in London might ignore the noise of a busy road. Gunfire was as much a part of their life as the weather. If they stopped every time there was shooting, they would only rarely finish a game. It seemed as much of a reason to call off the game as drizzle might be in Manchester. We drove back along the seafront. Swimmers enjoyed the waves. Men were dressed in modest loose-fitting shorts; the few women were fully clothed even in the water. The rapid sunset was a few minutes away. The skeletons of an amusement park and holiday hotels suggested what might have been. Fayed smiled sadly and then shrugged as he saw me looking at the rusting bumper cars. 'I used to take my boys there, but now…' His voice trailed off as the sun sank into the Mediterranean.

My task as a journalist was not going to be easy. But I relished the challenge. I would have to write about political and military developments of course – probably finding myself being shaken awake by air raids in the middle of the night. I wanted most of all to write about the people here. I wanted to tell anyone who would listen what life was like in this strange land. What did the boys playing football think when the shooting started? Or were they, even in their primary school years, already immune to the violence and hatred which divided them from their neighbours in the settlement? Why had my landlord returned from Sussex? Later, when the way the territory was divided had more meaning, I came to understand that the issue was home: to have one, and to hold on to it.

For now, I was plagued by the journalistic challenges which lay ahead. How could I remain objective? The Israelis are extremely efficient at keeping an eye on everything that is written about the region. Deciding to report from 'Hell' for a year would mark me down in their eyes as a Palestinian sympathiser. I would have to fight for my principles, to struggle not to take sides. I knew that my colleagues in the international press corps in Jerusalem were under huge pressure. They mostly lived in west Jerusalem and shared the Israeli population's fear of suicide bombers. One told me of an attack where the bomber's head had ended up in the playground of a school for expatriate children. Another spoke of the bakery at the end of his street being destroyed, and with it, he suspected, the friendly baker. Despite this, many of the foreign reporters were loathed by the Israelis and by Jewish lobby groups around the world. Streams of abusive faxes and emails poured into their offices and inboxes. 'Jew haters and flaming homosexuals' was among the more colourful insults. Another foreign correspondent had the words 'Arab licker' traced in the dust on her car.

I spent that evening in the hotel trying to make sense of what I had seen. When I woke the next morning, the sun was already high and hot. The light played on the water as it would in a tourist resort somewhere on the shores of the same sea. These normal details often struck me as strange in conflict zones. For some reason, I almost expected the natural elements to reflect the human battle. There were a few small fishing boats out trying their luck – many more were tied up in a harbour a short distance away from the hotel.

During the night, the Israeli Army ('Israel Defence Forces' – IDF) had attacked and destroyed a factory on the eastern edge of Gaza city. The IDF apparently believed that it was being used to manufacture mortars. They had come into Gaza under cover of darkness, set explosives, and blasted the place apart. No one had been killed, despite an exchange of fire between the soldiers and Palestinian fighters. Fayed wanted to go – and I was keen to get a taste of the sort of stories I would be covering. We took the armoured car which the BBC had provided for Gaza. Fayed drove. He had lived here all his life, and knew the city well. Although the factory wasn't on a main road, he had a good idea of where it was and quickly found it.

The factory – which seemed to have been little more than a warehouse or workshop – had been blown apart. The remains of a metal frame which had held the walls and the roof were all that was left. Still, the sight had drawn a crowd. They muttered their disapproval; tutted; smoked. Metal sheets which had presumably made up the walls and the roof lay around like playing cards cast to the floor after an argument over a game: this had been a powerful explosion. Beneath the skeleton of the building, machine parts and misshapen lengths of metal were strewn across what had been the shop floor. The destroyed machinery would have been all but impossible to replace. The factory's production days were over, whatever its product had been. A man who said he was one of the factory owners came to talk to us. He said that his business had been cutting stone and marble. He had a glossy brochure which he said showed his machinery before it had been blown up. In the wreckage, you could just make out damaged and dented versions of the tools in the publicity material. Special benches such as these, for stonecutting, were also used in Israel, but having the work done there, according to the man from the factory, cost considerably more. He accused the Israeli Army of wrecking his business so that Israeli factories could take his work. What to believe? I was quite relieved I had not yet formally taken up my post. I realized that, from what I saw before me, from what I heard in the conflicting Israeli and Palestinian accounts, that it was quite impossible to tell. They were secretly making weapons somewhere in Gaza. Why not here? As time went on I would get better, on the basis of my experience, at guessing the real story – but guessing it so often remained, unless you were close enough to see, and that was when it was dangerous. Small details could be indispensable in trying to piece together the events of the day, but concentrating on them too much could prove a distraction in telling the bigger story: the consequences of the divinely-inspired struggle for every small piece of land and water. It did not matter what the factory had been making. The Palestinians wanted to cut stone, and they wanted weapons. The Israeli Army's action that night had frustrated them in one or both of those enterprises, weakening them all the same.

We drove back to the office. It was Friday, and the streets were beginning to empty as the people of Gaza went to pray. From the office on the 10th floor, the scale of devotion was clear to see. Few people remained in the streets – even the water cart and fruit sellers who tried to pull in custom with annoying sirens (including, for some reason, 'Jingle Bells') had fallen silent. The sounds which rose up from the streets below were now quite different. Every imam in every mosque now seemed to want to make their voice heard above all other. I could not understand what was being said, but, after seeing the overcrowding and the destruction, I sensed anger and defiance in the words which rose from the loudspeakers. After a while, I noticed that I was alone. My Palestinian colleagues had disappeared – apparently to pray in another part of the building.

I almost smiled, reflecting that after a few months, the call to prayer would seem no more unusual to me than church bells had in Brussels or London. I wondered if I would ever feel at home here. I remembered an evening during a trip to Yemen the previous summer. Alone in my friend's house as night fell, I had been unnerved by the loudness and strangeness of the muezzin from the city's different mosques. I had woken with the dawn call to prayer for the first few mornings, wondering what it could be. Then I had become used to it. It became part of the landscape, which grew more and more familiar, until I almost came to think of it as home.

After prayers, Fayed offered took me out to see more of the Gaza strip. This time we headed north of the city. As we were about to round a corner along the coast road, he turned to me and said, 'You're from Brussels – let me show you some Euros.' He waved his hand at the remains of a stout perimeter wall which now enclosed only rubble. He smiled in anticipation of my reaction. This was one of the Palestinian Authority buildings, paid for by EU development grants, which had been flattened by the Israeli Air Force.

As we drove on, a settlement came into view. Already I was learning to recognise the red roofs and whitewashed walls. There was always an army position – usually a watchtower with an overlord's view of the area around – nearby. I tried to imagine what it must be like to live there. Even for a correspondent, the settlements were not easy to visit. There was no direct access to them from inside the Palestinian controlled parts of the Gaza strip. The settlers themselves came in and out along military roads. The Palestinians were not allowed to use these roads, and the points at which they could be crossed were only opened every few hours. A trip from the south of the Gaza Strip to Gaza City could take a day or more. The previous afternoon we had chatted to taxi loads of people trapped as they tried to travel around. So long were the delays that a stall selling falafel had been set up along the dusty road. In the distance, behind a concrete wall (even from here, the settlers' road was in kalashnikov range), we could make out the convoy speeding along. A normal civilian bus – transport for the settlers – was preceded and followed by army jeeps.

I realized that I would always have to tell this story from behind one fence or another. It would be like reporting on a football match from one section of the segregated crowd. The deeply prejudiced view of any decision would seep into and inform your view of what you saw. I wanted to go to meet the settlers, to try to understand what had brought them here. Religious convictions about historical, God-given rights to land that others had lived on for centuries was one thing. How did the people in the neat white houses live with the danger which they had put themselves, and especially their children, in? For the settlers in Gaza, a return to the ancestral promised land had become, in the idiom of their fellow Israelis, a descent into Hell. Life in Gaza was going to be tough, but I knew that whenever it got too much, I could leave and go and have a rest somewhere else. The people among whom I would be living had no such choice. I would have to be sympathetic and understanding while always reminding myself that there was a different point of view. The price of failure would be mistrust and loathing; possibly even physical danger.

As we drove back, we passed a score of people sitting out in the street drinking tea. A large white awning stretched over them, shielding them from the sun. Banners explained that they had gathered to honour a 'martyr' – either a suicide bomber, or a fighter who'd died in battle with the Israelis. Three – probably four – generations of the extended family sat together. From veiled women of indeterminate age to toddlers, they had assembled to mourn and celebrate, while neighbours offered condolence and possibly congratulation. Boys of four or five ran round the outside of the circle as they might do at any adult ceremony where their presence was required, but which they didn't fully understand.

A month later, I left Brussels for the last time. The train sped through Flanders, past the cemeteries for the dead of the First World War. The neat rows of white crosses had become places of interest for historians, tourists, and relatives curious about ancestors they had never known. The visitors might be sad, but not crushed by grief or crazed for revenge. Those European wounds had healed. Only the scars were left. The blood in the Holy Land still flowed freely. While in London waiting to leave for Gaza, I visited a museum. One of its exhibits was a recreation of a house destroyed in the blitz. It looked like the factory I had seen that Friday. Londoners had to go to a museum to see what Gazans found outside their door.

The Gaza Strip was to be my home for almost two years. It was also home to more than 800,000 Palestinian refugees from the 1948 Arab-Israeli war, and their descendants. They didn't think of it as home, but they were stuck there, dreaming of a mythical return to farms and villages, many of them long destroyed, now inside Israel. They shared the crowded coastal stretch with some 7,500 Jewish settlers. They also thought of Gaza as home, but the refugees who said they were not at home in Gaza said that it wasn't the settlers' place either. Who had the right to call where 'home' was the issue at the heart of the conflict. In order to better understand and report on that conflict, I made my home – temporarily – at the centre of it.

On February 19th 2003, the Foreign Office advised British nationals to leave Gaza 'while exit routes remain open'. I stocked up on tinned food, clean water, and cigarettes and decided to stay. I read the email from the British consulate after an almost sleepless night – kept awake by work and explosions. Eleven people were killed, all within a couple of miles of my house. The next day, the funeral crowds howled with a fury I had not seen before, screaming for revenge, calling down curses on Tel Aviv. The war in Iraq was only a month away. The world was preparing to largely ignore the Israeli-Palestinian conflict, and look instead to Baghdad. The absence of attention would be the opportunity for increased aggression.

CHAPTER 2
SACRIFICE

The hall was crowded. People had gathered outside, in one of Gaza City's main streets, waiting for the event to start. It was cold, and the sky was heavy: a warning that the seasonal sand storm, the *hamsin,* was about to blow in from the desert. Some dust had already drifted in from the street, making the hall seem shabby despite attempts to create a sense of grand ceremony. Rows of plastic chairs – vital for any public event in Gaza: wedding, wake, marriage announcement, or mourning – had been set out inside for families and well wishers. A picture of Saddam Hussein in traditional Arab dress hung at on the front wall, looking over the speakers. It was a week before the invasion of Iraq began. There was more and more fighting in Gaza. Many Gazans were convinced that the Israelis were preparing to occupy the territory completely while attention was focused on Baghdad. In the middle of February 2003, in northern Gaza, the military wing of Hamas destroyed an Israeli tank with a huge landmine. The tank's crew of four were all killed in the explosion. For the next month, the IDF hit back hard, seeking to punish those who were responsible for the deaths of the servicemen, and also, it seemed, others who might have supported the attack.

One evening, in the first week of March, at around 6pm, I had a call from the Israeli Army press office. The sun had already set over Gaza City. We were to meet at Erez at 9pm. North of the city, the feeble street lights gave way to near-total darkness. Entering or leaving Gaza at night was dangerous. The Israeli Army posts at Erez were frequent targets for Palestinian attack. Soldiers, nervous about what lay in the murk beyond their bunkers, might shoot at shadows. The crossing itself was floodlit so that they could see who was approaching. The Major from the Army Press office turned up just before 9, as did Alon Farago, the cameraman from Jerusalem. We drove along the road which borders the northern edge of the Gaza Strip: the Erez industrial zone on one side, sand dunes everywhere else. Any land here which wasn't irrigated soon turned to desert, briefly green only during the heaviest of winter rains. Suddenly, a short distance ahead, there were lights. 'That must be the army camp,' I said to Alon.

'That's not a camp. It's the column,' he replied.

The shapes of tanks and armoured vehicles became clearer. There were about 40 of them: armoured personnel carriers (apc's); tanks; and colossal 'D9' bulldozers which seemed as high as the houses they were designed to demolish. The force had been assembled between two sand dunes near the settlement of Dugit. From a distance, it would be completely hidden. The only lights were pale green. The Army didn't want their presence to be betrayed by a glow rising up into the desert night. For now, the soldiers lounged around near their vehicles. A senior officer with a head torch briefed the tank commanders. Feet weighed down by boots and body armour sunk into the sand. Stars shone in the clear night sky overhead.

Captain Eric Oken was in his mid 20s. It was hard to see what he looked like: the darkness and the camouflage paint he had daubed on his face obscured his features. He explained to his men in Hebrew the goal of the night's mission. They put the finishing touches to their face paint. The Army press officer told Alon and me of the night's objective. 'You're going to Jabalya,' he said.

Jabalya is a United Nations refugee camp on the edge of Gaza City. The refugees have been there since they fled the 1948 Arab-Israeli war. They and their descendants now number more than 100,000. The place still described as a 'camp' is no longer made up of tents, but of countless houses and shacks built of breeze blocks and corrugated iron. It is one of the most densely populated places on the planet, and a stronghold of the Palestinian militant groups Hamas and Islamic Jihad. The sense of the injustice suffered by their parents and grandparents inspires the younger generations to take up arms. If the Hebrew phrase 'Go to Gaza' means 'Go to hell', then, in the Israeli imagination, Jabalya is the place where the fires of that hell burn hottest: flames of hatred fanned by more than 50 years of Israeli-Palestinian conflict. The Israeli Army's mission that night was to extinguish some of the burning brands there forever. The aim was to 'arrest terrorists', Captain Oken explained. Most of those 'terrorists' were likely to choose death and the glory of 'martyrdom' over the humiliation of being taken alive by their enemies.

Despite the danger they faced, the soldiers seemed calm. Their foes might be fierce, but they were poorly armed by comparison. kalashnikovs, grenades, and home-made land mines rarely blew a hole in Israeli armour. The Israelis rarely sustained serious casualties on their night-time raids. The troops knew that. That was why the attack on the tank, in these same sand dunes three weeks before, had provoked such fury. The soldiers' task wasn't easy, but deep down they knew had little to fear. Shortly before midnight, the soldiers got into their vehicles and the column prepared to move off. There was a delay. Everyone had to stay inside the armoured personnel carrier. The soldiers passed the time by picnicking on bread, meat, and hummous – one part of the Arab world which the Israelis have embraced wholeheartedly. They shared their snacks with us – motioning and pointing as they passed the food around. The vehicle was built for combat not comfort. There was so little space that it was almost impossible even to shift in your seat. That was made worse by the fact that everyone was wearing flak jackets and helmets.

The column started up. Shortly afterwards, it stopped again. Alon listened to the radio network from the speaker in the apc. One of the bulldozers was stuck in the sand ahead and could not be moved budged. Had the Palestinians tanks, artillery, or helicopter gunships, the column could have been blasted to pieces as it paused. They had none. The soldiers sat, heads down, with the weariness of rush hour commuters resigned to a late-running train. Impatient and, to me, incomprehensible voices chattered and instructed over the radio. After a wait of another half an hour or so, the column was mobile again. It was impossible to tell exactly where we were, but soon we were on a surfaced road rather than on sand. From below, little was visible through the turret of the apc. Soon, though, overhead power lines and balconies came into view.

Then the shooting started. The people of the refugee camps have little to do at night. In consequence, the streets and crowded alleys of the shanty towns are usually silent after dark. Tonight was different. Gunfire seemed to come from all around. Palestinian fighters loosed off at the armoured column. The heavier guns mounted on tanks and apc's answered back. Empty machine gun shells rang as they hit the metal floor at Captain Oken's feet. The refugee camp, the only place its inhabitants could call home, had become a battle zone. This was where more than a hundred thousand people were born, studied, worked, got married and raised their families. Tonight, some of them would die, too.

The men in the vehicle were supposed to take over a house. They would use it as a firing position to cover their comrades who were moving in to capture the Hamas men who were the target of the raid. They were almost the only Israelis to walk the streets of the Gaza Strip now. The Israelis who have been to Gaza have usually come this way: in an armoured column in the dead of night. The soldiers opened the back door and sought the shadows. Although the night was clear, there was almost no moon and hardly anything could be seen. With the back of the apc open, the noise of the battle filled the vehicle. Bullets passed close by but none hit the armour. Eventually the soldiers who had left the apc returned, sneaking silently up to the open door, and clearly relieved to find themselves once again under the protection of the armoured shell. Still the apc did not move. There was a huge explosion nearby. Army engineers had detonated the charges they had placed on the house of one of the wanted men – the usual punishment for anyone suspected of having carried out, planned, or directed, attacks on Israeli targets. The homes of suicide bombers are routinely destroyed to teach their families and communities a lesson. It is a tactic which the Israeli Army copied from the British who ran Palestine between the two world wars of the twentieth century. Destroying a house punishes not only the alleged wrongdoer, but also his entire family. Demolishing a home is designed to make the rest of the family feel so powerless, helpless, destitute and defeated that none of them will want to rise up. Yet it often breeds resentment which drives revenge.

The operation was nearly over. Weak daylight came in through the turret of the apc. The windows of the houses above were closed and silent, but few people can have been asleep. Everyone, though, seemed to be resisting the natural urge to look out and see what was happening. A soldier only has a moment to decide whether the face at the window is that of a sniper or a disturbed sleeper. In Gaza, children and people with learning difficulties sometimes paid for their curiosity with their lives. Wiser friends and relatives kept them out of sight, and themselves stayed hidden. Homes in Jabalya offer little protection. The walls of the buildings are often too flimsy to stop bullets, and no house there is strong enough to resist bulldozers or explosives.

The apc rumbled on, driving over curb stones and bouncing over the ruts left by tanks. It was light now. The shooting continued. Then there was another huge blast. Alon translated the radio announcement. 'A bomb has gone off in a furniture shop,' he said. 'The shop was on fire and the flames set off the bomb.'

A bomb in a shop, said the Israelis. A tank shell launched as the troops were withdrawing, said the Palestinians. Members of the local fire brigade were among the dead, killed as the shop windows were shattered by the explosion. Television pictures of the incident were slowed down countless times in an attempt to decide what had caused it. There was no agreement. Each side stuck stubbornly to their version of the truth, the view which served them best.

By around 8.30, column was back at the point which it had left from the night before. The soldiers lit cigarettes and pissed in the sand dunes. They peeled off their body armour. The more religious of them took out sacred books, and began to pray, rocking their heads back and forward next to the tanks and bulldozers which had been their shelter for the sleepless night from which they were now safely delivered. The morning had brought warm, gentle, sunshine. The noise of engines and gunfire had gone. Captain Oken was exhausted. He struggled a little in his second language. He painted a picture of professional care and consideration when he described his men's taking over of the house. They had asked the family to go into one room while they secured the building, he said. No one had been hurt. The terror provoked by a group of soldiers, themselves nervous, bursting into your house in the dead of night while a battle raged outside can only be imagined.

11 Palestinians had been killed in the battle which had raged around the armoured column. Some were the targets of the operation, others, like the fire-fighters, were civilians. The Israeli Army suffered only a few wounded. Captain Oken wouldn't talk about the Palestinian dead. 'Don't ask me about civilian casualties,' he sighed, almost yawning, in South African accented English. 'The operation was a success. My men behaved professionally.'

Soon, buses drew up to take the soldiers back to their base, special services laid on to collect the night shift workers in Israel's 'war on terror'. Civilian coaches seemed incongruous next to the green hulks of military hardware. The night was over. The Army had done its duty protecting the Jewish homeland. In Jabalya, the flames from the furniture shop had been put out. More fuel had been added to the fires of 'hell' and hatred.

Once the U.S. led coalition went into action in Iraq, the situation in Gaza briefly became calmer. It later became clear that the Israelis had decided to strike at the Palestinian militants before, rather than during, the battle for Baghdad. Ten days after the raid into Jabalya, the crowd gathered at the dusty hall in Gaza City, waiting to see the 'martyrs'/ 'terrorists' rewarded by Saddam Hussein. Saddam Hussein had many supporters in Gaza. He was hailed as an implacable enemy of Israel who refused to be cowed by the United States. Through the 'Arab Liberation Front' – in effect, the Palestinian branch of the Ba'ath Party – he even sent money to the families of Palestinians killed in the conflict with Israel, and compensation to those who were wounded or suffered damage to their property. The money was given out at ceremonies in Gaza City: the last taking place just days before the fighting began. Everybody in Gaza knew the war was coming. In the main streets of the city, Saddam Hussein's smiling face looked out from almost every shop window. When the rush hour traffic built up, he could be seen in the back window of many of the cars. It was not an easy time to be British. When I went to the butcher across the road from the office, I passed a picture of the Iraqi dictator in the shop window as I entered. The friendly fat man in the supermarket, who often offered me a soft drink or some chocolate free with the rest of my shopping, took to lecturing me on why Washington and London were wrong to attack Baghdad.

I was one of the few British people they could speak to directly when they wanted to express their frustration. It would not be fair to say that I felt unsafe, just uncomfortable. However angered they were by the British government, the people I saw every day knew that I was no architect of British foreign policy. They knew, too, that there was almost no chance that Saddam Hussein would remain in power, although no one wanted to say so. The final ceremonies where Saddam's supporters handed out money to 'martyrs'' families were a chance to pretend that things were otherwise. A 'martyr' is anyone who has died in the conflict with Israel: anyone from a suicide bomber who blows him or herself up on a bus full of schoolchildren to a baby killed by an Israeli Army bullet. They, and everyone in between, are seen as having sacrificed themselves for Islam and the Palestinian cause. Consequently, they are revered as heroes. Their families suffer in their bereavement, but are respected in the street.

The Palestinian national anthem was played to mark the start of the ceremony. The old recording cut out, or was switched off, before it ended. It gave the whole ceremony a half-hearted feel. There followed rousing speeches praising Saddam Hussein, and cursing the United States, Britain, and Israel. The 'martyrs'' families may have been honoured by their peers, able to hold their heads high in scruffy street market or stinking refugee camp alley, but they were not Gaza's wealthy and powerful. They were shabbily dressed and looked poorly fed. Occasionally, a group of young men in the crowd would leap to their feet and start shouting 'Oh Saddam, oh my dear, destroy Tel Aviv!' but their rage seemed choreographed, and they themselves must have felt more powerless than anything else.

It was time for the cheques to be distributed. Ibrahim Za'anin, one of the leaders of the Arab Liberation Front, explained who received what. '$25,000 for those who carry out martyrdom operations (suicide bombings – JR), $10,000 for other martyrs, $5,000 if your house is completely destroyed.' The families queued up patiently. Each received a cheque for the appropriate amount, stapled to a certificate celebrating their relative's deed. There was only one cheque for $25,000. Since the beginning of the intifada, Gaza had been so tightly controlled that no suicide bomber had been able to make it out of the territory and into Israel. The sea was the only other way out. Some two months before, the Israelis had announced that one of their patrol boats had fired on, and detonated, a raft filled with explosives off the coast of the Gaza Strip. The army press release said that the forces believed that the raft had been unmanned.

Most militant groups would probably have left their enemy unaware that they had suffered a casualty. Not the armed wing of Hamas, the Izzedin Al-Qassam brigades. The incident had taken place early on a Friday morning. Just after noon prayers, the Al-Qassam brigades announced that the raft had in fact had one of their men on board. He was declared a martyr: the honour so great that he could not be denied it, even if it might have made the movement as a whole look less ineffective. Now his father, a sheikh with a grey beard, and the keen, bright eyes of a much younger man, left with a cheque for $25,000 concealed in his cloak. He would not answer questions. Whatever was said, he answered only by shaping his lips into a thin smile. Later, once he had been driven from power, and his money supply to Gaza had dried up in consequence, I would see how some of Saddam Hussein's dollars had been spent.

A week later the invasion of Iraq was underway. There were no more prize-giving ceremonies for 'martyrs'' families. There were demonstrations. U.S. and European Union citizens had already been advised to leave. I decided it was wise to keep a low profile, but I still had to see what was happening. After Friday prayers on the 21st March, a crowd of several thousand gathered in the square outside the Great Mosque in the centre of Gaza City. Their numbers might have been greater, were it not for the fact that watching coverage of the war on television was proving very popular. During the first war in Iraq, in 1991, Gaza was still under full Israeli occupation. Palestinian friends recalled a curfew which lasted 40 days. The only way to express one's feelings was to head for the rooftops to dance and cheer while Saddam Hussein's Scud missiles – clearly visible in the winter sky – headed for Tel Aviv. In 2003, people were free to demonstrate. They streamed into the streets straight from Friday prayers. Palestine Square, more usually a chaotic din of car horns, came to life with a different noise. Minibuses with huge speakers lashed onto their roofs drew up. The songs of Hamas blasted out. During pauses in the music, young men took turns to holler through the echoing microphone.

The procession moved off. The chanting was led by shouts from the top of the minibuses. 'Who is your God?' 'Allah!' 'Who is your leader?' 'The prophet!' 'What is your movement?' 'Hamas!' 'Who is your army?' 'Al-Qassam!' The Al-Qassam Brigades was Hamas's military wing, their name coming from Izzedin Al-Qassam, a guerrilla leader who battled the troops of the British Mandate in Palestine. With each chant, each marcher raised the first finger of his right hand to emphasize the one-ness of God, the unity of their movement, and the unity of their purpose.

This was a march for Iraq and for Islam. When George W. Bush and Tony Blair talked about 'civilization' and 'common values' their words were met with scorn. For most people in the Gaza Strip, and for the marchers in particular, the whole purpose of the attack on Iraq was the humiliation and occupation of more Arab territory by non-Muslims. One young lad carried a caricature of George W. Bush and Ariel Sharon. They were pictured as two monkeys embracing: Mr. Bush, the larger, mother figure, carefully cradling his baby, Mr Sharon. There were countless photographs of Saddam Hussein. A man with a long, thick, beard and a few words of English broke away from the demonstration to chastise me. 'We love the peace, but you, Bush, Blair, only want to kill all Muslims. You say all Muslims are terrorists. You are terrorists!' As the crowd passed down Omar Mukhtar Street, the main thoroughfare through the city, the balconies overhead filled with onlookers who had torn themselves away from the TV to shout slogans of support. The march ended at the Palestinian Legislative Council (PLC) building: its history a chronicle of the changing fates of those who have called themselves masters in Gaza. Built under the British Mandate, it was home to a Parliament granted limited powers under the Egyptians, then the residence of the hated Israeli military governor, then again a parliament building, but one which was rarely used as such. As the intifada wore on, the Palestinian Legislative Council met less and less often. About half the members from Gaza were refused permission to travel to the West Bank 'for security reasons'. The remainder often stayed behind out of solidarity. If there were a session in Ramallah, the Gaza members often sat glumly in the building here and watched it via video link. More frequently, as today, the PLC building was a venue for demonstrations. The people who marched had never been able to call the ground beneath their feet theirs. Today they came to support the Iraqis: another people, fellow Arabs, who were not being liberated, but losing their homeland to occupiers.

Dr Abdel Aziz Rantissi, one of the founders of Hamas, and at that time its most prominent spokesman, emerged from the crowd to speak. The domed roof of the PLC building rose behind him, the crowd stood in the yard between tall palm trees below. He wore, as usual, tinted glasses and an open-necked shirt.

His neatly-trimmed beard was greying. Sometimes, even when addressing a crowd, he spoke in calm and measured tones. Today, he did his best to stir them up: cursing the United States and Israel. Prophesying the direst consequences for the invaders, he called on the Iraqis to become suicide bombers: 'We believe that if the United States of America will occupy Iraq, then no choice, no option in front of Iraqis just to use martyrdom bombers, the same like here in Palestine,' he seethed, apparently having made not only the crowd but himself more angry during his speech.

The war in Iraq did not serve to persuade the Palestinians that the United States was serious about bringing freedom and democracy to the Middle East. It served as proof that the U.S. and Israel were fighting the same war: a 'war on terror' which was really a war on Arabs and Islam. When the pictures of Saddam Hussein's statue being hauled down in Baghdad were broadcast around the world a couple of weeks later, the pictures of the Iraqi dictator soon disappeared from butchers', barbers' and bakers' windows across the city. The back shelves of taxis were once again decorated with fake flowers and tissue boxes adorned with gold plastic. The 'solidarity tent', which the Arab Liberation Front had set up in the square in front of the PLC building, was empty. One reporter, going there for a reaction to the news from Baghdad, found only the tent's owner looking for unpaid rent. If the defeat was noted, it was not accepted. The friendly fat man in the supermarket told me confidently 'Saddam will return!' As the weeks went on, he seemed to become less sure. Saddam's return to power became first a matter which was open to question, and then dropped from the conversation altogether. His humiliation, and the occupation of Iraq, was still frequently referred to, and added to the list of wrongs which the Arabs had suffered at the hands of the United States, Israel, and their allies.

Saddam's millions may have dried up, or been frozen, but those who had been lucky enough to be rewarded before the war started could still benefit. Rateb Shabat was more talkative than the silent sheikh who had stolen away from the ceremony in Gaza City. A few days after President Bush had given his 'mission accomplished' speech, Rateb was working in his garden: supervising sons and nephews at work on the foundations of a new house. It was early summer, and the sandstorm-laden clouds of late March had gone. Beyond the wall of their garden, on the outskirts of the village of Beit Hanoun, scrubland stretched away to the fence which marked the northeastern corner of the Gaza Strip. Rateb and his family hadn't planned to move, but then his 18-year-old son had been killed in a gun battle with the Israeli Army. Now they were waiting for the Israelis to demolish their house as a punishment. To help pay for the new home, they had $10,000 from Saddam Hussein. To his family, Mohammed had been a quiet student. To his comrades in arms, he was a fellow member of the Al-Qassam brigades. Now he was a 'martyr'.

Rateb had two wives. His first wife bore him no children. He had married again and had nine children with his second wife. Now, after Mohammed's 'martyrdom', there were eight. It was only two months since Mohammed had been killed, but his parents showed no trace of grief. Rateb took me inside the concrete and corrugated iron house to show me the photographs of the funeral he had stored on his computer. The one of which he was most proud depicted him at the head of the procession waving a kalashnikov. 'I am proud that my son was a martyr, and I hope that one day too I will be a martyr,' he beamed. He took down a picture from the wall, taking it outside into the light where it could better be observed. In the centre, Mohammed, a puny youth with a wispy beard, stood holding a copy of the Koran, and an assault rifle. He was wearing combat dress and a green Hamas headband, bearing the Arabic text, 'There is no God but God and Mohammed is the prophet of God.' The photograph was mounted within the frame, and the mounting was decorated with a string of coloured plastic lights, like those on a Christmas tree. Mohammed's mother and father held the picture between them like a trophy. They could have been holding a university graduation photograph. 'Of course it would have been good if he had finished university, got married, and had a family,' Mohammed's mother conceded. 'But there is no greater honour than martyrdom.' They would always be able to hold their heads high as they walked through the shabby streets and scrubland of Beit Hanoun. Mohammed's 'martyrdom' guaranteed his family's social standing as long as they should live. Young men like Mohammed, with little or no military training, know that when they go on an 'operation' they face almost certain death. Unlike many warriors in the history of the world, these fighters pray for 'martyrdom' rather than for victory. Perhaps it is just a realistic acceptance of what they can expect when they stumble through the night, poorly armed and poorly trained, to face an enemy with first world weaponry.

For decades, until the Al-Aqsa *intifada*, the land around Beit Hanoun, beyond the house where Rateb and his wife now celebrated their son's 'martyrdom', was covered with orange groves. From the edge of the orchards, it was just a few kilometres to the Israeli town of Sderot, on a nearby hillside. The Izzedin Al-Qassam brigades used the fruit trees as cover while they set up their rocket launchers. Press reports of 'rocket attacks on Sderot' if literally true, were misleading. The Qassam rockets then were crude, home-made, devices which could not be aimed accurately. But they did cause panic when they landed in the hilltop town, and the Israeli Army responded. Tanks and troops occupied the town of Beit Hanoun for two months, closing the section of the main road which ran alongside it. The houses of militants and suspected militants were demolished, their ruins left as a warning of the penalty of angering the IDF. A house belonging to the Za'anin family, part of the same extended family as Ibrahim Za'anin of the Arab Liberation Front, was flattened by bulldozing and blasting. The family's 14 year-old son was killed by the invading troops. Perhaps the most serious long-term consequence of the invasion was the Army's uprooting of the orchards. The orange groves were gone. Splintered stumps and rotting fruit were all that remained of trees which had taken decades to reach maturity. The farmers struggled to salvage what they could for firewood. The landscape of the journey into Gaza City had changed forever. The new emptiness was a reminder of lost lives, and a monument to lost livelihoods – losses which even an unlikely eventual peace agreement could not reverse.

Before the intifada, Beit Hanoun was known as a place to go for relaxation. Away from the sandy streets of the town itself, past goats grazing on the sparse greenery sprung from seasonal rains, the orchards seemed a place of peace. The day after Ariel Sharon was re-elected as Israeli Prime Minister in January 2003, I had gone there to see what the people of Beit Hanoun made of the news. It was four months before the Israeli Army occupied the town and cut it off from the rest of the Gaza Strip. But the reprisals against the amateur artillery of the Al-Qassam brigades had already begun. The bridge crossing a wide ditch at the entrance to the town had been destroyed, and now lay in the shape of the ditch it was supposed to go over. The bridge had been knocked down to stop militants having easy access to their launching sites, but its absence meant that vans, cars, and carts were now forced to bump over the rough ground, down one side and up the other. The entrance to the orchard was through the town, and down a sandy lane. There was hardly anybody working there: just a man with a chainsaw slicing the uprooted tree trunks, and a guard. We walked up to the top of a rise from which we could see Sderot. Below us, in the dip which separated the two hilltops, a huge avenue had been cleared through the orchard. The open space meant there was no cover for fighters, and also that the farmers' crops were no more. In his hut near the entrance to the orchard, Ahmed, the guard, made tea. He brought out some of the things he had collected during his wanderings through the orange grove: the spent shells of heavy machine gun bullets fired from Apache attack helicopters. Ahmed was bitter, and pessimistic. 'We see nothing, no future, no hope, now that Sharon is back. Only more shooting and killing.'

Four months later many more of the orange trees around Beit Hanoun had gone, ripped from their roots by tanks and armoured bulldozers. Tanks blocked the main road from Gaza City to the Erez crossing. The constant passage of heavy armoured vehicles had torn up the paving stones of the central reservation. Its surface looked like pack ice, fractured by a mighty ship. Getting in and out of Gaza had become more and more difficult. With the main road blocked, all traffic was forced to take a detour through Beit Lahiya, a village on the other side of the main road from Beit Hanoun. The beginning and the end of the detour was along sandy tracks barely built for light cars, never mind trucks and overloaded shared taxis. In the late morning, when students returned from morning classes at the universities in Gaza City, the slope which led down to the main road was choked with vehicles: donkey carts, vans loaded with vegetables, minibuses. An Israeli tank sat twenty metres away, watching everyone who came and went. The 'Road Map' – the U.S. backed plan for peace between the Israelis and the Palestinians – had just been formally launched.

Since it had been presented to the two sides, life in this part of the Gaza Strip had actually got substantially worse, not better. One student, struggling to get home from her morning lectures, stopped to tell me what she thought. 'They say there is a *kharta tareeg*,' she began, using the Arabic for 'Road Map'. 'But look at this!' I asked her if she could begin again, saying 'road map' in English. She made as if to start, looked over her shoulder at the tank, and then burst into tears. Her college day had presumably ended with her wondering whether it would be safe to walk past the tank on her way back. Now she was too distressed to talk. A week or so later, the same tank fired at a car carrying two Swiss diplomats. They had stopped to check with the soldiers whether it was safe to proceed. Neither was hurt, but their experience showed the risks that the people of Beit Hanoun faced as they went about their daily business. While the Israeli troops stayed in Beit Hanoun, and along the main road, we foreigners got a tiny taste of what life was like for Palestinians: never knowing when or whether it would be safe to move. For a few weeks, our foreign passports counted for little. In any case, the soldiers struggled to see them from 20 metres away. I struggled to see their signals. Once I went past, mistakenly thinking that I had been given permission to continue on my way. When I returned, half an hour or so later, an apc drove up and blocked the road. I was given a lecture on waiting to be told I could move. No use arguing. They had the guns, and they would not hesitate to use them – misunderstanding or no misunderstanding. It was just a couple of weeks since James Miller, a British cameraman, had been shot dead by the Israeli Army in Rafah. Any sense I once had that being a reporter made me safe had gone.

One morning, about two weeks after the 'Road Map' was unveiled, the Israeli Army unexpectedly appeared to withdraw. Mahmoud Abbas – known locally by his honorific *Abu Mazen* – the first ever Palestinian Prime Minister, was new in his job. His post had been created as part of the 'Road Map', mainly because the United States would no longer talk to Yasser Arafat. Abu Mazen was due to come to visit Beit Hanoun to see the damage done in the first phase of the incursion. It was mid-May, but dark clouds hung over the northern Gaza Strip. The scorching sun had yet to claim its place in the summer sky. The main road out of Gaza City had been cleaned up for the Prime Minister's visit. An honour guard of Palestinian policemen, some proudly mounted on bran new motorcycles, had assembled at the junction where the road turned towards Beit Hanoun.

But there was something wrong. A couple of hundred metres away, people were sheltering behind the walls of their houses, from time to time peeking out from their hiding place. A short distance further on, along the road into Beit Hanoun, an Israeli tank sat among the tree stumps like a monstrous predator enjoying a snooze after gorging itself. An embarrassed deputy minister from the Palestinian Authority, who had himself come to welcome Abu Mazen, was left to hold a stand up news conference on the forecourt of a nearby petrol station.

He explained that the Israelis had refused to guarantee Abu Mazen's safety, and so the visit would not go ahead. The honour guard dispersed. The villagers gave up cowering behind their walls and went inside, out of sight. A few pedestrians made their way along past the petrol station, and tried to get to Beit Hanoun. Once it was clear that the Palestinians had accepted that the visit wouldn't go ahead, the Israeli tanks advanced further, moving to block the road altogether. A bulldozer began piling up earth and rubble to make the way impassable. Boys in their early and mid teens gathered to throw stones at the heavy, armoured, vehicles. The sky remained covered, but it was hot. Dust in the air and the throat made the overcast day worse. This non-event received little news coverage on the day it happened, but served to demonstrate to the people of Gaza that their Prime Minister was as powerless as they when faced with Israeli armour. Those few Palestinians who dared to believe that Abu Mazen's appointment might make a difference, might mark the start of a real peace process, probably smiled bitterly as they chided themselves for foolish optimism.

The Israelis ended their occupation of Beit Hanoun about a month later, during the period of a *hudna* – or temporary cease-fire – called by the Palestinian militant groups. There was great excitement when George W. Bush presided over a summit in the Jordanian resort of Aqaba. Very few people in Israel, the West Bank, or Gaza shared the optimism. The most they allowed themselves to do was enjoy the brief calm which followed, too wise to believe it would last. The road from Beit Hanoun to Gaza City had been torn up by tank tracks. It was a mixture of sand and holes. It remained that way for some months while the local authorities collected the funds, machinery, and manpower to put it back together. In this respect, the Israelis probably unwittingly aided some of the bombers they had come to destroy. The road's surface was an ideal place to conceal a home-made mine.

On October 15th 2003, a massive explosion hit an American diplomatic convoy which had just crossed into Gaza through Erez. Three security personnel were killed. A short while after the blast, their car lay on its roof at the side of the road. It was a silver-grey four-wheel drive vehicle. Its remains looked like the carcass of a metallic whale, harpooned by a bloodthirsty hunter so often that it was not just dead, but disfigured. The arrival of an Israeli tank, the aftermath of a helicopter missile strike, anything, in fact, which makes life in Gaza more dangerous, always draws a crowd. Males from the age of 10 upwards arrive like shoals of fish towards a source of food. If there are tanks and troops still in the area, they hide behind the flimsiest cover, out of the line of sight, occasionally darting out to shout insults or throw stones before being driven away by a burst of gunfire. The onlookers can be relied upon to turn up. The crowd at one incursion in Gaza City was even catered for by one gentleman selling flavoured ice. I had previously seen him plying his trade on the edge of crowds at demonstrations. The crowd today was aggressive. Young men swarmed around the car and the police who were trying to keep them away.

Some of them were bearded, lean, and hungry. Others seemed just to be the local disaffected youth who had come to watch the spectacle. It was chaos. The Palestinian police made no attempt to cordon off the area around the wreckage. They just engaged in the occasional shouting and shoving match with the bystanders. This degenerated into scuffles whenever the police tried to take one of the men away and were prevented from doing so by his clansmen and friends. Two Israeli tanks had taken up position a little further up the road, but well within shooting range.

The warmest part of the year had passed but the noon heat was still oppressive. Dust and sand thrown up by the explosion and the scuffles hung in the air. Into this anarchy drove another U.S. diplomatic vehicle, carrying American investigators. They went to look at the wreckage and the youths surged forward to encircle them. The crowd began chanting 'Allahu Akbar!' (God is greater) in celebration of what had happened. Then stones began to rain down, missing the sunglass-covered eyes of the Americans, and bouncing off the roof of their car. They made to leave. Suddenly, there was gunfire all around. No one was sure who was shooting. The crowd bent double and ran for cover. The bullets were the Palestinian police's first serious attempt at crowd control. As the police continued to fire, the Americans made their escape, a few final defiant rocks landing in the dust wake of their car. The jeering youths, their faces twisted from shouting, moved back and the crowd thinned out. An Israeli helicopter gunship clattered overhead, the tanks revved their engines. The grim show was over.

I had seen the Americans at Erez several times. They rushed through. Everyone else, including senior United Nations officials, seemed to have to wait. They were chummy with the soldiers and security guards on duty at the crossing. Only the bodyguards ever seemed to emerge from the four-wheel drive jeeps with blacked out windows. It was they who died in the explosion. The United States Embassy in Tel Aviv said that the diplomats in the convoy had been going to Gaza to interview candidates for scholarships to the United States. Whatever their business, the cars always seemed to pass in and out of Gaza at roughly the same time, and by the same route. They would have been an easy target for anyone who took the trouble to monitor their movements. After being driven away by the rocks of the mob, the Americans never returned to Gaza to continue their investigation. There were some meetings with Palestinian officials, but nothing seemed to come of them. The Palestinian Authority's 'Preventive Security' force tried to make some arrests in Jabalya refugee camp, but were driven back by gunfire from their quarry and their quarry's clan. Four months later, apparently frustrated at the lack of progress in finding those responsible, the U.S. Embassy offered a $5 million reward for information leading to the capture of those who had carried out the attack. A few days afterwards, without prior notice, the Palestinian Authority announced that it was putting four suspects on trial. It was as if they hoped to get the reward money. The trial was a farce and was soon abandoned. Even though Gaza's view of the U.S. administration was going from bad to worse throughout all this time, the people of the territory knew that whoever bombed the convoy had done further damage to the Palestinian cause. The P.A.'s failure to catch the culprits made matters even worse. The conspiracy theorists tried to explain it away. 'Do you think it's possible that the Israelis bombed the Americans to make the Palestinians look bad?' they asked in the streets and taxi ranks, knowing it wasn't, and that this had been an act not only of deadly violence, but also of gross stupidity.

The road which passed Beit Hanoun on its way to Erez was ripped up and then repaired more than once during the intifada. Destruction and damage recorded the deterioration in relations between the Israelis and the Palestinians. There were some, though, who tried to make things work. The Erez industrial estate at the northern edge of the Gaza Strip, near the crossing point, was one place where there was cooperation. To its supporters, it was an example of the two sides working together. To its critics: cheap Palestinian labour exploited by cynical Israelis. Whenever there was talk of a new initiative, a new attempt to start the peace process, an Israeli minister would go to visit the industrial estate – providing a photo opportunity for a dutiful press corps. The security for these visits was extremely tight. Once, my colleague Ian Druce and I were searched for 45 minutes after we arrived for a visit by the newly appointed Defence Minister, Shaul Mofaz. The search became even more thorough when they discovered that Ian was carrying some postcards showing Mandate era Palestine (i.e. the region before the creation of the State of Israel) which he had bought in Gaza. Once we were through, we waited in one of the factories for the minister to arrive. The company made sweets – unpleasantly sugary and sickly marshmallows covered in fake chocolate. They had put some out for the press to sample while they waited. They tasted as if they contained nothing natural, nothing which was not artificial. They looked good, but tasted bad. They were part of the spin; part of the photo opportunity.

The industrial estate was more interesting on a normal day. Reporters could only visit with a representative of the Army press office. On a wet morning in February, it was hard to see the place as a shining light of coexistence. The sand dunes, where the armoured column had gathered for its deadly advance into Jabalya almost twelve months before, stretched away beyond the barbed wire and concrete which marked the industrial zone's perimeter. Winter rain had soaked the edge of the desert. Here and there green shoots poked up through the sand. Major Assaf Librati pointed to the gate which, until recently, had been the Palestinian workers' entry and exit point. He was a slim, thoughtful, bespectacled man, probably in his early 30s. 'We call this place the island of sanity,' he said. 'It brings together the interests of both sides. We get the security and the Palestinians get the work and bring money.'

Two weeks before, that idea of mutually beneficial commerce had been dealt a harsh blow. Reem Al-Riyashi, a mother of two in her early twenties, had detonated explosives she was carrying at the entrance. She killed four Israelis as well as herself. Her exact motives remained obscure. Hamas leaflets said she was a dedicated 'martyr' who had decided that fighting the occupation was an even nobler calling than motherhood. Reports in the Israeli papers suggested that she had been committing adultery with a Hamas bomb maker. When the affair was discovered, she was forced to carry out the attack to save the family honour. This account was denounced in Gaza as Israeli propaganda, designed to destroy the honour of a martyr. It may have been the truth, or an Israeli attempt to deter future female suicide bombers by ensuring that too they would be suspected of marital infidelity. The wreckage of the x-ray machine which Reem Al-Riyashi had succeeded in avoiding stood abandoned to one side. Apparently she claimed to be disabled, and have a metal plate in her leg, when she set off the metal detector. She was allowed through, and then blew up.

'Hamas attack again and again these places,' the Major continued. 'With mortar shells, with suicide bombers like we saw last month, with shooting toward here, also shooting whenever the workers come. Some of them died because of Hamas attacks. They try to destroy this prototype to show that it's not going to work, and we try to show that it is possible.'

The winter rain battered down on the corrugated metal roof overhead. The desert became damper. The factories were at least working that day. Closures became more frequent and lengthy as the attacks on the industrial zone happened more and more often. On the shop floor of the Negba furniture factory, the call to prayer rang out from the radio, above the roar and whine of mechanical saws and sanding machines. The muezzin had a good voice, presumably why he was chosen for the radio rather than some of his less vocally gifted counterparts in the streets of the city and the alleys of the refugee camps. The workers didn't pause to pray. They toiled on, bent over their machines. One man sanded the rough edges of chair legs before they were sent on to become part of the whole. His bare fingers seemed to move dangerously close to the fast-moving belt of sandpaper. His skill kept them intact: confident in experience, wary of the poverty which would come with unemployment, the poverty which surrounded him in the refugee camp he left every morning to go to his job.

The workers privately complained of humiliating treatment. I had seen them on the other side of the gate, forced to wait in the sun while those in front of them went through the security screening. There was no shade. Some carried pieces of cardboard or newspapers which they used to keep the heat from beating down on their heads. . Those who were allowed to take up jobs there were strictly vetted, and every day, before they entered, they were forced to lift their shirts and roll up their trouser legs to show that they weren't carrying guns or explosives. Many found it humiliating, but they need the money. Once inside, they were glad of the work and the wages.

Major Librati called the industrial zone the 'island of sanity'. It felt more like another world. After more than three years of bitter bloodshed – let alone the century or more of suspicion, hatred, and sometimes open war – here were people who talked of the benefits of living and working together, of sharing the land. Valentine's Day had not long passed, and in the furniture company's main office, Israeli and Palestinian employees jokingly asked one another what they had bought their spouses. Upstairs, Haniyeh Majed, Negba's accountant, sat quietly in a tidy office. He was a calm man in his forties, wearing a freshly pressed shirt. Glasses gave him an air of seriousness. To look at him, he would have been an accountant anywhere in the world. Haniyeh had been unfortunate enough to be born in a region where even office-bound bookkeepers have a dangerous journey to work. It seemed unfair that it was so, but he was determined to be positive. There was a trace of resignation in his words, perhaps betraying a wish that things could be otherwise, mixed with an acceptance that they could not.

'This zone is owned by the Israeli government and the Israeli Army are responsible for security. Despite all of the difficulties which we face every day to go into this zone, we hope that this zone make a hope for the future because many Palestinians and Israelis work together and live together in this zone,' he said in the cautious tone a professional man who wanted to avoid controversy.

'How is it for you as a Palestinian working together with Israelis during the intifada?' I asked him. Major Librati was right when he said that Hamas wanted to undermine this rare example of cooperation between Israelis and Palestinians. What some saw as a desire to work with the Israelis, others condemned as a willingness to collaborate with the occupier. Haniyeh and his fellow workers were in a difficult position.

'I think I am as a Palestinian it is so normal to work with the Israelis,' Haniyeh replied, taking time over every word. 'Because both of us have to live here, and together. And we have to respect one the other, that's all.'

Negba's owner, Jamal Ajour, was a Palestinian from Gaza. Downstairs from Haniyeh's office, at the entrance to the workshop, he was chatting in Hebrew with Shlomi Levi. Mr Levi was a salesman offering glue to the furniture factory. The roar and whine of the machines behind drowned out their conversation, as if they were standing at the entrance to the lair of an angry wild beast, or trying to discuss daily business even as a huge storm headed towards them. The two men's working relationship went back 10 years, to a time of optimism when Mr Levi could just drive into Gaza and visit Mr. Ajour at his house. Now, in early 2004, making the journey in a car with yellow Israeli licence plates would not only have been illegal, but probably suicidal. Like Mr. Majoud the accountant, though, Mr Levi was determined to be hopeful. He was sad that sales were down: the security situation meant that Mr Ajour and his workforce could never be sure when they would actually be able to get to the factory. That meant that fewer customers were willing to rely on them to complete orders on time. That in turn meant that less furniture was being made, so there was less need for Mr Levi's glue.

'He want to work and to live and I want to work and to live,' Mr Levi said, gesturing at Mr Ajour, who stood next to him. Mr Levi was tall. His jet-black hair now grew only around the sides of his head, which was completely shaved. To any Palestinian, he was unmistakably Israeli. Mr Ajour was shorter, darker-skinned, and with the moustache of an Arab patriarch. To any Israeli, he was unmistakably Palestinian. Three years into the second *intifada*, it looked odd to see them standing so comfortably together. 'So there is no problem between us,' Mr Levi continued. 'It's difficult because he has a problem with workers who can't come from Gaza to here, and I have a problem that I can't sell him a lot of material because he doesn't have workers to do the work. But everything between this factory and me, it's ok.'

I asked him if there were any lessons in their cooperation for other Israelis and Palestinians. 'I can tell to all the men who working with Gaza and the West Bank – there is no problem between me and them,' he said, his frustration with the situation seemingly increased by having to explain it in his second language. 'He wants to work and I want to work. The most important thing that I think that if there will be peace it will be better, for him and for me.'

'Do you see that peace coming?' I asked.

'I hope so. I hope so. I don't see it coming but I hope so, because without hope nothing matters.'

Mr Ajour was more poetic. He hoped against experience that the day would come when the two sides could share the land they now fought over so bitterly. It must have broken his heart to see his business suffering so badly. He took me to his showroom, where beds, dining tables, chairs and wardrobes were all proudly displayed. Few seemed to be on the move. Rather they waited for the better times which Mr Levi didn't see coming.

'All of us – Americans, Israelis, Arabs, Europeans – came from this land. So we must live together on it,' he said, the philosopher among the furniture. 'We came from the land. We don't own the land, the land owns us.'

The conciliatory words of the furniture factory shop floor were rare. All around, the industrial zone was encircled with concrete and razor wire. The nearby Erez crossing was heavily fortified: gun emplacements, checkpoints, and barriers cried out saying 'we own the land'. From behind the walls of the industrial zone, I could see across the main road which led to Erez and into Beit Hanoun. The 'island of sanity', where Palestinians and Israelis worked happily together, couldn't have been more different from the dusty streets where they met mostly to kill each other. There, Israeli Army press releases crowed over the death of 'terrorists'; Palestinians glorified their 'martyrs'. The energy and determination which inspired Mr Ajour and Mr Levi to work together was nowhere to be found.

Two weeks before my visit to the industrial zone, I had spent another, different, day in Beit Hanoun. The road which had been ripped up by Israeli tanks, and blasted apart by a car bomb, was now long repaired. The Palestinian Authority found the money from somewhere, probably Brussels, and there was never any shortage of labour. With 70 per cent of the workforce – many of them skilled craftsmen – sitting idle, there was always a ready supply of eager workers. The road surface was now the finest in the whole of the Gaza Strip – the only place in the entire territory where a motorist could reach 100 kph, so they usually tried to. Taxi drivers wondered out loud when the Israeli tanks would tear up the road again, and reduce the race track to an obstacle course once more.

It was the beginning of February. The winter rains had threatened for a few days and then arrived spectacularly in the early hours of the morning before. Gazans were used to being roused from their sleep by explosions, but the thunder that came that night was louder than any bomb I heard in my entire time there. Rain battered against the windows so hard that it forced its way through the gap between window pane and wall. The heavy rain only falls for a few weeks a year, so the windows aren't necessarily built to keep it out. Puddles had spread across the bedroom floor by the time I woke. Now, 24 hours later, the air was clear. As the morning went on, it even became warm in the sunshine.

At 11, Fayed came to pick me up. We drove to the slaughterhouse in Beit Hanoun. On the way, the puddles – the rain which had fallen the previous night – were red with blood. It was Eid-al-Adha, the Muslim 'Feast of the Sacrifice'. The day commemorates God's sending a sheep to Abraham, or Ibrahim as the patriarch is known to the Islamic world, to be sacrificed in place of his son. The prophet Mohammed instructed Muslims who could afford it to remember the day by sacrificing an animal, and sharing the meat with the poor. Fayed had ordered a cow, but had apparently called the slaughterhouse a little late. 'The butcher was busy on the first day of the feast, so he asked me to come today,' he explained. Eid had actually begun the day before, the morning of the great storm. I had gone back to sleep after the thunder woke me in the middle of the night, only to wake again around 7am when a special call to prayer rang out across the city announcing the beginning of the feast.

In the slaughterhouse near Beit Hanoun, sheep, goats, and cows sat patiently in pens. A huge corrugated iron roof stretched overhead, but the structure was open at both ends. There was a strong smell of manure. Yehiya, Fayed's younger son, grimaced and covered his nose as soon as he got out of the car. The butchers were working in an area on the opposite the pens. The animals' throats were cut in a tiled area. The carcasses were butchered nearby, where mud, manure, and straw were tramped underfoot. There were piles of guts on the floor; blood on the walls; a cow's head on a tree stump which served as a chopping block. One of the butchers looked a bit like the man in the laundry near my house. Then I recognised Mohammed Aseel, the young lad who did the ironing there. It turned out that he was working with his uncle for a couple of days. The man who ran the laundry was the butcher's brother. The slaughtermen were covered in blood. The first one who shook my hand left behind a gory smear. They had knives hanging from their belts next to mobile phones and more knives stuck in the tops of their boots. I asked if I could take some pictures and the butchers, especially the younger ones, were keen to pose. One insisted on keeping a pair of bull's balls in his hand for the photo. Mohammed moved his fellow apprentices into position, all the while asking for a copy of the pictures once they were ready.

Fayed's cow was prepared for loading onto the back of a pick up truck. It was to be slaughtered and butchered outside his apartment block. Fayed and one of his neighbours, who also had a share in the beast, counted out wedges of shekels and Jordanian dinars. Any transaction in Jordanian dinars was an important, major, one. Shekels were the everyday currency for small purchases: taxi fares, vegetables, fruit, falafel. JD were the sign of a major investment, one that could raise your standing in your neighbourhood or refugee camp: land, property, livestock. We drove back to town at a crawl. The truck carrying the cow was old and slow. Fayed didn't want it to get lost. Outside Fayed's apartment block, a crowd soon began to gather. Ancient bearded sheikhs, their eyes dimmed by age, looked on with curious toddlers. Teenage boys from the wealthier families made ready with video cameras. An area of concrete paving was hosed down, and the truck backed up to it. The cow's throat was cut with a sharp knife. Blood gushed out, adding to that which was already caked on the butcher's jumper. The cow fell down, its legs jerking in the air. Its head rolled back and its tongue stuck out over its jaws. The corpse was dragged off the truck. Blood dripped through the sides of the truck onto the sand below. The carcass was swiftly and skilfully skinned, and then butchered. None of the kids, from toddlers upwards, seemed to show the slightest sign of revulsion. There was just one little girl who grimaced when she saw the severed head lying on the concrete paving. Even in the midst of the conflict, the Islamic rituals, the Palestinian rituals, were strictly observed. Even though 70 per cent of Gaza's workforce was unemployed, the butcher had too much work for a single day. Palestine might not exist, its people might not be free. Home was where Eid-al-Adha could be celebrated. The sacrifice served to remind people of their faith, one of the forces which bound them together.

That afternoon, the Israeli Prime Minister, Ariel Sharon, was quoted on the website of the Ha'aretz newspaper as saying that he had ordered a plan to be prepared for the evacuation of all the Jewish settlements in the Gaza Strip. 'In the future, there will be no Jews in Gaza,' Mr. Sharon told the paper. The man who had been behind the location of the settlements was planning remove them. Was he now ready to make sacrifices to ensure the future of his homeland? As time passed, and, after both cynicism and opposition, Israelis and Palestinians alike began to wonder if Mr. Sharon might be serious, one of the measures announced was the closure of the industrial zone. Major Librati's 'island of sanity' was on the list of sacrifices.

CHAPTER 3
'NO IDENTITY, NO NATION, NO COUNTRY'.

In the early mornings, the tunnel was stiflingly overcrowded. The sense of panic and despair increased as the sun rose and the start of the working day approached. If you did not make it to the other side before the gates closed for the day, the entire effort expended in getting up, then travelling to the crossing, would be wasted – along with the money you had spent to get there. In February 2004, Mohammed Al-Sheikh, a father of six in his early forties, was crushed to death. Approaching the gate in the early morning, after hours trapped in the throng, Mr. Al-Sheikh stumbled, and fell underfoot. He was taken to the open air at the Israeli side of the crossing, but it was too late. His life could not be saved. At that time, the Erez crossing between the Gaza Strip and Israel had frequently been closed completely. Everyone within sight of the gate had been desperate to get through it before it shut, taking away the chance of a day's pay.

The tunnel was a covered walkway, perhaps five metres wide and three metres high. The only light came through gaps below the roof, well above head height. Although the men who crowded in here every morning were going to earn money which would feed their families, there was a feeling of foreboding in the place. The floor and walls which boxed in these human cattle felt like the entrance to a slaughterhouse. From the Palestinian side, the tunnel stretched ahead straight for perhaps 150 metres. Then it curved to the right. For the person walking across, Gaza disappeared from view. To anyone watching them go, they had gone. Around the bend, the corridor continued, leading to metal gates and turnstiles. Here, there was razor wire even on the walls, closing off the only gap which allowed in daylight, and casting a shadow. The wire was hung with jackets and plastic bags, presumably discarded by their owners as they rushed to be allowed through, or thrown aside for fear that they might slow progress through the metal detectors. The torn clothes and tattered wrappings hung overhead, like rubbish on the beach that had been washed above the usual high water mark. It was as if, one day, the human tide had surged in so strongly that those at the front had been tossed into the air, hung on the wire for a while, and then been dragged back into the current. The next wave had pushed them forward, finally through the gate, and to the other side.

The Erez crossing was dangerous. It was a trip to make quickly, and to avoid completely after dark, when Israeli soldiers might shoot at shadows, or Palestinian fighters might emerge from the murk to start a gunbattle. It was always safer to be away from there before sunset. The Palestinian labourers going to jobs in Israel didn't have the choice. If they didn't live in the north of the territory, their journey to get to work at 6 or 7 in the morning began before midnight. They had to allow enough time to cross the Israeli checkpoints which controlled the roads as they made their way northwards, drawn towards wages like fish swimming through dark water towards a light. In the Rafah refugee camp, at the southern edge of the Gaza Strip, they sometimes had to listen, then look out their doors, to see how much shooting there was. It was a bit like someone in Manchester peering out to check if it was raining. Here, though, it was a matter of death not damp and discomfort. Half asleep, they crammed into shared taxis and battered minibuses which took them to Erez. The working day was long, hard, and humiliating. The rewards, by Gaza standards, made it just about worth it. The men – most of them working as bricklayers, plasterers, painters, and agricultural labourers – earned 200 shekels a day (about £30). It was about three times what they could expect to make doing similar work in Gaza, if any such work could be found. From Autumn 2002 onwards, the Palestinian ministry of Labour put the unemployment rate in the Gaza Strip at around 60 or 70 per cent. It was hard to get a permit to go into Israel. In September 2000, there were more than 100,000 Palestinians allowed to enter Israel to work. Two years later, only around 12,000 Gazans had permits. That number remained just about steady as the third year of uprising turned into a fourth. Unmarried men, and those under 35 years old, were barred altogether. These were the criteria the Israelis used to judge who had the most to lose, who was likely to be the most hot-headed. Some days, when the Israelis decided that the security situation demanded it, no one was allowed though at all. The Israelis used to say that they would like to let more people through, and make the passage easier. While the threat of suicide bombers remained, that never happened. During Jewish holidays, following attacks inside Israel or on Israeli targets in Gaza, or whenever the Israelis believed such a strike was imminent, Gaza was closed off completely. More people were trapped, left with nothing to do except think about how much they hated it.

Even when the system was functioning as it was supposed to, there were often long delays at Erez. Everyone came as early as he could, not wanting to miss the chance to cross. 'Since the intifada, we leave our homes at midnight, we come here, then sleep for two, three, or four hours at the checkpoint. The situation is very difficult,' one builder, whom I agreed to call Ahmed, told me. No one wanted his real name used. A permit was hard enough to come by. Criticizing the system might lead you to lose it. 'You can only get a permit if you have no relatives who are martyrs, and you've never been in prison,' Ahmed went on. 'You have to satisfy all the security requirements.' When the crossing opened, the workers poured into the tunnel that led to the other side. Foreigners and 'VIP's' were allowed to cross in the open air. Sometimes it made you feel exposed, but at least you could breathe. The security precautions, the searches to stop suicide bombers, made the labourers' daily journey almost unbearable. 'We suffer a lot on our way to work,' said one of Ahmed's fellow builders. 'Here at the checkpoint, the Israelis sometimes beat us with sticks. It's all really tough. I think the lives of dogs, of animals, are better than ours.'

As the intifada continued, life became more and more difficult for the workers, both those crossing Erez, and their counterparts in the nearby industrial estate, where Palestinians worked in factories owned mostly by Israelis. Both the industrial zone and the Israeli positions at Erez were attacked more and more. On Sunday 8th June 2003 it was already very hot by 9am. It always was in the summer. But when dawn broke around 5am, it had been cooler. Condensation had formed during the night. At first light, it rose from the ground as a thick mist. Sunday is the beginning of the working week in Israel, and the labourers were already heading towards the crossing.

The night before, there had been a meeting at the Palestinian Legislative Council building in Gaza City. All the Palestinian political groups had been represented. It was the latest in a series of meetings between the 'National and Islamic Groups' – the whole Palestinian political spectrum from the most secular to the most devout. From a news point of view, these talks were usually desperately dull. They took place every so often, with the aim of reaching a common view on what the Palestinians' approach to the conflict with Israel should be. The public statements at the end always seemed to be the same, irrespective of which group gave them. 'We had a very useful dialogue with our Palestinian brothers, and we have agreed to meet again'. Nothing of substance ever seemed to be resolved. When the meetings in Gaza failed to produce any progress, they even had similar rounds of talks in Cairo, hosted by the Egyptian government. They proved to be equally fruitless. This hot Saturday night in Gaza was different. There was a great deal of speculation at the time that the armed Palestinian groups might be ready to call a cease-fire. The 'Road Map' had been formally launched in Aqaba just a few days before. President Bush had come to the Middle East for the grand occasion. Eventually, it amounted to nothing more than a photo opportunity. Then, though, some people seemed to think it could be the start of a process which really could bring an end to the conflict.

All eyes were on the Palestinian militant groups. Their representatives trooped up the steps of the PLC building, then moved out of the hot, humid, June night into the air-conditioned cool of the room where the meeting was to take place. A couple of hours later, they filed out again: the usual quotes; no decision taken on the cease-fire. One thing, though, felt out of the ordinary.

None of the senior figures seemed to be present; none of the people who might have had the authority to take the decision to suspend the armed campaign. Abdel Aziz Rantissi of Hamas was the most notable absentee. When the Road Map had first been unveiled a few weeks before, I had gone to talk to him for a response. He was critical of anyone who seemed ready to talk to the Israelis while the occupation continued. That included the Palestinian Authority.

'They are really leading the situation in the wrong way,' he had said in his usual measured tones, his English not faultless, but clear. 'We are under occupation, and we must resist that occupation. We will not surrender in front of the aggression of the Israelis. And we said many times, as long as there is occupation, there will be resistance.' So where was Dr. Rantissi that night? Why wasn't he at this apparently important meeting? He was hard to track down, but Hamada, one of the BBC's local producers in Gaza, eventually got through to him on the telephone, and asked him about the results of the meeting.

'Which meeting?' Dr. Rantissi asked in his turn. 'There were two.'

His reply explained the apparently junior rank of the delegates attending the publicly announced talks. The whole thing had appeared rather staged. One of the members of Yasser Arafat's Fateh movement had thrown his arm around the shoulders of a Hamas man, and jokingly announced to the press corps: 'So you see, Hamas and Fateh are together!' They hadn't seemed serious, and there was no reason for them to be so. The real meeting was taking place somewhere far less public than the PLC building. Its results would be announced not with empty words that had been said countless times before, but with deeds that marked a new departure, and a new stage in the Palestinians' military campaign against Israel.

As the workers moved towards Erez in the mist of that summer morning, three fighters, disguised in Israeli uniforms, hid among them. When they were close to the industrial zone, they moved out of the crowd. They opened fire on an Israeli Army position at the edge of the industrial zone. Four soldiers were killed. The attackers themselves were all gunned down when the Israelis returned fire. That would have been expected by those who sent them, as well as by the men themselves. Their last words had perhaps been a whispered prayer, designed to speed their way to heaven as martyrs. They would not have expected to come back from their mission alive. The Palestinians were rarely able to kill so many Israeli soldiers in one go. They had been able to do so by working together in an unprecedented way. The three fighters were all from different factions: one each from Hamas' Al-Qassam brigades; Islamic Jihad's Al-Quds (Jerusalem) brigades; and Fateh's Al-Aqsa Martyrs' Brigades. If the political groups had been unable to agree on a unified approach to dealing with Israel, the military wings had managed to overcome their differences. From then on, 'joint operations' became more and more common. The realisation that the political and diplomatic process had simply stopped working spread further and further, and the militants began to cooperate more and more. Abdel Aziz

Rantissi had presumably been at the meeting where this unprecedented attack was given the green light. As the Road Map, and talk of a cease-fire, gathered momentum, he became increasingly outspoken in his dissent, and predictions of failure. More and more, he preached criticism of Israel and rejection of any peace process while Israeli troops remained on the West Bank and in Gaza. Two days after the attack on the army post at Erez, the Israeli Air Force made their first attempt on his life. He survived. In April 2004, with Dr Rantissi the leader of Hamas in the Gaza Strip, they tried again. Abdel Aziz Rantissi met the martyr's death which he had previously urged so many others to strive for.

The cease-fire did eventually come, but it was short lived. The violence returned, and the hatred grew stronger than ever. The Erez Crossing, and the industrial zone – Major Librati's 'island of sanity', became an ever more frequent target. The response, usually in the form of military escalation, generally ensured that more Gazans lost what little faith they had in negotiation – and some of them, young men especially, became more willing to take up arms. The labourers were caught in the middle: mistreated by Israeli soldiers nervous of potential killers hiding among them; penniless when the crossing was closed off completely. There was once a story, told only in the Israeli press, that the workers had detected a suicide bomber in their midst. They reportedly beat him and drove him away. This may have been true, or it may just have been Israeli propaganda. It is not hard to imagine that the workers wished only to be able to travel to their jobs in peace. To think that way, though, was one thing. Actively to intervene against someone engaged in the intifada was quite another, and could be interpreted as collaborating with the occupiers: potentially a very dangerous thing to do. Collaborators risked severe punishment from the militants, and brought shame on their family.

Every day, or at least every day when they were able to leave, at around four o'clock in the afternoon, the workers trudged back through the tunnel. Their faces were weary; their clothes splashed with paint and plaster. Returning, as leaving, they were subjected to the most thorough checks. They had to lift their shirts and roll up their trouser legs before they were searched. Being forced to display bare flesh was particularly humiliating for conservative Muslims. A photograph in a Palestinian newspaper once showed a man, perhaps in his forties, stripped naked and forced to sit in a stress position in an open area in front of a check point. 'If this is my father, tomorrow I am a suicide bomber,' commented an onlooker who saw me staring at the picture. The workers were not allowed to bring so much as a lunchbox or a packet of cigarettes, in case it might somehow be a bomb or other weapon. Instead, they had to buy food and drink in Israel, at higher prices which further cut into their wages. The only light entering the tunnel was sunshine filled with dust. The men seemed too tired to lift their feet, too tired even to talk. Almost no one smiled. The only sound was that of shuffling feet, thousands and thousands of them. The noise echoed off the concrete walls. Some were burdened not only with the fatigue of backbreaking work, but also with ancient television sets, obsolete hairdryers, and battered children's bicycles: gifts from Israeli employers, or bargains snapped up to give the family a treat. There seemed little sense of release, of relief that the working day was over. This was not a happy or contented workforce. 'The Israelis look at us in a very bad way. They look at us as a people who have no identity, who have no nation, who have no country,' Ahmed reflected on his return one day. 'We all think a lot about stopping. But there's nothing else to do. Everybody here has 11 or twelve kids at home. There's no food, there's no money to support them. What else is there to do except go to Israel and work?'

These men were among the few Palestinians who had any contact with Israelis other than soldiers. Where these relations might have been cordial, if sometimes uneasy, before the intifada, now there seemed to be nothing but hostility. 'The attitude of the Israelis makes it very hard for us Palestinians now,' said one man, his eyelids drooping after a punishingly long day. 'It's changed from before. Now I can't even take a bus in Israel. I can't go to a shop to buy something. If I want to go to the shop, there's a security guard, who'll kick us out. If we do manage to get in, they put the prices up because we're Arabs. And inside Israel, they write 'Death to Arabs' on the walls, and slogans asking the government to kick the Arabs to Jordan because this isn't their country.' Impotent rage burned through the exhaustion. This man had accepted being treated as a second-class citizen and suspected terrorist because he needed to feed his family. He also had to put up with being told that there he had no right to live between the River Jordan and the Mediterranean: the land which, probably for centuries, his family had thought of as theirs.

'These days, we spend four hours at the checkpoint on our way to work, and three hours on our way back. It's harder than the work itself!' He was warming to his subject, beginning to show the anger he bottled up when he was near the Israeli soldiers, the people he really wanted to see his anger. 'If I could find a job here which paid 30 shekels a day, I'd stop working in Israel,' he concluded, and trudged off.

Salem Haboush lost his work permit for Israel in October 2000, just after the intifada started. At that point, he'd been building houses in Israel for 20 years, helping to build the Jewish homeland. In the autumn of 2002, following a security review, he got his work permit back. After three days, he'd had enough. The October afternoon was warm, as was the breeze blowing up Omar Mukhtar Street from the sea. The sky threatened early rain, but it never came. Bits of paper and shreds of plastic tumbled along the pavement, driven by the wind. There was sand in the air, and it settled in piles next to the kerb. Salem sat behind a desk in the shop where he worked, the door before him open onto the street. The shop sold satellite dishes. Even though the popularity of Arab TV channels such as Al Jazeera and Al Arabiya was booming, business was not. A satellite dish was a luxury and few people had any money. After giving up his 200 shekels a day, Salem now earned about a third of that. That was on a good day. Often, he said, his wages were about thirty shekels, or £5. He said he would think about going back to work in Israel if things returned to the way they were before the intifada, but there was little prospect of that. His words echoed Ahmed's feeling that the Israelis looked down on the Palestinians as people who had neither nation, nor country. 'I tried working there for three days. I saw a lot of strange things there. I lived in fear there. Even if I asked somebody the time, he would look at me and just ignore me. They look at us as if we come from another planet.' Salem said that he had been driven away by the treatment, the working conditions, which so angered those who continued to go. 'All these things prevent me from going to Israel. I prefer to die here rather than to work and to be insulted like that.' Salem's pride had come to mean more to him than money, even when he was on the breadline. 'A man's dignity is above everything in life,' he said. 'If you earn a lot of money and don't have dignity then you are nothing. You don't make a lot of money here. The most you can do is provide food for the family. We can manage with that.' So there he sat, poor and underemployed, barely able to provide for his children. The afternoon passed in a haze of chat and cigarette smoke as a succession of idle friends, and even the occasional customer, dropped into the shop.

At around the same time, the workers at Erez, Salem's former companions, were emerging from the tunnel. In an open area where taxis and minibuses waited to take them on the final leg of their journey home. Drivers touted for trade – crying out the names of the towns and villages they were bound for. Fast food stands – at Gaza prices – tempted the hungry labourers. Second hand electrical items, old shoes, and cheap clothes, were sold from an improvised market on the car park. The workers faced the decision whether to sell what they had been given by their employers, and put more food on the table, or take that old TV set home and see their children's faces light up as it struggled into life. Some didn't get that far. 'A lot of people you see here at the checkpoint just go and get their sandwiches and sleep here for a few hours before going back to work,' Ahmed's companion explained, pointing round the car park. 'It's an insult. I don't want to stop going though, because it's the only way I can make money.' Those who did have the time and energy to get back to see their families, even for a few hours, squeezed themselves into the waiting vehicles and headed south: past the entrance to the industrial zone, past the destroyed orchards outside Beit Hanoun, over the road repaired after Israeli incursion and land mine explosion. Then the road rises slightly. At the crest of the hill, you see Gaza City.

Each landmark on the road to Gaza City is a reminder of the conflict. The morning after an Israeli raid, the kerb stones at the edge of the road and along the central reservation would be cracked where tanks had crushed them. Palestinian workers speedily set about the task of repairing the power lines which had been torn down as tanks crashed into electricity poles. They knew they may have to do the same thing again in a few days, or weeks, time. The road surface was scored with the marks of tank tracks. These were just small, superficial, signs of the greater destruction which the night had brought: hints that people had been terrified by the armoured column which had shaken them awake. Some of them had opened their eyes for the last time.

Jabalya itself, where I spent that night in an Israeli armoured personnel carrier, stretched away from the road: down and to the right from the hilltop a short distance from Erez. Its ramshackle breeze-block buildings with their flat roofs were a patchwork of dull colours – grey, sand coloured, or shades in between. In the flat light of midday, there was little contrast. Crammed together in their thousands, they reached all the way to the beginnings of the city itself. Welded on, but even if the join seemed almost invisible, it was there. Jabalya's people came as fugitives. After more than fifty years, in their hearts, they still saw it as a temporary home, even if secretly, in their heads, they knew it had already become permanent. The crowded conurbation which built up after 1948 stood as a monument to the conflict which created the state of Israel, and thousands of refugees. Gaza City was not huge. It had a population of about 400,000. From the top of the hill, though, you saw just how packed with people it and Jabalya, clinging to its outskirts, had become. In the centre of the city, the buildings were taller. In the gentle sunsets of spring and autumn, the outlines of minarets and apartment blocks stood out in the dusty glow. Beyond them lay the sea – one of the limits of the Gaza Strip, and even harder to move than the fences which marked the other boundaries. Down the hill, the route into the city led through the back streets. The turn off the main road was next to a falafel shop which was destroyed by the Israeli Army. The Israelis often destroyed workshops which they alleged had been making weapons. The reason for blowing up a takeaway was harder to fathom.

That operation began on a Thursday in September 2002, shortly before midnight. Apache attack helicopters clattered overhead. The people of Gaza pronounce the word fearfully: fearfully, and unusually. There is no 'p' in the Arabic alphabet, so 'Apaches' became 'Abaches'. There was nothing to see. The Apaches hunted without lights. If you fear that you might be their quarry, this must add to the sense of powerlessness. Helicopter gunships, heavy machine gun fire, explosions, and you could not know where your attacker was. Even the noise was deceptive. It was not clear whence it came. For most of the people of Gaza, though, who have no involvement with armed groups, this was something which could happen any night. That night, the battle continued until about three in the morning. Three Israeli soldiers were wounded. Their tank drove over an 'explosive device'. It was probably hidden in one of the piles of sand which sprang up in the streets on the outskirts of Gaza City whenever an Israeli raid seems likely. Many of them supposedly had explosives inside them: removed during the day when the swarms of bored kids might accidently set them off; then replaced at night, switched on at bedtime like a suburban householder's burglar alarm. That night, the Israeli Army killed two people: a man with learning difficulties, who apparently ignored warnings to get off the street, and a 25 year old off-duty policewoman. The mentally ill, or the hard of hearing, were especially at risk during Israeli Army operations. Even if the troops bothered to shout before they shot, a warning was no use if it was not understood.

The next morning, after the tanks had gone, people went out to look at the damage. On the opposite side of the main road from the ruin of the falafel shop, a sandy track led to a destroyed house. About twenty men sat along, then across, the road on plastic chairs. A younger lad brought tea. This was where the man with learning difficulties had been killed. The men were his relatives. They had gathered to talk of the night before, and to mourn. The man had gone outside to see what the noise was, they said. When he didn't respond to the soldiers' warnings to go back in, they shot him dead. The ground floor of the house had been smashed up by a tank. Just next to the track were the remains of a workshop. Could it have been a weapons factory? Possibly. It was away from the town itself, down the sandy road: a quiet place where you could get on with your work without fear of interruption. An ostrich poked about in the scrub – a bizarre remnant of more hopeful times when farming the creatures promised prosperity. All the targets seemed to have been well identified beforehand. The intelligence must have been pretty good – even if did appear on this occasion to have led to a falafel shop being blown up.

Now the ruins of the shop marked the turning off the main road. The back streets were narrow and crowded. The shop fronts were open onto the road. The owners perched on plastic chairs in the doorway when business was slow. Some shops were full; packed to the ceilings with goods. Stacks of washing powder, sweet fizzy drinks, fruit, and vegetables reached to the door. Other stores were pitifully empty. The owners were not making enough money to buy much new stock. Falafel were cooked in basins of bubbling oil and sold to passers-by. Washing machines were repaired or offered for sale. Car engines were stripped apart and reassembled by men in grimy vests. The oily workshops spilled out onto the pavement. There were children everywhere. The average married couple in Gaza then had more than six offspring. Fishermen, for some reason, had a reputation for having even bigger families than the average – and, at least for the few I met, this seemed to be true (one said he had fourteen children). With little room at home, and gardens or even small yards the preserve of the rich, the street was their playground. Frequent speed bumps stopped motorists from going too fast. In any case, that was usually impossible. There were too many other obstacles: donkey carts, concrete mixers, delivery trucks. The games the kids could play in spaces like this are limited, but there was lots of running and shouting. In the summer school holidays, kites were a favourite. Any wide street or waste ground open enough to admit a breeze became a launching spot. During the school summer holidays, the power cables which criss-crossed the alleys of the refugee camps were decorated with the wrecks of kites which had become entangled and did not make it back to earth.

The walls were covered with graffiti; nearly all of it political, anti-Israeli. The slogans praised the fighters and bombers of Hamas and Islamic Jihad, promising death to the Zionists, and an advance on Jerusalem. They illustrated with spray-painted pictures. The Dome of the Rock, the place on Temple Mount (to the Jews), or the Noble Sanctuary (to the Muslims), from where Muslims believe the Prophet Mohammed ascended into heaven was a favourite subject, as was the nearby Al-Aqsa mosque. They were often shown with two kalashnikov assault rifles crossed above them. Palestine as it was during the British Mandate had a sword handle growing out of its northern border so it comes to resemble a scimitar. Israeli tanks were shown exploding in violent flames of orange and red. The soldiers thrown into the air by the force of the blast had streaks of blood running from their wounds. Some had been decapitated. 'Martyrs' were remembered in posters tacked to electricity poles or pasted to walls. Those from wealthier families were portrayed in specially commissioned pictures which dominate the streets. The Al-Aqsa mosque, which the younger of them can never have seen, stands in the background. Like the city walls of Jerusalem, in a renaissance painting of a scene from the Bible, it was out of proportion – its size chosen to reflect its importance more than its actual appearance. It was the iconography of *intifada*, the rhetoric of the longed-for return. Everyday life may have been filled with more pressing thoughts of how to survive until tomorrow, but when it was time to dream, this was the pictorial language of the dreamer.

One Saturday in February 2004 – an exceptionally cold day by Gaza standards – there was a prize giving ceremony at a Boys' school in the Jabalya refugee camp. The winter wind whipped at the faces of the pupils as they sat obediently on the cold tarmac of the playground, the only place big enough for the whole school to gather, listening to speeches and music. The ceremony had been put off from two days before because the pupils had been on strike. They had walked out of school in protest at an Israeli incursion which had left blood in the streets, and houses in ruins. One teenager sang unaccompanied. His thin voice was distorted by the imperfect public address system, and by the wind. His message was clear.

> Fadi, a child of the revolution, says to his teacher:
> 'Teacher, Teacher, where is my homeland?
> I heard them talking about our absent homeland
> About our fields, our olive trees,
> And a land which has been stolen by the occupier.
> All my friends tell the story of the homeland
> Which they dream of
> And which isn't here.'
>
> 'One day you will grow up Fadi.
> You will be in the land of Palestine

And you will see the soldiers of righteousness together,
Surrounding the Al-Aqsa mosque.
Don't be sad. The way is long.
And if today you are far away, tomorrow you will return.
Your land, my son, is calling you
And it will see you as a hero.
And one night in Jerusalem,
The Occupier will be threatened with the greatest fire.'

'I don't understand the meaning of exile
Or the reason for exile.
But I have a list of names written in my heart:
Jerusalem, Haifa, Acco.
My home has a beach, and a port.'

'Well done, Fadi.
You gave your listeners a good lesson
In how to love your homeland.'

The boys applauded as the song came to an end, and the singer took his place back among his classmates. 14-year-old Mohammed Saleh was the school's star pupil. He conducted the ceremony, introducing singers, speakers, and prayers. Mohammed spoke of the *intifada*. It was, he said, on every child's tongue, part of a history of Palestine perfumed with blood and tears. Mohammed had grown up in Jabalya, in its suffocatingly overcrowded streets and alleys. He had seven brothers, and four sisters. Jabalya was the only home they had ever known. Away from the crowd, Mohammed was quietly spoken. His dream of return, his vision of a homeland he had never seen, was just as strong as that of Fadi, the pupil in the song seeking to know the story of his people's exile. Mohammed had been born more than 40 years after his family had fled from the war which created the State of Israel. The time that had passed was not important. The sense of injustice was still vivid. It had not faded during four decades when new generations had been born away from the land. The story was told and retold, a story which everyone knew, but had to hear again and again so that it could not possibly, ever, be forgotten. In any case, the story was unfinished. The noise of battle could still be heard from time to time in the narrow alleys of the shantytown. During the prize giving, a group of boys had prepared to perform the 'dabka' a traditional Palestinian dance. Just before they started, the headmaster had told them to stand down. Three days earlier, the Israeli Army had moved into a neighbouring district. Some of the men of Jabalya had raced across the city to join the fight against the invading force, and been killed. It was not appropriate to dance while the 'martyrs' were still being mourned.

Mohammed excelled at most subjects. He hated his education being interrupted by the conflict.

'When the Israeli soldiers go in the camp and shoot fires and rockets I can't learn. Sometimes I feel scared…yes scared,' he replied, when I asked him about life at school.

Very few of the Gaza Strip's 800,000 or so officially registered refugees would say they were from the territory. It was not 'home'; it was just a place where they happened to be living at that moment. Mohammed was no exception. His home was not in Gaza, but in Brer, a village in pre-Israel Palestine which was now little more than a few ruins. It no longer existed, except in the past, and, in the dreams of the refugees, in the future.

'My family come from Brer' he explained. 'The Israeli occupation get out them in 1948. And they come here, to Jabalya.'

'The Israeli occupation'. For Mohammed, and the hundred thousand or so other refugees who lived in Jabalya, 1948 was not the founding of the State of Israel, but of 'the occupation'. The 1967 war, when Israel captured the West Bank and Gaza, was just another stage. What followed was what most of the world knew as 'the occupation'. To Mohammed, it was all the same. The existence of a Jewish State on part of historical Palestine was all an 'occupation', whether or not international lawyers called it that, or Israel. 'Now I want to get back to Brer,' Mohammed said softly. 'It has farms and it will be beautiful,' he said, recounting faithfully the bedtime story he had heard all his life.

'Why do you think about Brer as your home? You have lived in Jabalya all your life.'

'Brer is my country. My grandfather and grandmother was living there. And my father and my mother tell me that Brer is a very nice country. Yes I live in Jabalya, but I hope I will return to Brer. I hope we will get out the Israeli soldiers and return to Brer.'

Ahmed Abdullah, the school's headmaster, listened, not interrupting to correct Mohammed when his English faltered. Mr Abdullah, a short, balding man with the smile of a good schoolmaster, and bright eyes, embodied the history of the Palestinian refugees. He had come to Gaza aged just eight months. 57 when we spoke then, he was as old as the exile. His story read like the plot of an opera. It would probably be dismissed as unbelievable were it to be submitted as a proposal for a Hollywood movie. I often spoke to Mr Abdullah during my stay in Gaza. We usually met at his school, after morning lessons. Once, during the summer holidays, I went to see him at his home in the refugee camp. The room where we sat was sparsely furnished. The only decoration on the wall was a portrait of Gamal Abdel Nasser, the former Egyptian president, and ardent Arab nationalist. The day of the prize-giving, once the ceremony was over, Mr. Abdullah invited me to talk in his office. The winter wind moaned round the corners of the school building, muffling of the call to prayer from the many mosques in the refugee camp.

In 1948, Mr Abdullah's family left Al-Lighat, just twelve miles from Jabalya, heading for anywhere they thought they might escape the fighting, until it was safe to return. More than half a century later, that time had not come. For his siblings – five sisters, and two brothers – it never would. As Mr Abdullah told it, they had all been killed by a bomb thrown as they fled. Only he and his mother survived. She ended up in an Egyptian military hospital; he was left for dead. His uncles prepared to bury him with the corpses of his siblings. Over the years Mr Abdullah had pieced together his story, a very personal story, and yet one in which countless Gazans would recognize part of their own: part of the chronicle of Al-Nakba, the catastrophe, as Palestinians call their 1948 flight from the land they still long for. Then, as an infant, Mr Abdullah was nearly among the dead. His uncles dug two graves: one for the girls, and one for the boys. His sisters were buried. His two brothers lay in the grave in which he was to join them, his body placed on top of those of his two dead brothers. They were already in the grave. One of his uncles, picking him up to put him in the ground, touched a wound, causing him to cry out. Suddenly, they came under fire. The uncles ran for their lives, leaving him where he lay. The injured infant was abandoned, and only saved by a neighbour who had been late to flee.

'I spent that night in the wild: an injured child, bleeding, wild animals, cold at night. I was lucky that I didn't die,' Mr Abdullah recounted, describing the events almost as if his eight-month-old memory had retained them into his sixth decade. 'Next morning, an old woman was still in the village. She left the village, and she had to come that way. She found me, and she thought that I was dropped from a family or something, because all the people were in a hurry. She took me and began to ask until people recognised who I am. She gave me to my aunt.'

Mr Abdullah was eventually rescued and reunited with his mother, who was lying severely injured in hospital. The two lived by collecting dung and selling it as fertiliser. They slept under trees or next to walls until the United Nations Agency for Palestinian Refugees, UNRWA, offered help. For the first time, Mr Abdullah and his mother had shelter. 'They gave us a tent. It was a small tent, ok, but for me it was a castle, because this is the only home I know.' Exceptionally severe winter weather hit the warm shores of the Mediterranean. Never before and never since in Mr Abdullah's memory, but that year it snowed. The little boy's 'castle' may have saved the life he had already so nearly lost as a baby. The cold was severe enough to kill some of the older, the younger, and the weaker refugees – living as they were under canvas and without heat. Slowly, as the years passed, Mr Abdullah and his mother became more comfortable. In 1953, the more permanent 'camp' began to take shape, and they got a house: one room, 9 metres square, with no toilet, running water, or electricity, but 'better than the tent'. Jabalya grew –still called a refugee camp, because the 100,000 or so people who lived there then, in 2004, were still classed as refugees (there numbers are even greater now), but the tents were gone. Over the years, they were replaced by concrete and breezeblock houses with corrugated iron roofs. It came to resemble a poor suburb of any Arab city. There were streets, some sandy, some with hard surfaces, shops, and a market. Its 'camp' status was given away by the blue United Nations signs which hung over clinics, food warehouses, and schools. As Jabalya grew, and became established, so did Mr Abdullah. At the end of the 1960s, he qualified as a teacher. He ran, rejoicing, home with his first pay packet. Mr. Abdullah's mother had worked as a cleaner and a washerwoman to support herself and her son. But the money they had lacked throughout his childhood and adolescence was not really what she had missed. 'She looked at the money this way and that way,' Mr Abdullah mimed his mother's disdain as he told the story, pulling a face as he looked at an imaginary bundle of notes in his empty hand, 'and she threw it away.' The headmaster in his fifties seemed briefly to turn back into the newly qualified teacher in his twenties as he recalled his mother's words: 'Ahmed. I brought you up for one reason. You are the only son I have left and I want you to bring me my family back again.'

Mr Abdullah understood that his duty was to marry and have a family to replace that which he had his mother had lost. 'I got lucky,' he said. Married a little earlier than he had planned, but with no regret: five daughters and three sons – the same family as his mother had had, and seen die – were eventually born to him and his wife. He stopped short of naming his own offspring after his siblings, but his mother could not resist. 'She insisted to call them with her sons' and daughters' names, so everyone has two names in our house.'

Mr Abdullah may have been able to give his mother a new family, the same number of boys and girls. He was never able to help the elderly lady back home. She died in 2001, never having seen again the land she and her son had longed for during more than half a century in a refugee camp. 'When she died I lost some of my roots,' Mr Abdullah sighed. The generation which actually remembers what it was like before 1948 was rapidly disappearing, worn out by old age, hardship, and disappointment. 'But I feel strong that she left me something. She left me how to live, and how to love. How to live until the day we are back again at the grave of her husband, which we left in our original village, the grave of her sons and daughters, our land. She left me the title deeds. This is the only thing she left me. This is her treasure, just the title deeds. She told me: "Maybe these are papers, but they mean a lot to me." I have told my sons how they are dear for me, and to take care of them.'

The counterparts of the 'treasure' which Mr Abdullah's mother left at her death –the British Mandate title deeds to land long lost – are carefully guarded in countless corners of refugee houses which were only intended as temporary shelters, but which had now become long-term residences to successive generations. The numbers of people who really knew this fabled homeland of Palestine, who could still recall the scent of the soil and the citrus trees, might be dwindling, but the idea of 'the homeland which they dream of' was still indelibly strong. The decades since 1948 had not weakened it. Mr Abdullah at 57, and Mohammed his pupil at 14, sensed it equally: an article of faith. Faith, too, was what sustained the hope that one day the dream would come true. Mr Abdullah felt that it was getting harder to stop the younger generation from hating.

'I never lost trust in God, and keep loving people. What happened to me, I don't like it to happen to anyone, even to my enemy. I bring up my children to forgive, and my students at school how to forgive. But unfortunately sometimes my plan is damaged because of the behaviour of the Israeli occupation. I cannot tell the students how to forget, because they live it. They live in a refugee camp, in a small house, small alleys. They have nothing to live for. They see the killing every day: the snipers, the tanks, the helicopters, they live in a violent atmosphere. They come to school; they find their classmate is shot dead. They see their father shot. I cannot teach them how to forget.'

Even if the dream of the homeland remained strong, daily reality of life in the camps meant that the Palestinians were not foolish dreamers. Mr Abdullah saw little around that encouraged him, and the pupils he taught, to expect much from the future. 'In the early 50s all the people were living in hope, that maybe next month, next year, we will return. They would never think that they would be refugees for more than 50 years. If they thought they would be a refugee for more than 50 years, they'd prefer to die in their homeland. They are already dead now. Even they are living but they are already dead because they have nothing. In the early 50s, all the people were living in poverty, but they had hope to live for. Now they began to lose the hope. This is dangerous. We'd like to give them the hope. They cannot see a light at the end of the tunnel. I have been a teacher since 1969. The students of that time were more serious because education was one, or maybe the first way to change the way of life. Maybe a person who was well educated would get a good job, and he can look after the family. Education was the most important thing for the family. Parents were serious about education. The students themselves were more serious than the students nowadays. The students see many of their brothers and sisters have been educated, graduated from university, and have no jobs. Some of them are not as interested as before, because they have no jobs, because we have no plan.'

The sense of lack of purpose, of lack of vision for the future, was only compensated for by the dream of return. Mr. Abdullah had lived in Gaza all his life, more than five decades. It was still not the place he was 'from'. 'Jabalya is not a home. It's a place where I live. I'm living here waiting a day to return back. It is not a home. My homeland is inside Israel now. It is not Jabalya. Jabalya is a place where I live. Temporary, until I return back to my homeland to live permanently. That was my homeland. I never forget it. Never. We teach our students, we teach our own sons, not to. This is something we cannot forget.'

Israel's overwhelming military might, and the unswerving support of the United States, would not change this, according to Mr Abdullah and countless thousands of others. This was a part of the world where the events described in the Bible and the Koran were as significant as if they had happened only yesterday – a world view which was hard for outsiders from less devout societies to understand. With that sense of the eternal, came a more patient view of time. Half a century sometimes seemed so little. 'The Israelis themselves said, that three thousand years ago, they were here,' Mr Abdullah argued, becoming more passionate. 'You'd like me to forget after 50 years? I cannot. That's one thing. Secondly, my father, my grandfather, more than three thousand years living on this land. They want me to leave this for a Jew coming from United States, from Russia, just because he's Jewish he has the right to live here? What about me?'

Time had not diminished the sense of injustice. No plan, or process, for peace between the Israelis and the Palestinians, had yet dared to tackle the question of refugees. It had always been one of the issues which was deferred, until 'final status' negotiations. For hundreds of thousands of Palestinians, it was – and still is – a basic question, not a matter to be put off until some distant future round of talks. Mahmoud Abbas' failure to mention refugees at the Aqaba summit in June 2003 meant that, in Gaza, the 'Road Map' was declared dead even as its birth was triumphantly announced. Mr Abdullah believed emphatically that the question would have to be tackled. Without giving Palestinians the freedom to move, there could never be a meaningful peace. For many in Gaza, a peace agreement had to include the idea of a chance to return home. Otherwise, it would be worthless; not a real peace at all.

'They cannot escape from our problem. The international community, they cannot escape. They cannot hide themselves. This is a problem. They must think of a solution to this problem. Maybe they will say: "Ok. The right of return. You Palestinians can forget the right of return, it is not the reality. Where will the Israelis go? This is their home." This is not the reality. The reality is that the Palestinian was forced to leave his country.'

While uncompromising in his view that the injustice suffered by the Palestinians will have to be corrected, Mr Abdullah seemed more moderate than some of his fellow refugees when it came to the idea of sharing the land. He said he would like to live with the Jewish people in one state – but seemed unsure whether that might be possible. 'This is not my problem. This is the problem of the Israelis. They want a Jewish state. For me, we would like to live in a secular state: no difference between Jewish, Christian, and Muslem. This land is wide enough for both of us if we make our hearts wide enough for love.'

Mohammed heard it from his parents, Mr Abdullah from his mother, and he has told the story to his children. The homeland of the dream was a wide land perhaps because the refugees lived in such intolerably cramped conditions, and were not even allowed in and out. Farms and open spaces, an idealized pastoral existence, were the defining characteristics of the homeland. 'We spent all our life in tragedy, and in sadness, unhappy. The only happy days for the Palestinians were before 1948, so this was the bedtime story from our parents to us, and from us to our children, and from our children to their children. The only thing we would like to give our children is the hope that, please, one day we could have a farm, and animals, cows, we could go everywhere…we were able to go to Jaffa, and to Jerusalem, on a donkey, on a camel, with no passport, and no one would stop you.'

Mr Abdullah worried that the disaffection and cynicism he saw among the coming generations would lead only to deeper hatred and disaster. The dream of farms, open spaces, and livestock seemed to be becoming more and more remote; so remote that they no longer provided the comfort they once did. He spoke of this hopelessness as a dangerous alarm which, were it not responded too, could turn all Palestinians into suicide bombers. It was as if dealing with the day to day reality were bad enough, but just about bearable while return remained a dream. Without the dream, and the hope it bore, the threat of a more terrible, merciless, destructiveness was summoned up. In the meantime, the prospect of the dream's coming true diminished daily. Mr Abdullah seemed to understand this, even if he did not wish to admit the fact. 'It is not the reality to bring a Jew from Russia (a picture of the checkpoint sentry and his 'Arabs are animals,' warning flashed through my mind here), and from Ethiopia, to live in my home and say, "That's ok, this is the reality." This thing happened by force!' It may not have been right, but it was certainly real – just as, it seemed then, the only realistic prospect which the refugees had of redress might be that one day they would receive some money in recognition of their loss of land, and home. Mr Abdullah was firm that compensation would not do. This was a tenet of the Palestinian refugee's beliefs, which no one dared to contradict, at least in public. In 2003, a polling organization in the West Bank published a survey suggesting that a large percentage of refugees would settle for compensation. The organization's offices were attacked by a furious crowd. As an infant, Mr Abdullah was nearly buried in the land which he held so dear. After living in a refugee camp for more than half a century, he hoped to be laid to rest in the earth he still longed for. He explained that he had written in his will that, should he die and be buried in Gaza, he had asked his heirs to take his body 'home' to pre-1948 Palestine if and when that were possible. The wind continued to howl round the empty playground outside. The cold made thoughts of home, and the warmth and comfort associated with it, seem all the more inviting. Outside the school gates, the market was beginning to close. The shouts of the stallholders faded away as they packed up fruit and vegetables, loading their wares onto donkey carts. Live chickens that had remained unsold continued to squabble in their cages, unaware, perhaps, that they had at least managed to live another day. Further down the street, a gang of workers toiled to finish a new road surface, repairing and improving the one which had been ripped up in a recent Israeli raid. Washing hung from balconies and window ledges overhead. Gangs of kids took turns to try to leap onto passing trucks and horse carts and steal a ride. Jabalya, and its population, continued to grow. But the two were joined only by necessity, and the refugee camp could never inspire the same feelings of love and longing reserved for the homeland of which Fadi, the schoolboy in the song, dreamt – and which wasn't there.

CHAPTER 4
LIFE DESIRE, AND DEATH DESIRE

The panic spread through the crowd as through a shoal of startled fish. It was just after 8am. The pupils of the first school of the day had begun lessons just an hour before. Now they fled in terror, streaming out through the school gates and into the playground and street beyond. Two Apache helicopter gunships hovered overhead – high above rifle range – while their crews checked to see if they had hit their target. They had. Ibrahim Al-Maqadma, a founding member of Hamas, had been killed along with his bodyguards as they drove across Gaza City to the Islamic University, where Dr. Al-Maqadma was due to deliver a lecture.

It was a Saturday morning in March 2003, at the time of year when the weather could suddenly change from spring sunshine to winter storms. Just as unpredictably, the streets could change from a shopping area to a bomb site. The boys who had just run away would be missing a day's lessons, as would their counterparts who were due to start school around midday (overcrowding in the schools in Gaza was so great that each building was actually home to two schools. One set of lessons began at around 7am, the second at about noon). The attack had been sudden; a surprise even when air strikes were frequent. The helicopters had fired from high in the sky. The first anyone had heard were the explosions themselves: four of them, coming from the centre of the city. Only afterwards was there a clatter of the rotor blades as the Apaches lowered themselves closer to the roof tops, hovering like monstrous mechanical wasps deciding whether they needed to sting again to kill. The people in the streets looked skywards in fear. Anyone wearing uniform, especially the police officers guarding the nearby Egyptian consulate, made for a place they could hide, then nervously peered upwards. These were the times when the streets of Gaza felt more unsafe than ever. The suddenness with which Ibrahim Al-Maqadma's life had been cut short were a reminder to everyone of their own mortality. If one day you might be killed so quickly, what was the point of staying at school? This was what Mr Abdullah had in mind when he spoke of his pupils, a couple of miles away in Jabalya, beginning to lose hope. A good education would not make you immune to a missile. The children raced out of school, then, when they thought that the helicopters had gone, gathered in the street to shout defiance and set fire to tyres. The smoke rose in noxious clouds from behind the schoolyard wall. Later in the day, all that remained were jet black scorch marks, ash, and thin strips of metal from the tyres, the bones of a weaker creature that the crowd, unable to confront its real enemy, had attacked from frustration. The only lessons learned at school that day had already been taught ad nauseam: how to fear, and how to hate.

Hamas described Ibrahim Al-Maqadma as a political leader. Abdel-Aziz Rantissi warned that the assassination of would 'launch a new stage of war against the Jews'. At the funeral, mourners vowed that the Al-Qassam brigades would cut off 100 heads in revenge. The Israeli defence minister, Shaul Mofaz, said that Dr Al-Maqadma, who had at different times been imprisoned by both Israel and the Palestinian Authority, was an 'arch-terrorist'. The missiles hit his car as it moved through the Sheikh Radwan district of the city, a Hamas stronghold. Israel's ability to do this, the accurate human intelligence they had obviously received, indicated their total military superiority. Hamas' threats of revenge were often wishful thinking. This time was different. The killing of Ibrahim Al-Maqadma did lead to a new tactic in Hamas' suicide bombing campaign against Israel, but that would not become clear until a year after his death, long after the new tactic had been used against the softest of civilian targets.

The schoolchildren who ran from the helicopters which killed Ibrahim Al-Maqadma got home safely. 14-year-old Tareq Al-Soussi's body ended up in the branches of a tree on one of Gaza's main streets. He had been on his way home from Saturday morning school too – a year after the attack on Dr. Al Maqadma, and in the middle of a new wave of strikes. Israeli jets suddenly tore through the sky above Gaza City. The noise was so loud that no one heard the approach of the helicopters. This was a tactic which the Israelis increasingly used as the intifada continued. Their targets had worked out that their mobile phones were often what gave their position away. They would leap from the vehicles they were travelling in, hurling their cellphones in the opposite direction, as soon as they thought they were being followed. Israeli warplanes frequently flew low over Gaza City. That in itself was not necessarily cause for alarm. By sending Apache helicopters at the same time, the Israelis seized back the element of surprise.

The front of the white Peugeot 205 was completely wrecked. Aziz Al-Shami from Islamic Jihad was the target. He lost a leg in the attack and died later in hospital. His car had been hit in Al-Wahda street, one of the three which ran east to west from the centre of Gaza City towards the sea. The BBC office was just a few hundred metres away. The back half of the car was strangely intact. There was even still glass in the back windscreen. The front was a mess of twisted metal, electric wires, and engine parts. As always, a crowd had gathered.

There was a bigger than usual security force presence. The car had been passing a court building when it was hit. The policemen guarding the court had rushed out. The street was wet with water from the fire fighters' hoses. The puddles immediately next to the car were red with Aziz Al-Shami's blood. Policemen and civilians alike stood and stared. There was nothing else to be done. A low-loader soon arrived to take away the wreckage so that the street could be opened once more. The noise of the engine roused the crowd from its reverie. Policemen shoved the civilians out of the way. The civilians shuffled off to the side of the road. The moment of death was over. Gaza tore itself away from the contemplation of mortality, and went back to what passed for normality until the next time.

As the second intifada continued, the leaders of the Palestinian militant groups lived in greater and greater fear. Publicly, when they were not in hiding, they scoffed at the threat they lived under. In any case, they could hardly have said they were afraid to die when 'martyrdom' was considered such a noble calling, and one which they exhorted others to seek. Abdel Aziz Rantissi was assassinated in April 2004, about a month after I had left Gaza. In the time I was there, he was my main source from Hamas. I interviewed him both at his house in Gaza City, and in a secret location when he was in hiding after the Israeli attempt on his life in June 2003. I was always nervous about going to interview anyone from Hamas. As the only foreign correspondent based in Gaza, I felt especially vulnerable. To begin with, there was the chance that the Israeli air force might just choose to strike when you were with the Hamas man. This was highly unlikely, but not impossible. Just before I arrived in Gaza, the Israelis had killed the leader of the Al-Qassam brigades, Saleh Shehada, his bodyguard, and fifteen civilians who happened to be in the same apartment block. 'Collateral damage' was not something which seemed to trouble Israel too much if the attack hit the intended target. Apart from the risk of a direct strike, there was the fear that something might happen to your interviewee in the 24 or 48 hours following your meeting with him. Then the risk was that you would be suspected of passing information on his whereabouts to the Israelis. Collaborators in Gaza were usually punished with death: either after a trial, or before. It made little difference. Being caught passing information to Israel, especially information which leads to the death of a militant leader, was an unforgivable crime.

The Hamas leaders seemed to live in an atmosphere of death: their statements glorified the deaths of 'martyrs', their own deaths at the hands of the Israelis could happen at any moment. Going to interview Abdel Aziz Rantissi about the 'Road Map' in April 2003, I passed the spot where, a month before, Ibrahim Al-Maqadma's car had been blown apart. The scorch marks were still visible on the road. Less than two months later, I would see a similar sight after Dr. Rantissi himself had survived a missile strike. A year later, he himself would be dead.

It was a few weeks before the 'Road Map' was presented to the Israelis and the Palestinians. Hamas had dismissed it out of hand, deciding that there was nothing in it for them. Their strategy was probably based on the fact that, despite diplomatic expressions of optimism in Washington and the capitals of Europe, few people in the region it was supposed to bring peace to gave it any chance of success. Once it failed, Hamas would be in the position of being able to say 'Well, we never thought it would work anyway.' In any case, the 'Road Map' talked about 'two states, Israel and Palestine'. Hamas' main policy was the destruction of Israel, and the creation of a single, Islamic state of Palestine.

The taxi stopped outside the modest house in one of the modest areas of Gaza City. I was never sure if Dr. Rantissi actually lived there. He always seemed to appear from another part of the building once we had been shown into a room and asked to wait. One of his sons opened the gate to the house. We went up two flights of stairs, past one tiny room which housed two huge armed men: Rantissi's bodyguards. The night before, the Israelis had moved into the Rafah refugee camp in search of suspected militants. Six Palestinians, including a fifteen-year-old boy, and one Israeli soldier, had been killed in the battle which followed. This, for Dr. Rantissi and Hamas, was what the new U.S.-backed peace plan was all about. 'It's the real application of the Road Map: killing, massacres, demolishing of houses, destroying Palestinian life. It's the real Road Map of the U.S,' he began, earnestly.

The room we were sitting in was plainly furnished, and sparsely decorated. Dr. Rantissi may have been one of the most important political figures in the Gaza Strip, but he didn't live like an Arab chieftain. Many members of the Palestinian Authority (PA) and the security forces lived in opulent mansions and villas, the fruits, ordinary people observed, of corruption. As the intifada continued, Hamas' popularity grew. People responded to their implacable opposition to Israel, and respected the fact that Hamas leaders lived as they did, in simple houses in the refugee camps and poorer quarters of the city.

'We believe that it's just a security plan,' he went on, 'through which the U.S. and Israel aiming to make pressure upon the Palestinians to make them surrender, in front of the aggression and oppression of Israelis, to accept the Israeli solutions for the Palestinian issue.'

Dr. Rantissi might occasionally smile when talking to his aides before an interview began. Once his remarks were being recorded, he was deadly serious. He leant forward slightly, and his glare was challenging, even through the tinted glasses he always wore. His clothes were simple, yet smart. Whenever we met, he was wearing an open-necked shirt and a jacket. These, though, were not the tailored European garments which graced the backs of some officials in the PA. Dr. Rantissi's clothes looked as if they had been bought in Gaza, in places where anyone with a few shekels might be able to afford a shirt or a pair of trousers. His analysis of the situation in the conflict was the same as that heard in taxi rank and takeaway food shop: the Israelis just weren't serious about peace. I put it to him that the Israelis were talking about scaling down their troop presence in the occupied territories, in order to give the 'Road Map' a chance. He returned to the deaths of the night before:

'While the Israelis spoke about these things, they invaded Rafah, and they massacred our people there. So all the time they are saying something, and doing another thing. I believe that they are going to escalate their aggression to our people, and we haven't another choice just to continue resistance, and struggle. Without that, we will not reach or achieve any goal.'

I pointed out to him that one of the main conditions that the PA was supposed to satisfy as part of its obligations under the road map was an end to Palestinian violence. Here again, in Dr. Rantissi's view, the Israelis were to blame:

'I believe that the thing which should be ended first is the cause of violence. The cause of violence is the occupation. Without ending the occupation, nothing will be changed. We are fighting for independence, for freedom, and we will continue our fighting, to get our freedom for us, and for our land, and for our holy places. Without that, we will continue resistance. So they should say to the occupiers, you should end your occupation.'

When the 'Road Map' was launched at the end of April, the Palestinian Prime Minister, Mahmoud Abbas (better known to both Palestinians and Israelis by his honourific, Abu Mazen) held a series of meetings with Hamas and Islamic Jihad to try to persuade them to call a truce. They responded, eventually, by breaking off negotiations. They continued to meet each other, and representatives of the other Palestinian groups. The attack on the guard post at Erez, in which 4 soldiers were killed, was plotted and carried out. Two days later, the Israelis tried to kill Abdel Aziz Rantissi.

It was Tuesday the 10th June, a still summer morning. The stillness made the city bake as the sun climbed higher into the clear Middle Eastern summer sky. I had been supposed to go to Deir-el-Balah, in the centre of the Gaza Strip, where the United Nations were handing over new houses to refugees who had been made homeless again in the conflict. I did not go. I was ill during the night. Stomach upsets – from mild food poisoning or dehydration – were the only illness I suffered while I was in Gaza. That morning I was feeling particularly ill. At 11am, I was still in bed, the curtains drawn against the hot, bright, sunlight.

There was a loud explosion a few streets away – at the edge of the Beach refugee camp, I guessed. I could see brown smoke rising up. Could it have been a 'work accident' (the euphemism employed when home-made bombs or landmines went off prematurely, while they were being assembled)? Then there was another blast, then another, six or seven in all. There was now white smoke rising from behind the houses too. Then the helicopters passed overhead as I stood on the bedroom balcony – two of them, looking mean as ever, seeing if they had hit their target. They had, but not hard enough. Dr. Rantissi survived the attack, but two of his bodyguards, and two civilians, didn't. He spent the rest of the day making the most of it: giving interviews from his hospital bed. He told the Arab satellite channel Al-Jazeera that he wished he had been a 'martyr'. He told us that this was the 'real road map'. His fellow Hamas leader, Mahmoud Zahar, gave a memorable quote: 'Now it is eye for an eye, nose for a nose, politician for politician.' What he meant to suggest, I suppose, was that Hamas now felt that Israeli politicians were legitimate targets for revenge attacks. I didn't really understand where the phrase 'nose for a nose' came from. 'In the Bible,' I said to Fayed, 'they talk about "an eye for an eye, and a tooth for a tooth"'. Fayed said it was the same phrase in the Koran. The origin of 'nose for a nose' remained obscure.

That week the Israelis attacked Gaza relentlessly. The day after the assassination attempt on Dr. Rantissi, there was a suicide bomb in Jaffa Street in Jerusalem which killed 17 people. Less than half an hour after the news broke, there were helicopters in the air over Gaza. They fired at a car passing the market in Shijaia in the east of the city. It was the early evening, a busy time for shopping. The strike killed two Hamas members and at least five civilians. That night, around 12, there were helicopters over Gaza again. Suddenly, a missile streaked across the city sky – a line of white light illuminating the clouds which had built up since sunset. There was a flash and then a loud bang as it hit its target. More white light tore through the deep blue of the Middle Eastern summer night. At the centre of the explosion, there was a carload of Palestinian fighters apparently on their way to attack the Jewish settlement of Netzarim, south of Gaza City.

As before the war in Iraq, it became clear with hindsight that the Israelis probably were expecting the Palestinian militant groups to declare a truce, even if it was only a temporary one. The militants themselves were already planning to make such a declaration. In the meantime, in the first half of June 2003, both sides tried to step up their strikes, to show that they remained serious. Later that month, the *hudna* – an Arabic word for a temporary truce was called. A *hudna* is always called for a clearly defined period, but it can last for a long time, even for generations. If, however, the side which called it feels that its enemy is not keeping to the law or the spirit of the *hudna*, it can immediately break it off.

The 'Road Map' had been launched. President Bush himself had come to the Middle East and spoken alongside Ariel Sharon, Mahmoud Abbas, and King Abdullah, who hosted the summit in the Jordanian Red Sea resort of Aqaba. The four sponsors of the 'Road Map': the United States, The European Union, Russia, and the United Nations, all spoke optimistically about the future, about 'two states, Israel and Palestine, living side by side in peace and security.'

This optimism was almost nowhere to be found among the people who were actually fighting each other, or who were victims of the conflict. Looking at the situation from the Gaza Strip, there seemed to be two main reasons why the truce was called in the summer of 2003. Firstly, both sides were exhausted. The intifada had been going on for almost three years, and there was absolutely no sign of it ending. Secondly, the United States had decided to get involved. This involvement soon turned out to be short lived, once the administration realised how difficult the problem was to solve, and once the occupation of Iraq turned into a disaster in election year. Neither side wanted to be blamed by Washington for the collapse of the 'Road Map'. Everybody on both sides, from Prime Minister to peasant, seemed to expect the process to fail. Some wanted it to, and worked towards that end. The root causes of the conflict were still there, and the 'Road Map' had no new ideas as to how they might be addressed. If the fighting stopped for a few weeks, it was only to let the two sides, two exhausted street brawlers, one bigger and stronger, the other determined not to give in, catch their breath. When they'd done that, they would soon begin trading blows again.

Abdel Aziz Rantissi went into hiding after surviving the assassination attempt on June 10th. After the *hudna* was declared, he returned to public life. The Israelis never formally agreed to the *hudna*, but they did scale down the number of strikes they carried out. The Israeli military and security establishment continued to make it clear that they believed the Palestinian armed groups were just using the truce to rearm, and reserved the right to strike at the 'infrastructure of terror' as they saw fit. The PA, for their part, were supposed to confront the militant groups, or 'dismantle the terrorist infrastructure' as the 'Road Map' put it. There seemed almost no chance that this would happen. A couple of weeks into the *hudna*, some television pictures emerged apparently showing members of the Palestinian Preventive Security Force in Gaza searching cars and confiscating weapons. Everyone in the Strip immediately dismissed the footage as having been staged for the cameras. For the Preventive Security to act in earnest would simply have been too provocative. Even if the comparative calm brought welcome respite from the conflict, the time had not yet come when ordinary people would accept the sight of militants being disarmed. The PA fought shy of 'dismantling the terrorist infrastructure,' fearing that individual disputes could escalate into armed clashes, and wider conflict. Hamas were fully aware of that.

I went to see Dr. Rantissi a few days after these pictures had been aired. He still had a bandage on his leg from the assassination attempt. His son, Ahmed, was in a wheelchair as a result of his injuries. He had been in the car with his father when the missile hit. Dr Rantissi restated Hamas' opposition to the 'Road Map': 'a security plan for occupiers and settlers', as he now called it. He knew very well that Hamas' weapons caches were safe.

'I believe that PA will not take this measure against Hamas and other Palestinian organizations because it will be very difficult for them to do that,' he explained, half-stating, half-threatening. 'Palestinians will not accept that, and we in Hamas will not give up our weapons, and so it will make the situation inside Gaza and West Bank very difficult.'

It was a hot day. Even inside the dark interior of the house, the heat was unpleasant. The humming of the fan that stirred the still air (no PA office air conditioning here) was an uncomfortable echo of an attack helicopter – a reminder of the dangers of being in the same place as a Hamas leader, even during a *hudna*. Dr. Rantissi made it clear that the truce was unlikely to last. Hamas and the other militant groups had placed conditions on their cease-fire: most notably, the release of Palestinians detained by Israel. That morning, before coming to meet Rantissi, I had watched a demonstration by prisoners' sons. This was the kind of summer holiday activity which Hamas arranged for schoolchildren. Boys of primary school age gathered in the square outside the PLC building, then marched up Omar Mukhtar street carrying pictures of fathers, uncles, and older brothers, many of whom had been neither tried nor convicted, but were instead simply held for unspecified 'security reasons'. The release of these men was a condition of the cease-fire, but even then it seemed impossible to believe that it would be satisfied. The Israelis never agreed to these terms, but they did set some prisoners free at the beginning of August. The fact that there was no real pact between the two sides was ignored by the 'Road Map's sponsors, in public at least. Nobody wanted to admit that the emperor had no clothes. Dr. Rantissi, like the Israeli Generals who were sure his organization was simply planning more attacks, was blunt. He doubted that the *hudna* would last. Less than a month after it had been declared, he was already blaming the Israelis for its inevitable collapse. The Israelis would blame Hamas. Quite simply, neither side had the will to make the plan work. 'If it will last for the three months it will be very strange,' Dr. Rantissi said, the fan clattering in the background.

There were a series of incidents on both sides. Then, on August 19th, a bus bombing in Jerusalem killed 23 people, including several children. Hamas said they did it. The *hudna* was over. Dr. Rantissi and his fellow leaders went into hiding, while Israeli did its best to kill them. Mahmoud Zahar, originator of the 'nose for a nose' threat, narrowly escaped death when his house was bombed. His son was killed. Abdel Aziz Rantissi disappeared again from public view, rightly fearing for his life. I did not meet him again until one evening in November. I got a phone call from a Palestinian contact. I was driving, so I stopped the car to talk. It soon became clear that this was not a conversation to have on the phone. Of course, I never knew who might be listening to my telephone conversations but there was enough anecdotal evidence to suggest that several different organizations might be interested, especially when there was news on the whereabouts of a fugitive Hamas leader. I just had to assume that nothing said on the telephone – mobile or landline – remained private. I told my contact I didn't want to discuss anything to do with 'a senior Hamas leader' on the phone, so we arranged to meet in the street.

'I'm not sure I should go,' I said. 'I will be the only foreigner there, and if anything happens to Dr. Rantissi in the next few days, I will definitely be suspected of passing information to the Israelis. It could be very dangerous for me. If they attack his car after he leaves the interview, I may be blamed for telling them where he was.'

'Don't worry,' said my contact. 'It's not as if we asked for this interview. We have been invited. If we had tried to find him, and then something happened to him, it might be different. But Hamas are asking us.'

We went to the building where the meeting was due to take place.

Rantissi emerged from the murk of a November night in Gaza like a conger eel, poking its head out of a dark hole in the ocean depths and flashing its teeth. He seemed to be in good health. The bandage he had worn following the assassination attempt in the summer had gone, and their seemed to be no sign of permanent physical damage. The Palestinian reporters fawned over him as if he were a hero: perhaps this was just Arab tradition of honouring those older and more senior than oneself, perhaps it was genuine, deeply felt admiration. He lapped it up. There was something of a celebratory atmosphere, even a few jokes. One reporter, whose agency had wrongly sent out a newsflash in the summer saying that Dr. Rantissi had been killed in the missile strike, was told by one of the Hamas aides that while all the other correspondents would get an interview, he wouldn't. How, the aide asked, could Dr. Rantissi give an interview to an agency which said he was dead?

Until the *hudna*, there had existed on both sides a hope that there might be calmer times ahead, even if they weren't going to last. That had gone. There was just the merest hint of compromise that night, one which passed unnoticed in the increasingly violent and desperate atmosphere of the conflict, one which the Israelis would simply not have thought worth taking at face value in any case.

'We are looking for something else, avoiding civilians, but we are not looking to accept *hudna* because we are under Israeli aggression, demolishing of houses, destruction of Palestinian life, assassinations, massacres,' he said, referring to the death toll from recent Israeli military incursions into the Gaza Strip. 'Under this kind of aggression, we can't speak about *hudna*. We are ready to speak about avoiding civilians.'

This seemed like a half hearted gesture, one which Dr. Rantissi knew would be ignored by the Israelis. Perhaps he already also knew that they would not allow him to live much longer. He used the interview to condemn a peace process which his movement had never been a part of, and which they saw only as a means of further oppressing the Palestinians.

'I believe that the terrorists are the Israelis who occupied our land, and are killing our people. And so they should have to destroy the infrastructure of Israel, because we are under aggression, we did not did not agress anyone, we are just defending our people, defending our issue, defending our holy places, and I believe that no one can speak about destroying the infrastructure of resistance movement in Gaza Strip and West Bank, so when the United States and Israel speak about this, they are just putting obstacles in front of the negotiations and peace process.'

The United States were to blame for the Palestinians' plight, he went on, because of their steadfast support for Israel. 'All the time the United States are giving the chance for Israelis to practice more aggression against Palestinians, and to create new situations on the ground which put obstacles in front of building a Palestinian state. I believe that the United States of America is backing all the time the Israeli terror and the Israeli aggression to our people, and they are not stand with our rights at any moment in the future.'

A little over five months later, Abdel Aziz Rantissi was dead, silenced finally by the attack helicopters of the air force which had almost killed him in June. His was the latest death in a series throughout the second intifada, as the Israeli military worked through a list of people who had been founders, or prominent members, of Hamas. Sheikh Ahmed Yassin, the movement's spiritual leader, was killed just weeks before Dr. Rantissi. Mohammed Deif, the leader of the military wing, escaped assassination in September 2002, and went underground, reportedly having lost an ear and an eye in the helicopter strike which was meant to kill him. He had become leader of the Al-Qassam brigades after the death of Saleh Shehada, in July 2002. The attack which killed Saleh Shehada sent a shock wave across Gaza City, and a message that if they had a prime target in their sights, the Israelis did not always take care to see that civilian casualties were avoided. Saleh Shehada's bodyguard was killed too. So were fifteen civilians, who just happened to live in the apartment block where Saleh Shehada was spending the night.

The Israeli Air Force dropped a one tonne bomb on the house and destroyed it completely, taking it like a rotten tooth from the row in which it had stood. The rubble stood there for months afterwards, a playground for bored children who picked among the fractured masonry. Remnants of a comfortable home life lay strewn across the ruins: odd shoes; torn strips of cheap dresses and shirts; pots and pans; schoolbooks. The houses which stood either side of the one that had been destroyed were still largely intact, but barely habitable. There were huge holes in the walls which they had shared. The idea of home as a sanctuary, of Arab family life as something private, not to be shared with outsiders, was destroyed. At the back of the empty lot, angry graffiti were scrawled across the bare, blasted wall. Most of them were in Arabic, but there were two in English, just in case international television crews and photographers hadn't got the message: 'This is the Israeli peace', and 'This is the American weapon'. The only other decorations on the wall were posters of the many 'martyrs' who had died that night. The gaudy pictures were pasted next to, and sometimes over, the pock marks left by the shrapnel which had been flung outwards as the house was blown apart. Boys in their early teens were happy to act as guides, pointing to spaces in the void and giving the names of the families whose apartments had once been there. The survivors had gone. Dispossessed and homeless, they had spread out across the nearby districts of the city, taking shelter wherever they could find it. 24 year old Hanna Al-Mattar sat with her husband, Rami, on the floor of an apartment they had rented a kilometre or so away. The young married couple had both survived the raid, although Rami's face was scarred from injuries he had received that night. Their infant daughter, Dina, had died from severe head injuries she received when the walls of the flat fell in. Hanna looked into the distance when she spoke, as if she saw not the bare concrete walls of her temporary home, but flashes of fire tearing through the deep blue of a Gaza summer night.

'I saw terrible things,' she began. 'We have 3 storeys in our house. I live in the second storey with my husband Rami and my daughter Dina. I were dressing Dina and washing her then I hear a terrible thing, a terrible thing, from the window. Then I saw a fire. After that, all the things, the wall, the cupboard, many things, fall on me. Then I can't see anything. I were in my grave.'

Speaking in her second language seemed to make reliving the events of that night even more difficult. Her voice wavered. An ambulance passed in the distance as she spoke, its siren helping to recreate the horror of that night.

'I were in my grave, under these things, then I can't hear, I can't see anything. I were under all these things. Many things were on me.' Even with the windows of the flat open, letting in the hot summer air, Hanna could still clearly recall exactly what it felt like to be trapped. 'My husband Rami was in a dangerous situation,' she continued, turning to him. Along with a couple of his brothers, he sat listening to Hanna's account. I'm not sure how much they understood, but there was little else to do for unemployed young men, and, in any case, it would not have been extremely improper for Hanna to talk to a man who was not a relative without her husband there. 'Something fell on his head from the explosion but *al-hamdulillah* (Praise be to God), God see to him, and he's good now as you see.'

Rami didn't actually look particularly good. Aside from the scars on his head, he seemed to have suffered mentally, too. It was impossible to tell whether his physical wounds had damaged his brain, or whether he was suffering psychological scars from his experience. In any case, sitting in an overcrowded rented flat in Gaza City, with no job, his prospects of recovery didn't seem good. Even if Rami had survived his injuries that night, he and Hanna still had the worst realization ahead of them.

Once freed from her 'grave', Hanna could think only of her baby. 'I was crying, 'Where's Dina? Where's Dina? I want Dina. I want Dina. But they can't do anything, my family, for me because Dina died in the explosion. Dina was on my bed. She died as you know. She was injured in her head. Dina was a beautiful baby.' Dina was only two months old. As her mother spoke these last words, her voice trailed off. She was no longer in the room, with the hot summer air coming in through the open window, but back in the smouldering ruins of the house that night, realising that her only child was dead.

A few streets away, in another apartment which echoed because of its emptiness, Mahmoud Al-Hweti sat, chain smoking. Mahmoud was thirty five, and looked as if he'd seen enough to last him his three score years and ten and more. His brown arms were scarred from shrapnel. Another a scar ran parallel to the curve of his left eyebrow. Like Hanna Matar, Mahmoud had lost his home when the apartment block was bombed. Mahmoud's 30-year-old wife, Mona, and two of their five children, were killed. Mahmoud shared the flat with his remaining three children: their mother and siblings remembered in garish 'martyr' posters, the only decoration on the wall. Mona, 4-year-old Subhi, and, Mohammed, 6, now stood proudly in front of the Dome of the Rock in Jerusalem: transported in death by a computer programme to a place the Israeli Army would never allow them to travel in life. Mahmoud had come home at about 9pm on the night of the attack. Mona had made him some supper, then he had decided to go to bed.

'I was sleeping. I heard an explosion. I thought it was the gas bottle.' There's no mains gas in Gaza. The bottles used for cooking are not always properly connected. Accidents are fairly frequent. Mahmoud's voice rasped from tobacco smoke and tears.

'Then I was under the walls of my house. My hands and face were wounded. I could hardly stand up. I went around the rooms trying to find my children. I heard my daughter shouting 'Daddy, Daddy, I'm here'. I tried to move the walls and the rubble, but I couldn't. I kept trying to move the rubble from her body. I kept shouting to the neighbours 'Come and help me!' Then they came into the house to help. They moved me to the hospital. That night, I felt in my heart that I had lost two of my children, but I didn't know whether my wife was still alive or not.'

The next morning, the doctors confirmed to Mahmoud the news that he had feared. Mahmoud started to talk about how life had been in the month since the night he had lost half his family. He couldn't. He began 'Well, you see...' but then gestured at the pictures on the wall, said simply, 'I can't' and started to weep quietly. We left him to his grief, left him with the half of his family which had survived, and what passed for a home, a rented flat decorated only with pictures of the dead.

Dr. Fadel Abu Hein of the 'Gaza Community training centre and crisis management' (Palestinian non-governmental organizations often had names which probably sound prestigious in Arabic, more verbose in English) treated the survivors of the attack. He outlined the general problems of mental health in the Palestinian territories, a place where mental illness is often still viewed as a weakness of which both the sufferer and his or her family should be deeply ashamed. For children who had been caught up in the conflict, Dr. Abu Hein said, typical symptoms were loss of concentration, sleeplessness, nightmares, fear of darkness, and a need to cling to their parents. Worst of all, there was none of the hope and enthusiasm for life which childhood should bring.

'If you ask Palestinian children, 'What do you want from the future?' He can answer you 'Nothing,' Dr. Abu Hein said on a quiet afternoon in his office in Gaza City. 'A lot of Palestinians you ask about the future will answer, 'I want to die.''

He continued, 'We have inside each of us two desires: life desire, and death desire. If you are opening a channel, or a way, in front of the life wish, now we are seeking the life wish, and developing the life wish. What is happening in front of Palestinian children, they are destroying every resource of their life. They are killing their childhood.'

This, he feared, was something which would affect Palestinian children and their Israeli counterparts throughout their lives. Among Palestinian children, it meant a complete loss of dreams or ambition. 'Maybe 20 per cent of them want to be lawyers, doctors, teachers, but more than 70 per cent of them ignore what the future means.'

Dina Matar only had two months of her childhood. Mahmoud Al-Hweti's surviving children had in effect lost theirs. Dr. Abu Hein said that the suffering the survivors of the bomb were going through simply defied description: 'I visited those families twice. If we are talking about trauma, it's not enough to say trauma. When you read any of the psychological and psychiatric dictionary, you can find among those people more than you can find in any dictionary.

A month or so later, I went back to try to visit Mahmoud again. He was out, walking with his children in Omar Mukhtar Street. Perhaps he had returned to his job as a labourer with the municipality, and had got some money. Omar Mukhtar street was Gaza's main shopping street, leading from Midan Falasteen (Palestine Square, the city centre) down to the PLC building. The street was named after a Libyan who rebelled against Italian rule in his country between the two World Wars. As the street approached the PLC building, it split, with the two sides diverging around gardens, and then around the Legislative Council itself. In the gardens, known as Midan al-Jundi ('Soldier square'), stood a statue of a militia man, pointing north, towards the rest of Mandate Palestine, the former homeland which is now Israel. When the Israelis occupied the Gaza Strip in 1967, they knocked the statue down. It was replaced with the advent of Palestinian Autonomy in the mid 1990s. People in Gaza did not stroll along boulevards; Gaza then was not that kind of city. Had it been, they would probably have strolled down Omar Mukhtar street. As it was, most of the people who did go there to see and be seen were gangs of teenage boys. In the winter, although it was never very cold in Gaza, the street emptied early. The wind from the sea blew rubbish around; shop signs creaked on their hinges. There were few lights – the odd takeaway food shop, and a tawdry amusement centre where the teenage boys who had tired of walking up and down the street stopped to spend a few shekels. At any time of year when an Israeli raid seemed likely, the streets were deserted after dark. When the days first began to lengthen in April and May, Omar Mukhtar Street sometimes came to life, if people were feeling safe enough to go outside. The shops stayed open late: clothes shops, shoe shops, ice cream parlours, jewellers, chemists, photographers, mobile phone centres, kitchenware. One of the photographers' window displays had family portraits which looked more than 50 years old, showing families in the homeland, in Palestine before they came to Gaza. The pictures seemed not just a record of the past, but a glimpse of the dreamland which was gone, the place which four generations of refugees still thought of as theirs. The sons and daughters of the few wealthy people who remained in Gaza looked at the latest fashion items: shoes labelled as having been made in Italy, but which, according to local legend, were manufactured on the West Bank, or shirts and jackets with slogans which appeared to be in English, but which made no sense in that language. Fashions spread quickly among Gaza youth. One winter, no self-respecting man between the ages of 19 and 25 could be seen without a black plastic jacket. Each would-be dandy would insist he wore leather when visibly he did not. Nearly everything on sale there seemed incredibly cheap compared to Israel and East Jerusalem, and certainly compared to Europe. In Gaza, though, cheaper did not mean affordable.

The father, probably in his mid-thirties, stood with two little boys, one holding each hand. They were probably aged around 4 and 6. The toyshop was near the amusement arcade, which always seemed to manage to attract a few customers. Tinny electronic music and cigarette smoke drifted out into the street, showing that there was life inside. The toyshop was usually empty, even around feast days when gifts were usually exchanged. The father and sons stood silent, looking at the cheap plastic playthings in the window. This was the week in June when Abdel Aziz Rantissi had survived the assassination attempt. Even though they lived in terror of helicopter gunships and tanks, the little boys of Gaza seemed to love these toys above all other. Perhaps it gave them an escape into a fantasy world where they controlled who lived and who died, who was fired on, and whose house was destroyed. The two boys were smartly dressed in shorts and shirts, their hair neatly brushed. Perhaps this was a special occasion, a birthday. Perhaps they were just out for an evening stroll with their father, enjoying the comparative cool after the stifling heat of the day. Whatever had led them to pause in front of the toyshop window, that was as far as they were going. All three of them looked at the toys, the boys with a sense of longing, the father with a feeling of failure and inadequacy. None of the things before them cost more than a couple of pounds, but that could be half a day's pay, or money that simply wasn't there if father was out of work. Sometimes, these trivial scenes seemed more heart-breaking than the violence. For the violence was a big thing – deadly, and apparently unstoppable without the involvement of potentates such as the President of the United States of America. That week, there had been a suicide bomb on a rush-hour bus in Jerusalem. Civilians had been killed in Israeli missile strikes aimed at militant leaders. In the middle of the deaths, this father and his boys, like Israelis on the other side of the fence, were just trying to life a normal life, but even a few pounds, which might have bought the joy of a new toy, could not be found. You could understand why the violence could not be ended – there were any number of reasons of evil, and folly, and hard-headed *realpolitik* – yet it seemed harder to explain, even in the midst of that, why these boys could not have a football worth a dollar or two. These were the children whose childhood was being killed, as Dr. Abu Hein said. I imagined Mahmoud Al-Hweti's shopping trip a few months before being similar, hoped that he had managed to scrabble together some money from somewhere to give his motherless children something to play with.

When the boys and young men in their teens and twenties became bored of the amusement arcade, or when the weather was too warm, they would wander across the road and sit in the gardens next to the statue of the soldier. They smoked fruit-flavoured tobacco through water pipes which could be hired from the roadside. The soldier stood over them, a reminder, even in this rare moment of pleasure seeking, that the issues which clouded their day to day life hung over their future. In May, the square filled with demonstrators, many growing old, who urged the youth never to forget where they came from, and where they must strive to return.

The Israelis marked the date according to the Hebrew calendar, celebrating 'Independence Day' – the declaration of the State of Israel. The Palestinians remembered it according to the secular, international, calendar. So on May 15th, they rallied to recall *Al-Nakba*, 'the catastrophe'. While the Israelis had barbecues and ball games in the public parks, the people of Gaza had a small but noisy demonstration in front of the Legislative Council. Rousing speeches and rebellious songs were accompanied by bursts of automatic gunfire – fired into the air by puny youths who fancied themselves as fearsome freedom fighters. The highlight of the rally was supposed to be a recorded message from Yasser Arafat, relayed over a telephone line from his compound in Ramallah. A few times the crowd was asked to be silent and the speakers hissed as if they were about to burst into life. When they did, it was to broadcast the sound of a phone ringing. You almost expected to hear it picked up by one of the Palestinian leader's aides, who, unaware that a crowd of thousands was listening, would say that Mr Arafat was busy. Eventually, they got through, and the message began. It began by talking about the first Zionist Congress, held in 1897 in Basel. Mr. Arafat's audience were then treated to a lengthy historical discourse. The sense of a great injustice suffered remained strong. At the demonstration, people held up cardboard keys with the legend 'Right of Return'. School children had painted pictures which they carried as banners at the rally. They showed an idealised pre-1948 life where Arabs sat happily in their homes: old village homes of cool stone which protected them from the sun, not the shaky breeze block buildings which did not keep out bullets. In the schools of Gaza, the maps on the wall showed the whole of Mandate Palestine as their home. The towns and villages had their Arabic names, and Israel doesn't exist. But they know themselves that Israel really did exist, it had existed for 55 years, and that their old homes were gone. Knowledge did not mean acceptance. 88-year-old Yuda Abu Rukhba was among the most angry and animated members of the crowd. Age, the frailty which came with it, and the passage of time, had not calmed his fury. He spoke in broken English, old enough to have learned the language when British troops were the controlling power in Palestine, before Israel. He lived in the north of the Gaza Strip, near Beit Hanoun, so close to the site of his former village that he could see it. For Mohammed Saleh, the star pupil of Jabalya boys' school, the beautiful farms of his forefathers existed only in dreams. Mr Abu Rukhba remembered the reality. 'I am here for our troubles what happened in Palestine,' he explained in a quiet corner away from the crowd. 'Today is the first day of what happened in Palestine.' He still wore the traditional Arab dress which was so rare among younger men. His clothes placed him in one of the idealized stone houses the schoolchildren had depicted in their drawings. This was where he dreamed of going back to, even more than half a century after he had left. 'I want to go home to my country. Nothing more. I don't need money, I need to go back to my country, to grow oranges and flowers on my land.'

He became even more agitated when asked more about compensation. 'Money, what I want money for? For nothing this money. Money is garbage bin. I need my land, my flowers, 150 dunams in Demra village! For me, not for Israelian! I have to go to my home, to my land not to stay in Gaza here. Why to say in Gaza here, for bad life we is in?'

Only when he could leave Gaza would Mr Abu Rukhba accept that there should be peace. For Mr. Abu Rukhba, as for Mr. Abdullah, the next generation, and even for Mohammed Saleh two generations on from that, peace was not about a 'two state solution: Israel and Palestine living side by side in peace and security', as the 'Road Map' would have it. Peace meant an end to fences and borders, an army that kept them from the lands their families had lived and died on for hundreds of years. Peace meant the right to live where they wanted, and to get back what they and their families had lost. To settle for a 'peace' which offered anything less meant accepting defeat, and formalising the humiliation they had felt so keenly for more than 50 years. That was no peace at all. The 'Road Map's' authors either knew this and chose to ignore it, or simply had little idea of how strongly the sense of loss and being conquered was still felt. Those who spent hours, days, and months drawing up the document in comfortable, climate controlled offices, should perhaps have spent just a few minutes in the dusty, hot, noisy alleys of the refugee camps.

The demonstration eventually dispersed, as it had done for so many years on 'Al-Nakba,' and the crowd left for houses they would not, could not, call home. As the second *intifada* continued, more and more people lost their houses again: demolished as a punishment, destroyed to clear land and deprive fighters of cover. Mahmoud Al-Hweti and Hanna Matar lost their homes, and their children, because they lived in the wrong block of flats. Half of Mahmoud's family were killed by Israel, but he didn't see them as the only ones to blame for the plight of the Palestinians. Like many people in Gaza, he wasn't fooled by rhetoric about Arab and Islamic brotherhood. 'I blame the Arabs. They haven't done anything for the Palestinian people. Secondly, I blame the Jews,' he told me bitterly when I left him to his misery. All he wanted from the Israelis, he said, was 'Salaam, salaam,' ('Peace, peace'). Hanna, too, like so many people just wanted the fighting to end. 'It's enough to do war. I'm not ready to lose any children in the whole of Palestine; I'm not ready to lose any child in the future. It's enough to kill, it's enough to do war, it's enough.'

Mahmoud and Hanna's children didn't survive their infancy. Many children who do in Gaza say that they want to die fighting the Israelis. Dr Abu Hein talked about the trauma suffered by children caught in the conflict. Nine months after we spoke in his office on that hot August afternoon, he found himself at the centre of it. The Israeli Army surrounded his family house. Three of his brothers, members of the military wing of Hamas, refused to give themselves up. Eventually, they died fighting. The house was demolished, and Dr. Abu Hein was detained without trial on suspicion of involvement in militant activities.

CHAPTER 5

'THEY WANT THE LAND. THEY DON'T WANT TO SEE ANY POPULATION.'

The house still stood three storeys high, but none of the storeys was complete. Shells had smashed sections of the outside walls. A dresser, in heavy, dark wood, lurched in one corner of the room, perhaps about to fall over. The floor below it looked unsafe. There were cracks in the inside walls too. The wallpaper still clung on, a reminder of the family life which had once gone on beneath it. The wallpaper was yellow with a pattern of brown curves. In one corner, the pattern was broken by the dried blood and brains which were splattered across it. This home, in the final hours before it was made uninhabitable, had been the scene of a battle which had left attacker and defender exhausted. The Israeli Army eventually decided to blow it up. They had fought for hours, all the time trying to persuade Ayman, Yusef, and Mahmoud Abu Hein to give themselves up. They wanted to take them alive. The brothers refused, choosing to die in the house where they had grown up, and where they may or may not have received sympathetic visitors from the United Kingdom.

The day before the Israeli troops surrounded the Abu Hein family house, in Shijaia, at the eastern edge of Gaza City, the 'Road Map' had been formally presented to the Israelis and the Palestinians. The day before that, Tuesday 29th April 2003, there had been a suicide bombing at 'Mike's Place', a beachfront bar in Tel Aviv. The two attackers carried British passports. Asif Mohammed Hanif blew up at the entrance to the bar. His bomb killed three people beside himself. Omar Khan Sharif's body was found a few days later, floating in the sea. They had visited Gaza before carrying out the attack. Now, when the people of the city should perhaps have been thinking about what the 'Road Map' meant, and what were the prospects for its success, they looked out from their windows to see a column of black smoke rising from the east of the city, and helicopter gunships high in the sky overhead. Explosions shook the city centre throughout the morning. Gazans went to school, college, and where there was any, work, wearily familiar with the sounds of war. No one in Gaza expected the 'Road

Map' to change that, and it did not. It was the time of year when the midday heat first began to be uncomfortable. The sand and dust which seemed to get everywhere in Gaza were no longer contained by winter moisture. Thirst struck after even a short time outside. The sights and sounds of the battle centred on a single house away to the east reached the tops of the taller buildings in the city centre. All this was familiar, and happened frequently. As if to reflect that the atmosphere had changed, as if to mark the publication of the 'Road Map', something was different.

When the Israeli Army decided to go after people they wanted to capture or kill, they usually did so in the dead of night: capturing or killing their quarry, demolishing their house, and withdrawing around day break. The targets of the raid were usually ordered to give themselves up. They almost never did. Then, normally around an hour later, there was a warning that unless they came out, the house would be blown up with them inside. It frequently was. The Israelis moved on the Abu Hein house at about 2 am. Dr Fadel Abu Hein gave a series of telephone interviews to foreign media while his brothers loosed off at their enemy. As the heat of the early summer day grew stronger, the fighting became fiercer. The Israeli raid was not following the usual pattern. Instead of just blasting the house, they proceeded step by step. Only when it became clear that resorting to overwhelming force, and destroying the building where their enemy was holed up, was the only way they could claim victory, did they decide to do so. By then it was late in the afternoon. Even the crowds of boys and youths who had gathered to throw stones at tanks were beginning to tire of their game, which was almost like a version of a bullfight. They teased the tanks as far as they could then, when the tank responded with a burst of gunfire, jumped out of the way – behind a corner – as quickly as they could. With the under 16's only spending half the day at school, university classes mostly in the morning, and almost no jobs, there were always plenty of willing participants. Incursions drew bigger crowds than football matches in Gaza, and even had some of the same street traders. An enterprising man selling iced drinks from a handcart had set up his stall just out of the firing line: at exactly the point where a thirsty young tank-baiter, having just taken cover, might just begin to think of a cold drink to drive the dust from his throat. The ambulances were normally parked as close to the fighting as it was safe to go. Their fearless crews could always give advice on the situation. Only the brave, the foolish, and would-be 'martyrs' readily went much further forward than the places the medics had decided to wait until they felt it was safe enough to go about their grim work. That did not mean they stood at the front of the crowd. The boys and young men – given Gaza courage by intoxicating talk of the honour of martyrdom – knew even less fear than the ambulance crews. Tank-baiting was not an after school activity for cowards. As the afternoon wore on, the area seemed to become more and more dangerous. A helicopter descended to take a closer look at the house where the Abu Hein brothers continued to fight. More hovered higher. 'That one belongs to Abu

Mazen,' said a grubby youth, looking up at the Israeli gunship, and giving the Gaza assessment of the document which the new Palestinian Prime Minister was preparing to begin working on. Thousands of words were written about the 'Road Map'. That short sentence managed to say more than all of them about the way the plan was seen in the alleys of the poorer parts of Gaza City. It was a non-starter; a collaborator's charter. Shortly after 4 in the afternoon, when the battle had been going on for more than twelve hours, concluding that the Abu Hein brothers would not be taken alive, the Israelis lost patience. A huge explosion rocked the streets of Shijaia. It was heard across the city. Shortly afterwards, the Israeli troops withdrew, leaving the ambulance crews to stub out their cigarettes and approach the ruins of he house which had been at the centre of the battle. The corpses of two of the brothers were found inside the crumpled building; the third in a nearby alley.

For days, relatives and neighbours helped those who had lived in the house to salvage what they could. The main staircase was still intact, but the walls and ceilings looked as if they might fall in at any time. If you did not want to take the stairs, you could just clamber up to the first floor on the mountain of rubble which lay next to the wrecked house. Water pipes and power lines dripped and hung uselessly from the outside of the ruin. The thin alley which separated the Abu Hein house from the next property was choked with broken masonry and blocks of concrete. Many members of the crowd who had turned out to watch the raid now joined in the post-raid assessment of damage, pointing to cracked and crumbling walls and shaking their heads. One relative or neighbour babbled in a mixture of English and Arabic about what had happened. He seemed to have been driven insane by his experience. These were the sort of symptoms which Dr Abu Hein had meant when he said 'When you read any of the psychological and psychiatric dictionary, you can find among those people more than you can find in any dictionary.' But Dr. Abu Hein wasn't there to offer advice or treatment. He had been taken from the house, the house where his brother's brains were spread across the wall, to an Israeli detention centre.

Two days before, Dominique Hass' body parts were spread across a car which was parked outside the bar where she had worked. Asif Mohammed Hanif's head hung from a trellis outside. 'Mike's Place' was the target chosen by Hanif, or perhaps by Dr. Abu Hein's brothers. Hanif, and his accomplice Omar Khan Sharif, had both visited Gaza before they carried out the attack. The raid which the Israelis mounted on the Abu Hein family house was linked by Israeli security sources to the bomb on the beachfront in Tel Aviv. A month or so later, a couple of days before President Bush met the Israeli and Palestinian Prime Ministers in Aqaba, I went to Mike's Place, to see what recent victims of a suicide bombing made of the summit, and of the 'Road Map.' It was a warm summer day, and the Mediterranean can hardly ever have looked more inviting. It was hard to believe that this stretch of beach, where women walked in bikinis, and couples kissed, was only a short distance up the coast from Gaza, where if women swan at all, they did so clothed from head to toe. The contrast could not have been greater, and could not have emphasised more sharply the way that Israelis and Palestinians used the same beach. It was less than 100km to the beach at Gaza, but it might as well have been on the other side of the world. The young people who lazed in the sand here had no idea of what their counterparts in Gaza were like, and the boys who baited tanks in the alleys of Shijaia would have been amazed to see a girl in a bikini. If it had been a female relative, they should have stopped throwing stones at tanks and hurled them at her instead, furious at the shame her immodest clothing was bringing down on the family.

Assaf Ganzman was having a quiet morning preparing the bar for a big night ahead. A warm breeze blew in from the beach, rustling the pictures of the suicide bomber's victims which were stapled to a board outside, a makeshift memorial where fellow workers and bar customers had lift candles and left flowers. Assaf was probably in his mid-30s, with long black hair tied in a ponytail. He seemed to stand for all the people in Israel who just wanted to live a life considered normal in western Europe or the United States: run a bar and play blues music for friends and customers. He spoke of how hard it had been since the attack, but allowed himself to be a little optimistic about the future. 'If you don't take the first steps, you're not going to get to the end of the road,' he reflected, as we chatted in the quiet of a slow lunchtime. I went back to see Assaf, and his brother Gal, a few months later, and they were still happy to talk. At the end of the year, I wanted to interview them again. They flatly refused. It seemed that by then they had had enough of talking about what had happened, and their hopes for the future. Their hopes for the future had probably gone altogether. They had reached the end of the road, and stayed there, making the best of it, the party atmosphere of their bar tainted by violent death, and the fact that the happy beach crowd would now all have to be searched by a security guard when they wanted to enter 'Mike's Place.'

The recruitment of foreign passport holders to the Hamas cause was a new tactic, one which enabled the bombers to circumvent the strict control over Palestinian entry and exit to Gaza. It meant that all foreigners, whatever their business, would now find it more and more difficult to get in and out of Gaza. A week later, the Israelis decided that any foreigner wishing to enter or leave the territory had to get permission to do so from the Israeli Army. The move followed not only the suicide bombers visit, but also the deaths of foreign nationals in Rafah, at the southern edge of the Gaza Strip. Announcing the new restrictions, the Israeli Army press office claimed, 'there is no intention to limit or encumber the passage of diplomats, UN and Red Cross personnel, international and humanitarian agencies, journalist, or the like.' Signing a form absolving the Israeli Army of any responsibility became a condition of going into Gaza. Many organizations, such as Amnesty International, simply refused to sign. United Nations staff were eventually exempted. I had a choice: refuse to sign the form and sit in Jerusalem, or sign it and carry on with my work. I signed it, but the sentence 'I am aware of the risks involved and accept that the Government of the State of Israel and its organs cannot be held responsible for death, injury and/ or damage/ loss of property which may be incurred as a result of military activity,' always filled me with dread. It became known among the expatriate community as 'the form which says it's my fault if they shoot me'. The Israelis clearly had a point about trying to stop suicide bombers. For most of the foreigners living in Gaza, though, or those who simply felt bold enough to go to see for themselves the occupation and the intifada at first hand, this was nothing more than an attempt to prevent people from going into the territory. Many of the Palestinian non-governmental organizations relied on foreigners, especially native English speakers, coming to assist them either as volunteers or for low salaries. That source of help was cut off, limiting their ability to work, and to communicate effectively with Europe and the United States. For those of us foreigners who lived in Gaza, the new restrictions removed an important psychological crutch. We knew that, whenever the situation got bad, we could leave: either for a few days, to take a break, or for good. A week later, the occupation of Beit Hanoun began, and the main road from Gaza City to Erez was blocked off. The sense of being trapped, of there being no way out, became stronger and more unsettling. It felt like an attempt to drive as many internationals out of Gaza as possible. It would prevent their giving assistance to the Palestinians, or bearing witness to the appalling humanitarian situation there, and it would remind the Palestinians who was in charge. Some weeks earlier, before any of these restrictions were introduced, I had arrived at the crossing point at the same time as a group of British Muslims. We chatted as we walked. 'We never get any idea from the media of what it's really like here,' said a young man of about 20. He wore a skullcap over his close-cropped hair. He had grown the bushy beard beloved of devout or angry young Muslims the world over. Like his companions, he carried framed Koranic verses under his arm, a souvenir of their visit. I protested that at least the BBC was trying, by basing a correspondent there. We agreed to differ. When, a few weeks later, the Israeli police issued the passport photos of Asif Mohammed Hanif and Omar Khan Sharif, I saw in them two faces who would have fitted in easily with this group of young men from the Midlands. Now, following their lethal actions, even fewer people would have any idea of 'what it was really like' in Gaza. The waits would be longer; more people would be flatly denied entry or exit. It was about this time that a new graffito appeared on the first Israeli sentry post you came to when leaving Gaza. It was a concrete cylinder – documents and words passed through a narrow slot in the front, where the soldier's face appeared. Just below it, like the caption on television which gives the speaker's name, was scrawled the word 'cunt'.

The sense of being trapped led to a certain feeling of solidarity among the expatriates in Gaza. United Nations staff rarely had any problems for long, neither, as a journalist, did I. The worst that happened was being held up for a few hours from time to time. Complaints to contacts in the Army press service rarely produced rapid results. It was military intelligence, not the IDF, who were in charge. Around the time the new restrictions were brought it, I spent about 5 hours waiting to leave Gaza. As I sat – fortunately in an air conditioned waiting area, not in the sun like the Palestinians – I fell into conversation with a British man who had been in Gaza to attend a conference on water resources. Since the suicide bombing at Mike's Place, British passport holders were subject to even greater delays than other foreigners. Soldiers and security guards I had been talking to regularly for months now pretended not to know me. The falsehood of this fake friendliness was exposed. An officer whom I did not recognize – there were many new faces at this time, all trying to catch the next terrorist – came out from a back room, and asked the man I was talking to to come with him. Fifteen minutes or so later, he came back, bemused. 'They took me in there,' he said, 'and showed me pictures of the two suicide bombers. Then they asked if I knew them!' The Israeli security personnel must have known that their chances of catching anyone associated with the bombers at that time was minimal. Their real purpose in asking questions of British water experts was not to help in the investigation so much as to say: 'We are in charge here. If you don't want to have to answer our questions again, don't come back.'

With getting in an out of Gaza becoming more difficult, I travelled less frequently to Jerusalem, only going when work required. I came to think of Gaza, of my flat there, more and more as home, albeit a temporary one. When the occupation of Beit Hanoun began in mid-May, I felt relieved that I heard the battle from a distance, knew at the same time that the fighting lay directly along and across my road out. By then, I had lived in Gaza for nine months or so, and I was able to take comfort from my surroundings. When the Israelis moved into Beit Hanoun, the battle began in the middle of the night and lasted well into the next afternoon. It was May, so already the windows of my flat were open, and would not be closed again until the end of October. The explosions, the bursts of gunfire, carried all the way from the dusty edge of the Gaza Strip to my flat in the city centre.

In between the noise of the fighting, I listened to sounds which had become familiar to me, the sounds of Gaza. My next-door neighbour kept chickens on the roof. The crowing of the cockerels occasionally interrupted my radio broadcasts, so I learned to close the window before I went on air. The first morning I arrived, I was woken about 4.30 by the dawn call to prayer, with the first glow of warm sunlight covering the town. The sound seemed almost to take on a physical shape, rising like an orange ghost in the dawn. Smaller phantoms formed further away, in proportion to the strength of the sound which was reaching me. Later, I slept until the city stirred at about 7. I became used to life in Gaza, with its restrictions which at first seemed so odd to a European. Relations between the sexes were strictly controlled. I was expected to kiss my male Palestinian colleagues on the cheek when I returned after a long absence. I could walk down the street hand in hand with them if we felt that our working relationship had developed into one of firm friendship. But I could never show any public affection for a European female friend, and having any sort of relationship with a Palestinian woman would have been out of the question. Almost the only Palestinian women I spoke to were people I interviewed. A British friend who returned to Gaza from a wedding in Sussex described how he felt when he saw the Saturday lunchtime crowd enjoying the sunshine outside a country pub. 'She'd better cover up,' he had thought, seeing a woman with bare shoulders. He was also worried that the public consumption of alcohol would provoke the wrath of the villagers, until he remembered where he was. It had all seemed so decadent, he concluded.

Over time, the view from my window lost its strangeness. In my first weeks here, it all seemed so alien. I had only been to the Middle East on short visits before, and to begin with I felt that this was just another trip, not a longer term stay. Eventually, the view from the balcony had a comforting familiarity. I was lucky enough to have open ground beneath my fifth floor flat. It was a rare privilege in Gaza. Directly below the balcony was a playground, built with funds from the Norwegian government. There were slides, a climbing frame, and brightly coloured tyres for the kids to clamber over. Tyres seemed an important part of the Palestinian street kid's leisure time. Whenever there was an Israeli attack during the night, the next day the children set fire to tyres as a sign of protest. The politically inspired pyromania took its toll on the playground, too. The nearest swings to my flat were burnt to the ground, leaving only charred marks on the sand. Beyond the playground was a school. Twice a day, the sounds of exercises and a rendition of the Palestinian national anthem rang out from the open-air assembly. Twice a day, because of the overcrowding which led to one school's being held in the morning, and another in the afternoon, all in the same buildings. Sometimes, as on the first day of the war in Iraq, or the day when Ibrahim Al-Maqadma was killed, school closed altogether, and the pupils, having arrived promptly at 7.30, rushed out of the gates again a few minutes later to enjoy their enforced leisure, burn tyres, or join anti-Israeli or anti-American demonstrations.

To the left of the playground as I looked down from my balcony was an area of sandy wasteland. In warm weather, when the windows were open for weeks on end, the floors quickly became covered in dust. Even a short barefoot walk left the soles of your feet black. I lived in a spacious apartment in a tall white building, but I couldn't escape the dust that covered everything in Gaza. In the winter, the rain which battered on the windows brought much needed water to the Gaza Strip, but it also brought more dust, running in dirty streaks down the window. The empty ground was an occasional football pitch, and a training ground for the Palestinian security forces. A sadistic-looking man with a stick and a paunch, and a smaller, wiry man with a beard and an assault rifle, drilled boys in their late teens. On hot afternoons, several of the recruits would collapse or faint. They were propped up against the fence at the edge of the playground until they recovered.

Further to the left lay the football stadium. A huge picture of Yasser Arafat hung at one end. On summer evenings, sprinklers watered the pitch. The senior leagues did not function when I was there, but the under 18 teams were important enough to claim a share of this scarce resource. The players celebrated victory in important games with hugs and backslapping, then knelt side by side on the touchline to pray. Beyond the football stadium was a mosque. Its tall, slim, minaret punctuated my skyline; its call to prayer punctuated the days I spent at home. It was the call to prayer which, eventually, no longer woke me.

There were nine apartments in the block I lived in. My landlord and his family had built it in the mid 1990s, in the optimism of Palestinian Autonomy. They had presumably hoped that the nascent state in waiting would draw foreign contractors and business people who would need comfortable accommodation. For most of the time I lived there, from August 2002 until March 2004, I was the only non-family member in the house of nine flats. Two Turkish journalists moved in a few months before I left. The house, I believe, had seen better, fuller, days. My landlord once told me that the basement of the building contained the possessions of European contractors who had been working on the Gaza seaport. They had left when the intifada began, withdrawn by a company who knew the work couldn't continue in a time of war. The progress they had made, the foundations they had laid – all was destroyed as the fighting continued. Perhaps one day it would be completed, when finally it became clear who was in charge in Gaza, whose home it was, and who had the right to say what would happen, and what and who could come in and out. I was fond of my flat. I had never lived anywhere so airy and spacious. For someone who grew up in the Manchester area, and who in adult life lived for years in Moscow, the light and warmth of the Middle East was a luxurious pleasure. From the end of April until November you could comfortably sit outside in the evening. You knew you would not need a jacket. You knew it would not rain. Memories of childhood days out and summer holidays in the Lake District or Scotland, when the whole family hoped it would 'stay fine', and said so, brought a smile.

The road outside the flat was sand in summer, often mud in winter. It climbed the slope towards the football stadium, scarred with ruts carved during January downpours. Opposite the front door was the playground, which doubled as an occasional grazing ground for goats. To the left of the door was a small shop, of the kind which were numerous in Gaza, selling little to people who did not have much money to buy. The shopkeeper sat outside most of the day, watching life unfold in the street. In winter, he and his friends lit fires of cardboard boxes and odd sticks to keep then warm as they passed the evenings in conversation. To the right, at the end of the sandy road, was Al-Thawra ('Revolution') street. I usually felt pretty safe here. During the anger over the war in Iraq, I decided to keep a low profile, but generally it did not feel dangerous. In Gaza, though, you never knew when it might suddenly turn that way. One Friday lunchtime, as the city lazed after prayers and lunch, three armed men took up positions at the corner of the street. They wore no uniforms, but all cradled assault rifles. They looked as if they were waiting to ambush somebody. I was about to go out, and did so anyway. They ignored me as I drove past, and I tried not to catch their eye. I had no idea who they were. That did not matter. By the spring of 2004, Gaza was becoming more and more lawless. Almost anyone who felt like it could take to the streets with a gun to resolve whatever needed resolving. They only had to make sure that their clan was powerful enough to protect them and itself against whatever might follow as a result.

Down Al-Thawra St. a turn to the left led to one of the cross streets which joined Al-Thawra St. to Al-Wahda St. Here were two of the staple sources of a quick dinner on a busy or a lazy day: 'Extra Baguette' bakery, and 'Palmyra' restaurant. 'Extra baguette' seemed to bake fresh bread morning, noon, and night. The ovens were in the rooms to the side and rear of their shop, and the smell drifted out through the open doors. The bakery had vans which delivered to the supermarkets across the city, and sometimes beyond. 'Extra' was apparently hard to transliterate into Arabic script, so the sign outside announced 'Ikstra' baguette. 'Bakery' appeared as 'backery' where it was written in English on their delivery vehicles. Inside, the selection varied depending on what was selling, and what kind of flour was available. Sometimes, during times of high tension, the freight crossing between Gaza and Israel would be closed for days, even weeks. Once, Extra Baguette ran out of the flour to bake the loaf from which it took its name. The entire stock of bread grew less and less day by day, finally dwindling to a few packets of biscuits. At other times, the stock grew old. There simply weren't enough people in the city who could afford it. The cheapest loaves there cost 2 shekels – about 30p – while 5 small pitta breads sold for half a shekel.

Across the road from Extra Baguette was Palmyra – a restaurant and takeaway which sold the best shawarma in Gaza. From late morning until around midnight – exceptionally late by Gaza standards – the cooks sweated in front of the electric grills which browned the pillars of chicken and turkey, the meat layered and spiced. The lights from Palmyra gave the whole street a warm glow, and a scent of tasty food. The grills were out the front of the shop. On busy evenings, queues would form, the people waiting entertained by the hectic, hot, work of carving the portions from the rotating spit, giving them a final fry, and then wrapping them in bread. You could either have a small pitta, or a larger one, about the size of a pizza base before it was rolled up, known as Iraqi bread. The men at Palmyra came to know me by sight. Ahmed was slightly built and wore small, round, glasses. He looked as if he should have been studying science instead of serving sandwiches. He always gave me a great welcome. As my Arabic improved from non-existent to basic conversation (that is, providing the subject didn't change) we got to know each other's names, and I managed to tell him where I lived, why I hadn't got my car that night, etc. During the humid summer evenings of July and early August 2003, Palmyra was busier than ever. The extra dining room which had been built during Ramadan – when it was closed – was full to overflowing, and the pavement was packed with hungry customers. Ahmed toiled away, his face to the furnace-like heat of the rotating grill. It was with relief that he paused from slicing the sizzling and spitting meat to turn aside for a moment as he passed the fresh slices to his colleague, who made up the sandwiches. Sweat trickled down his temples, making him lift his glasses and wipe it away with a shirt sleeve before he paused to sharpen his carving knife, and then turn his face again to the grill. He worked so fast on busy nights that sometimes he seemed to have more than two hands: it almost looked as if he could sharpen his knife, slice the meat, and shake hands with a passing friend or new customer all at the same time. As the summer went on, he seemed to work harder and harder, but he was always able to look up from his work to greet people as they passed, whether on foot, or weaving through the traffic jam which Palmyra and its double-parking customers usually seemed to cause in the narrow, pot-holed, street. Palmyra always did pretty good business, but this was exceptional. The *hudna* – the temporary cease-fire – had been declared. More people were able to go to their labouring jobs in Israel, so there was more money coming into Gaza. The lull in the fighting made people want to build and to work in the territory itself, too. Most importantly, the calm and the summer evenings brought people out onto the streets. On the winter nights of the intifada, Gaza city fell silent shortly after dark. People had no money to go to restaurants, it was cold, and the Israelis might attack at any time. Society also frowned on any large parties or celebrations while people were dying almost every day.

For a few weeks, it was different. The beach came to life. For the first time for three years, local businesses got together to hold an evening of entertainment at one of the cafés on the sand. A crowd of more than a thousand people gathered to listen to a band – unbelievably loud, as Gaza amplification always seemed to be – and wait for the results of a prize draw. The Sunset café was one of several which came to life every summer on the seashore. Crowds this large in Gaza were almost always at either funerals or demonstrations. Nothing dedicated to pleasure would ever normally attract so many people. The combination of conservative Islam, and the inappropriateness of pleasure during the *intifada*, prevented that. Now that no one had been killed for a few days, the atmosphere was suddenly more relaxed, affording the briefest glimpse of how pleasant this long stretch of sandy coastline could be if only it were not one of the borders of a battlefield. The road above the Sunset café was packed with chaotically parked cars. The seats beneath the shade put up for customers, and those outside, nearer the band, were all taken. Children made themselves comfortable on the sand. The waves broke just a short distance away, and the setting sun coloured the water pink and orange as it sank, out to sea. There was a slide for the younger children. The descent began through the mouth of a huge plastic monkey's head, brightly painted, a fairground amusement set up in a war zone. I had noticed the monkey slide standing idle on wet winter afternoons, when the rain poured down, and when crowds in the city mourned the recent dead. Now it seemed to have been set up almost as a flag which defied the fighting, and announced that things were different, if only for a while. Pools of sticky, fizzy, drinks lay on the plastic tabletops, the sand not stable enough to stop them spilling. The sweet smell of fruit flavoured tobacco smouldering in water pipes mingled with the harsher scent of cigarette smoke and humid sea air. Dozens of children raced along the gaps between chairs and tables, enjoying the space, light, and freedom that came with an evening away from their cramped houses. Sometimes, in the winter, when people lurked in their homes because Palestinians felt that 15 degrees was too cold a temperature to go to the beach, or because they were afraid to go out, the sands were almost empty. You could wander for more than a mile without meeting anyone, seeing only the vast, open sea, which seemed impossibly huge after the cramped city and refugee camps. The long stretch of sand was like a window which could be opened to ventilate an insufferably stuffy room – going for a walk on the beach was the equivalent of fighting your way through a crowd to take a breath of clean air. Plastic bottles and other rubbish were strewn along the shoreline. Whole, weighty palm-tree trunks rolled in the surf after being washed up. At certain times of year, huge jellyfish lay dead where they had beached. Fish which had been flung out of the surf lay stiff, but still shiny. For a few months, the corpse of a horse rotted below an abandoned building which had been hit too many times in the fighting to make its sea view an attraction any longer. Sand drifted over the dead animal, and as its flesh decomposed, its ribs stuck out above where the rest of it lay. The horse had perhaps died at its work, expiring after waiting in the sun to carry home the meagre catch of a family of fishermen trying their luck with nets from the shore. On this summer evening, though, the beach was a place of rest and recreation, not death and toil. There was great excitement as the crowd waited to hear the winning numbers in the prize draw. The music fell silent, the master of ceremonies took up the microphone. 'Let us remember the prisoners and detainees in Israeli jails,' he began. Even in the midst of this rare evening of leisure, of escape, it was not appropriate to forget that the *intifada* still continued. That would have been wrong, almost an acceptance of defeat.

Summer was wedding time, too. During the *hudna*, they seemed to be celebrated with more boisterousness than the year before. Every evening, for weeks, pipers and drummers played as loudly as they could from the back of trucks which sped through the main streets to the hotels and wedding halls on the seafront. There was one group in particular which seemed to make a regular appearance. They seemed to play almost every night for a different couple. There were four of them, all men in their early to mid 20s, dressed in maroon shirts and black trousers. Three of them played different kinds of drums. One of them had huge drum, like the lambegs beloved of Orange men in Northern Ireland, strapped to his chest. It would have looked more at home in a military parade than a wedding procession. I saw them in action close up at the wedding of my Palestinian colleague, Rushdi Abu Alouf. The drummers pounded away for all they were worth, and the piper blew so hard that his cheeks looked as if they were stretched to breaking point. Rushdi's family were refugees. He was in his mid 20s, so he was proably only the second generation to be born away from the homeland. His family had prospered sufficiently to move out of the camps, and now they lived in Sabra, an area of Gaza City. Once, from the office window in the city centre, we heard a loud blast, and then saw smoke rising from Sabra. Three members of Hamas had blown themselves up in their home-made bomb factory. Rushdi's engagement had been announced during the winter. One Friday, after prayers, all the men of the neighbourhood, the heads of families, whose responsibility it was to digest and spread news, gathered on the ground floor of the apartment block where Rushdi lived. It was an open area. There were about 300 men there. There was a long reception line. As he arrived, each man shook hands and greeted all of Rushdi's male relatives. Rushdi himself, his father, and prospective father-in-law (who was also his uncle – many people in Gaza married their first cousins) stood in the centre. When everyone was seated, Rushdi, his father-in-law to be, and the imam from the local mosque seated themselves on a dais at the front of the hall. Their chairs were decorated with plastic flowers. The imam explained that Rushdi and Shireen would soon be married. 'It's so that they can walk in the street together without people saying bad things about her,' the man sitting next to me said quietly, by way of explanation. Without the imam's sanction being explained to all the men of the district, so that they could then communicate it to their families, the two young people walking in the street together would have provoked outrage and scorn, and brought shame on Shireen and her family.

Some six months later, in July, it was the wedding day. At midday, it was Rushdi's duty as the groom to feed the men of the area. Huge vats of mutton and rice were set up in the street, and males young and old arrived for their share. I arrived with some colleagues from the BBC in Jerusalem. There were two women in our party, so we couldn't join the open-air feast. Instead, Rushdi had arranged lunch for us in the kitchen of his new apartment. Before we sat down to eat, he proudly showed us round the home which he had spent months, and thousands of dollars, preparing. Each week between engagement and wedding seemed to bring a new expense as he prepared a place for himself and his new wife. Rushdi's mother came from the flat opposite to say a brief hello. Even if he was moving out of the family home, he wasn't going far from the family. As we left – at about three in the afternoon – the women were gathering across the corridor. There was music and dancing, from what little I could glimpse through the open door. Barbara and Jacqueline, the two women in our party, were allowed to go in for a look, but no male eye could look on the secret celebration. We returned to the house at about six in the evening. The piper and drummers were already belting out loud and lively music, and Rushdi and his young male friends and relatives danced in the street. His hair was newly and neatly cut, and he wore a white shirt and dark suit, which fitted closely around his well-built frame. Hamada – always the snappiest dresser – had shown him to tie a windsor knot. A circle of dancers moved around with one or two taking turns to shine in the middle. The sun was well past its hottest, but the sandy streets and concrete walls had stored the heat of the day, and now radiated, so sweat poured down the dancers' faces. The drums were extremely loud, the noise bouncing from drum skin to wall to ear. A bus pulled up outside the house, ready to take the groom's party to the wedding hall on the seafront. Soon it was ready to depart, and a convoy of cars followed it to Shireen's house, where Rushdi was to collect his bride. The musicians were already in the street, and there was more dancing and deafening drumming. After a short time, Rushdi and Shireen came out. The wedding dress was hooded, with a veil covering the bride's face. The bride's mother wept. The couple and their closest relatives climbed into a brand new Mercedes which had been hired for the big day. The convoy followed at high speed: overloaded cars scraping over speed bumps. The route led along the coast in front of the Beach refugee camp, a collection of miserable, cramped, hovels with a view of the Mediterranean which would have made them worth a million dollars each if their location and the circumstances had been different.

As it was, many of the dilapidated dwellings on the seafront were places whose inhabitants were not envied. Never mind that the dream of home in historical Palestine was unattainable: even getting out of the overcrowded camp was out of the question. Beach Camp was so called because in the 1950s it had been set up on the sand outside what were then the limits of Gaza City. Like Jabalya, the home of Mr. Abdullah the schoolteacher, it had never been intended as a long-term arrangement. More than five decades had passed, though, and no other solution was in prospect. Beach camp now sprawled from the built up edge of the new districts of the city (until the 1950s, and the arrival of the refugees, Gaza City had been much smaller, and further back from the seafront) to within a few metres of the sea. The camp's hardworking donkeys and horses were occasionally treated to a salt water bath in the waves, before a night's rest somewhere in the dark alleys of the camp, a place so cramped that man and beast alike could barely hope for enough space to stretch out and take their ease. It was a bright summer evening. Some of the boys of the camp were playing a noisy and energetic football game on the street at its edge. The setting sun lit up the waves which stretched away to the horizon beyond and below them. In the winter, it was harder to imagine a place more miserable than Beach Camp. From the centre of Gaza City, the land sloped down towards the shore, so Beach Camp caught the filthy floodwater which ran down the hill. Ever growing families had led the residents to take every inch of space they could. Alleys which had once been wide enough for a cart to pass down were now so narrow that even a child could stand in the middle, and touch the walls of two separate houses with their outstretched hands. Most of the people here lived on handouts from the United Nations. At the allotted time on the allotted day, a representative of the family would go to the warehouse to collect the due amounts of rice, cooking oil, flour, and chickpeas. In the January rain, this was an especially pitiful sight. Sometimes the only thing which seemed to make life bearable in Gaza's refugee camps was the sun. With that gone, the food queues took on an even more hopeless and miserable aspect. Flip flops were fine footwear for Gaza most of the year. They were not made for walking though winter mud to the UN warehouse. Just to look at the feet of the ill-shod refugee was to feel cold and hungry. Marwan and Itaf Sa'ati lived a short walk from the warehouse. They – like many Palestinian refugees – had six children, ranging in age from 12 years to three months. Marwan was unable to work. A leg injury ten years before had left him lame and virtually bedridden. He lay on a mattress in the one main room of his family's shelter. The rain pounded on the corrugated fibre glass roof above his head. Damp patches marked the walls where the water was running through. The family relied completely on UN handouts. With Marwan unable to work, they had no prospect of improving their lot. Even if he had been fully fit, there were no jobs to be found. 'Without the UN, we would just have to trust to God,' Itaf sighed. At the time, the UN were worried that they were running short of money to feed the refugees. Itaf hadn't heard this, because she rarely left the house. 'We'll just have to trust to God to provide,' she repeated. This was her life, the life she shared with a crippled, unemployed husband. Not only were they trapped inside the Gaza Strip, cut off from the land which their family had once called home, they were trapped in Beach Camp, trapped in this hovel, where the rain came in through the door, and through the roof, and the baby coughed and bawled because it just never felt warm. The whole family lived in the one room. The adjacent corridor, which led from the door, was home to a stove, the only source of heat in the place. Marwan was in his mid-thirties, Itaf a few years younger. Neither was old enough to have lived in the homeland, but no wonder they and countless other refugees dreamed of it, when this was where they lived instead.

Perhaps that summer evening, as Rushdi's wedding convoy passed, Marwan had made his way outside to enjoy some heat and light. Perhaps he was playing one of the countless games of backgammon which wiled away long evenings in the camps. If he was not playing, perhaps he was one of the crowd of spectators offering unsolicited advice on tactics to those who had to decide how to respond to the roll of the dice. Perhaps he was relaxing after being fed by a neighbour who was himself getting married. The car carrying Rushdi and Shireen stopped at the Gulf Hotel, a pink building at the edge of the refugee camp. There was more dancing. A couple of celebratory shots were fired into the air. The couple quickly went inside. Rushdi was the only man inside the wedding hall. All the other men would sit outside while the women danced.

After a couple of hours, they were allowed in. Male relatives had been in shortly before, then friends of the groom followed. The bride had already left. The wedding hall was a big open space, filled with plastic chairs. On the stage stood a series of red chairs, almost like thrones. White drapes flowed down from a wooden or plaster crown above the stage. Rushdi greeted all his male friends. They slipped him money in their handshakes. His left fist was clenched around a bundle of notes, as more came into his right. There was more dancing. Rushdi's friends wheeled around him, their arms waving in the air, their feet moving in circles. He looked happy, but tired. It was time to leave the groom to his first night of married life. 'That's it. He's captured. He's under occupation,' said a Palestinian friend as we left. The language of the *intifada* was never far away, even at a time of celebration. The heavy, warm, dark night had fallen, and the city was soon silent, the only sound here on the shore was the waves softly washing to and fro, lulling Gaza to sleep. That summer it was a deep sleep, unbroken by the sounds of rockets or tanks, though no doubt there were nightmares of attacks gone by, and fears of more to come in the future. No one was convinced that this calm could last. In the early morning, before 8am, the only time when it was cool enough to be on the beach in July, different groups organized summer activities for holidaying schoolchildren. This was supposed to be the summer of cease-fire, an end to anger. The Palestinian Authority sent teams of cleaners, often protected by armed guards, to whitewash the walls of the city centre, and cover over the fiery slogans prophesying the destruction of Israel. On the summer beaches, though, thin men with long beards and burning eyes drilled boys of ten and younger, overseeing morning exercises beneath the flags of Hamas and Islamic Jihad which hung in the still air. The Gaza municipality could paint over all the slogans they wanted – the joke went that it was good of them to clear so much wall space for fresh graffiti – but they couldn't erase what was written in the heart of even the youngest refugee, and carved into his brain. The supervisors – in their twenties and thirties – knew that the victory, the return, the triumph for Islam and Palestine might not come in their lifetime. They still had to play their part in keeping the dream alive until the day when it would come true.

During the intifada, the road which ran along the shore – the Beach Road – was the only way for Palestinians to travel from the north to the south of the Gaza Strip. The main route, which ran through the centre of the territory, was blocked south of Gaza City, near the Jewish settlement of Netzarim. Leaving the city that way was a strange experience: the dual carriageway was one of the better roads in the whole of the territory, so it was odd to see it used by so few vehicles. The Palestinians called it the Salah-el-Din Road, named for the medieval warrior who battled the crusaders, captured Jerusalem, and who is remembered in English folklore and history as Saladin. The Israeli Army called it the Tancher Road, their lips perhaps reluctant to frame the name of an Muslim conqueror of the holy city. However it was described, it led nowhere. After the suburbs had slipped away – and with them any feeling of relative security which came with being in the city itself – huge cubes of concrete lay across the road. An Israeli army watchtower rose above the nearby scrubland, all it surveyed in firing range. Until the start of the second *intifada*, this had been a reasonably busy area. That quickly changed. Mohammed Al-Doura, the 12-year-old Palestinian boy who was one of the earliest casualties of the fighting in 2000, was killed nearby. The picture of him taking cover in his father's arms, shortly before he was hit by a fatal shot, was seen all over the world. Soon after, the road was closed. It was opened briefly during the *hudna* in the summer of 2003, and then quickly closed again when it became clear that peace was just wishful thinking. For the Palestinians who lived here, in the shadow of Netzarim, life became harder and harder, and more and more dangerous. Their plight was documented by the United Nations and other organizations, but nothing changed. That made them reluctant to talk to outsiders. They feared that the only real consequences of such exchanges would be punishment from the Israelis.

Barjas Al-Waheidi was bolder. He was one of four brothers, part of an extended family group living just a few hundred metres from Netzarim's perimeter. Theirs were the last houses before the wasteland which the adjacent fields had become. The Israeli Army had torn up the orchards, charging that they were being used as cover by Netzarim's attackers. Mr Al-Waheidi, like Mr. Abdullah in Jabalya, was in his late fifties, a little older than the exile itself. Fewer and fewer men in the Gaza Strip, even those in middle age and above, dressed in traditional Arab clothing. Mr. Al-Waheidi was an exception. He wore a plain white *kefiyeh* on his head, and a dark, ankle length *jelabiya*. He completed his outfit with a western style jacket. His moustache was white, as was the stubble on his cheeks. His brown eyes were bright. His was the gaze of a man who wanted his interlocutor to understand clearly how life was. He was sitting behind his house. It was the only place which felt safe. Even though it was winter, the afternoon sunshine was warm, but it was better to stay in the shade: out of sight, and out of the firing line. The arrival of any visitor attracted the attention of the soldiers in the nearby watchtower. If they felt curious enough, an Israeli military jeep would tear up to the far side of the concrete blocks for a closer look. It was quiet here in the afternoon, but it was not the calm of a peaceful spot away from the noise and grime of the city, it was the stillness of a place where it was dangerous to move. His children were scared just to begin their journey to school each day. Often, they just stayed at home. Mr Al-Waheidi and his family were simply trapped. 'Because of the Israeli tower we can't move from our houses. If we move they will shoot at us. They will kill us,' he said, gesturing towards the concrete cylinder on the other side of his home.

Bullet holes scarred the back of the house, like the symptoms of a disease which was spreading uncontrollably and incurably across a sick body. The olive and orange trees in the field beyond had mostly been reduced to stumps. Even where they weren't, Mr Al-Waheidi and his family didn't feel it was safe to go into the field, so their harvest was a fraction of what it had been in calmer times.

'There are a lot of difficulties, but one of the most important difficulties is the agriculture,' he said, drawing on a cigarette. 'For example, we can't move just behind our houses because the Israelis bulldozed all the land here, so nobody can grow anything on it. Our main source of life is agriculture. We have about 20 dunams (a dunam is about 1000 square metres) just behind our houses, and we can't work them.'

Mr Al-Waheidi pointed to where one wall of his garden had been destroyed: demolished, he said, by an Israeli armoured vehicle which arrived in the dead of night. Soldiers burst into the house. 'They made us all sit in one room,' he recalled, still angry long after the event. 'They ordered us to put our hands on our heads. Three soldiers stood there, pointing their weapons. They told us not to speak, and not to move.'

While Mr Al-Waheidi, his wife, and three of their four children, were held at gunpoint, their eldest son, Mohammed, was taken by the soldiers to accompany them as they searched the house. He was a slight youth of 17 with a wispy moustache, studying, when the situation allowed, for his school leaving exams. On the unfurnished, incomplete second floor of the house, he acted out with wild gestures of his arms the events of the night. He says the soldiers threatened to kill him. 'They said 'We've seen you on the roof,' (Mohammed said he'd been up there to try to fix the water tank, which had been holed by a bullet). 'If we see you up there again, we'll shoot you.' It felt as if the family were living in an ever-contracting space, as if their home itself were growing smaller and smaller. Mr. Al-Waheidi, like many people in Gaza who found themselves in desperate circumstances, tried to be optimistic. Even at a time when the 'Road Map' had been left to one side, and the fighting was getting worse and worse, he tried to see a better time ahead.

'*Insha'allah* (God willing), there will be peace in the future, and they will pull out from the Gaza Strip and the West Bank. And the Israeli state and the Palestinian state together can live like neighbours, according to the agreements to make two states, Palestinian and Israeli. And I hope it will be an easy life after that.'

Mr. Al-Waheidi saw no possibility of peace while the Jewish settlers remained in Netzarim. He described a situation where it was impossibly dangerous for him to visit relatives who lived 100 metres away, or to work the land which lay next to his house. During the time I was in Gaza, a number of Palestinians were shot dead while digging their land, on the pretext that they were suspected of being in the process of planting explosives. So while the settlers remained, Mr. Al-Waheidi and his family lived on a front line. Netzarim was not only a settlement, but an army base, from which Israeli troops mounted raids into the southern and eastern districts of Gaza City. Mr Al-Waheidi was resigned.

'At night the situation is worse than the day. Last night the tanks moved from Netzarim at four o'clock in the morning. And we couldn't move. Even our kids couldn't go to school that day. We couldn't move from our houses. And last Sunday, they were also next to that area, and no one can move from his house.'

I asked him if he ever wondered whether the army and the settlers weren't just trying to drive him out.

'Of course, they don't want to see anybody here,' he replied. 'They want us to move from here, because they want to expand their settlements, and to expand their lands. And they want to have more and more land. It's like what happened in '48, when we emigrated from our lands in '48 to the West Bank and Gaza Strip. They want the land. They don't want to see any population.'

'They' might get their wish. The land around Netzarim was becoming more and more sparsely populated, so even if the Palestinians were still there, few of them were visible. Mr Al-Waheidi got up from his chair and walked back towards his house. The day was ending, and he knew it was better to be inside after nightfall, when the family gathered at home, taking care to spend as little time as possible near walls and windows which looked onto the watchtower.

CHAPTER 6
'WE AT LEAST KNOW WHY WE'RE GETTING SHOT.'

As you left Gaza City, the ramshackle breezeblock houses thinned out and the southbound road bordered the beach. A few solitary villas, with views of the Mediterranean, had been built along the road, but by then no one was living there. Their facades had been broken up by bullets; corners torn off by tank shells. Behind the villas, there had been orchards, but, like the wealthy Gazans who owned the seaside properties, they had gone. The Israeli Army tore up the trees and crops on the left of the road. Whereas early Zionists strove to make the desert bloom, the Israeli Military of the 21st century sometimes turned blooms back into desert. To the right of the road, there was a strip of sand, and then the sea. The only features in the scrubland were ruins, tree stumps, and Israeli Army positions. The open ground stretched away, and slightly uphill, for about a kilometre. There, the eye fell on the reason for the wasteland: the settlement of Netzarim. If Netzarim had not been there then, Palestinians would have been able to move freely between the north of the Gaza Strip and its centre, assuming, of course, that the Israeli Army didn't suddenly decide to close the road anyway. But it was there: a symbol of Israeli strength and an object of Palestinian loathing. The area around it was declared a 'security zone'. No Palestinian was allowed to enter. If they did, they risked being shot. Most of those killed there after the land was cleared – to take away cover for potential attackers – were armed. Others have been deranged, hopeless, would be assailants, driven mad by their sense of humiliation. Yet another was a 75-year-old shepherd, shot in the neck as he rode his donkey towards his flock. Abdullah Shihada al-Ashab's neighbours said that he had been a familiar sight to the soldiers, who appeared to tolerate him. Perhaps the settlement guards had changed. There seemed to be no warning, not even any attempt to warn or merely wound the bold septuagenarian. A shot to the neck is a shot to kill, instantly.

In calmer times, Palestinians could pass close to the settlement. Some even worked there as labourers. Now they could not go near it. The only way in from the Gaza Strip was to leave the territory altogether and then re-enter through a crossing point reserved for soldiers and settlers. When the *intifada* began in September 2000, for a few weeks the only way in and out of Netzarim was by helicopter. As the fighting continued, the Israeli Army arranged convoys to escort the settlers. The buses were armour plated, but the protection only extended halfway up the windows, so the driver warned his passengers to keep their heads down. Most of the passengers were soldiers, heading for a tour of duty guarding the settlers. This was a source of debate and friction amongst Israelis: many of the more religious settlers were exempted from military service to allow them to pursue more fully their studies of the scriptures. Secular Israeli conscripts ended up protecting them, and occasionally taking a fatal bullet for them. Even the settlers themselves would admit privately that relations between them and their guardians were not as good as they could be, and, as one army officer once put it, 'I can't imagine why anyone would ever want to live there.'

'Now we entered to Gaza Strip. We crossed the fence. We use Netzarim road. This road, and Kisufim road, this is two routes that the IDF use to divide Gaza Strip for three parts – when there is need – after some terror attacks unfortunately, or something like this,' explained Eran Sternberg. A short, stocky man in his late 20s, already the father of a large family, Mr. Sternberg was the spokesman for the settlers of the Gaza Strip. He lived in Gush Katif, the block of settlements which lay along the southern third of Gaza's coast. We had met there before on a couple of occasions, but I had always been refused permission to visit Netzarim. Now, in February 2004, the settlers had agreed. The Israeli Prime Minister, Ariel Sharon, had announced that he had ordered the preparation of a plan to remove the Gaza settlements. Their inhabitants were keen to explain why they should say. Mr Sternberg pointed through the windows of the bus at the wasteland either side of the road.

'Once there was a lot of Palestinian houses here. The reason is because of the huge amount of the terror attacks that was committed from these houses. The Palestinians show you how much they poor, and how much they suffer from the IDF destructing their houses…but I want tell you how much terror attack have been committed from these houses.'

Mr Sternberg appeared to have prepared his words with as much careful thought as the most conscientious of tour guides. Points of interest were indicated en route, although everyone on the bus had to remember not to lift their head too high. After all, the windows were only armoured half way.

'Now you can see a very nice example of Israel counter-terror. You can see a bypass, a bypass that's made here, a detour, because of mosque,' Mr Sternberg continued, looking at a lonely building. 'Instead of the straight road, Israel make a detour because of mosque, isolated mosque, the houses around it destructed, and the mosque remain, because we are not dismantling holy places.'

It was difficult to appreciate the real virtue in leaving the mosque untouched if the houses of all those who worshipped there had been destroyed. No one was left living close enough to heed the call to prayer which used to ring out from its minaret. Mr Sternberg did concede that it was in a 'very bad situation because of the war' (it had clearly been hit more than once, and, in consequence, damaged) but he was nevertheless keen for its continued existence to be noted. Mr Sternberg was direct, efficient, and friendly in a businesslike way, although it was hard to imagine him laughing. The matters he discussed, the situation in which he found himself, were just too serious for that. He was keen to stress how dangerous the settlers' lives were, how they were put at risk by 'terrorists'. He traced the beginning of the trouble back to the Oslo accords: the agreement from the mid-1990s which provided for limited Palestinian Autonomy, and which threatened the settlers' view of the Jewish homeland as an Israel which included the West Bank and the Gaza Strip. Even just taking the armoured bus trip to Netzarim was hazardous – and it was now the only way to make the trip at all. Indicating the pager he carried, Mr Sternberg said that almost every day it relayed to him news of an attack on one of the buses. He described a picture of life before the accord, before Palestinian Autonomy, before the settlements were the fortified stockades they had now become.

'Until Oslo, Netzarim was guarded by two reservists, two reservists, that's all. So the battle today is not because of Netzarim, it's because of the Oslo agreement. We have to be accurate and to look straight at the reality,' he insisted. 'Every moment it can happen. Every moment some missiles can hit the bus. Nobody can promise nothing. Like every moment you can explode in Jerusalem by suicide bomber.'

This was the point which he emphasized time and again. According to Mr Sternberg, Gaza was a part of Israel just as much as Jerusalem, and, in the view of the settlers, living in Jerusalem with the threat of buses being bombed was just as dangerous as living in the middle of a wasteland, surrounded by barbed wire and more than a million neighbours who at best loathed your being there, at worst dreamed of killing you. The short bus journey was soon over. From the area which had been cultivated and then turned back into desert, we passed into a desert which had become an oasis. 'Now we enter to Netzarim and suddenly the landscape is changed: flourish garden, flourish settlements,' as Mr Sternberg commented.

Netzarim was a pleasant place. Where the surrounding area was a desert of danger and violent death, this was a haven of well-kept lawns and well-watered flowers. A group of kindergarten children sat in a circle on the grass listening to their teacher. Classes over, they got up to play on the swings and roundabouts nearby. Just a few metres away, at the edge of the playground, soldiers lounged in the shade of a palm tree. Beyond them, emptiness: a watchtower that commanded the wasteland the only landmark. Any eye scanning carefully the curves of the land would come to rest on a shape that didn't quite fit: the turret of a tank, half dug in, or an armoured personnel carrier hidden behind a sand dune. Nearly everything else was gone, even two tower blocks about a kilometre away. They were blown up after the Israeli Army decided that they had been used as a viewpoint to plan an attack in which three soldiers, two of them women, were killed. The shell of one of the buildings remained, a ruin on the skyline, everything between bulldozed or dug up to make any attempt to attack the settlers as difficult as possible. The outlines of a couple palm trees – also on the horizon – emphasized how empty was the rest of the land. Inside the settlement, it was quiet and calm. It was orderly and tidy: a huge contrast to the noise and chaos of the towns and refugee camps just a short distance away. It was as if part of one country had been dropped into another. For all the security concerns, the constant threat of attack, the international political controversy which the settlers' presence provoked and continued to fuel, this was something of a paradise. But you had to look selectively to see it as such. Standing near the entrance, where the kindergarten kids sang their songs, or played on the swings, you could lift your eyes and look towards the blue, blue, Mediterranean beyond. You had to make sure that, as your gaze jumped from lawn to surf, it didn't fall short and land in the wasteland, the monument to war. One lot of homes had been flattened in the name of protecting this lot of homes. The neat rows of white-walled, red-roofed houses could have come from suburban America.

Some of their owners had. Tammy Silberschein held the youngest of her five children, Shmuel, in her arms. She had fair skin and a bright smile. Her hair could have been light brown, or perhaps even a bit red. It was impossible to say because it was covered according to religious Jewish tradition. She wore a striped jumper, and a skirt which came down to her ankles. Nine month old Shmuel seemed content. He wore purple babyclothes and sucked a dummy. Only occasionally did he babble, or yawn, but he seemed to do so in support of his mother, not to contradict her. She spoke quickly, in perfect English, her accent revealing that she had come from the United States only eight years earlier.

'Coming to Netzarim was a fulfilment of the Zionist dream, out of ideological reasons, believing that it's our moral right and obligation, divinely to settle all parts of the land of Israel, and that's why we're here,' she said. 'We live history all the time, and we feel it and we feel that we're messengers of the people of Israel from its dawn, from Abraham, all the way through its future.'

Where Mr. Sternberg's description of the danger the settlers faced almost sought to glamourize their existence, Mrs Silberschein's was a little more frank. The sense of duty she spoke of, though, shone through every word, and was clearly an inspiration, succour through the dark nights when bullets flew over the rooftops where her five children slept, and mortars landed nearby.

'Yes it is sometimes a difficult place to live. There are definite limitations on our normal life here. But despite the limitations we're flourishing, we're growing, we're expanding our homes, we're bringing many children into the world, and we have a lot of new things here,' she said, brightly.

Mrs Silberschein also spoke of the neighbours she never met, the Palestinians. Many settlers seemed reluctant to use the word, which suggested the existence of a people, and therefore, presumably, a homeland. A lot of settlers preferred usually just to speak of the 'Arabs', a mass of people, indistinguishable one from the other, living all the way from North Africa to Iraq. Even if she had little or no contact with them, Mrs. Silberschein had an idea of what the hundreds of thousands of people around her longed for, and how it threatened the 'Zionist dream' she held so dear.

'Most of the Palestinians living in the Gaza Strip are refugees from places in Israel proper: places like Jaffa, and Acco, from Haifa and their intent is to go back to those places,' she began. (Her language was interesting: as well as 'Palestinians', she said 'Israel proper', a phrase usually employed by neutrals trying to make the distinction between towns and villages inside the state's internationally recognised borders, and those outside.) 'When they say that we don't have a right to be here, they don't mean here Gaza, they mean here in the entire state of Israel. They don't think that the Jews have a right to be in Israel at all. They're against our sovereignty and that's something that of course I can't agree with. I think that we have the right and obligation to be here, and that's something that's accepted by the world, it was voted by the U.N. and this is the Jewish state. We only have one homeland. There are many Arab countries that the Palestinians can go to. This is the only Jewish homeland that we have, and it's small and we need it.'

'Do you feel any sympathy for the refugees living around here?' I asked.

'I think that the refugee situation is terrible. It's something that we did not create. It was not created by the state of Israel. It was created by the U.N. and by Arab countries that had an interest in having refugee camps because they wanted hostile forces to erupt. I think it's terrible. I think they live in poverty that absolutely anyone with a heart would feel terrible about it and I think the solution has to be made. But the solution isn't kicking me out of Netzarim. I think that there are other solutions that we can come to.'

'What sort of solutions?'

'I think that...hold on one second, let me just ask Eran about it. Eran...' She broke off, and began to speak to Mr Sternberg in Hebrew. An Israeli friend later translated her words as follows. 'He's asking about the Palestinians, and I've said the usual things, that it's terrible and so on.'

Mr Sternberg intervened, in English. 'I don't have to provide solutions...ones who create the problem...'

'Exactly,' Mrs Silberschein continued, like an actor who had been prompted. 'The one who created the problem should create the solution. The UN, the UNRWA whatever it's called has to create the solution.'

We walked down towards the edge of the settlement, continuing to talk. Mrs Silberschein outlined further her reasons for being in Netzarim, and why she and her fellow residents should never have to leave. There are many examples in human history of people who have been willing to put themselves at risk, even sacrifice themselves, for a cause. How, though, did she feel about being a mother in Netzarim? Putting herself in danger was one thing. What about her children?

'I feel very good being a parent here,' she replied immediately. 'I think it's a wonderful place to bring up children.' She went on to concede that there were 'effects of war', but that these were 'minimal' to her children. In fact she suggested that living in Netzarim made it clear to her children who the 'Palestinian terrorists', were and, as a result, they were growing up ideologically strong. 'I think that in general my children are growing up healthy on all levels,' she continued, 'and again, there are effects of war, and we're dealing with those effects, whether it's fears, whether it's bedwetting, and we have a team of people that come and support us.'

The settlers seemed to see themselves very much as pioneers, people of the frontier, brave and committed enough to live where others dared not, thereby affording a degree of protection to their compatriots. Mrs Silberschein contended that all Israeli society was living in a war at that time, and that the dangers then faced by residents of Israel's urban areas – suicide bombs in shopping centres or on public transport – were terrors which her children did not face. As Mrs Silberschein continued to talk, the smallest sense of doubt appeared to creep in. I knew that people in the settlements conceded that their children faced big psychological challenges but it was she who raised the subject now – in the shape of the team of people that came to support – not I. This doubt though, whether it was there or I imagined it, was soon banished. Coping with it was just perhaps one of the difficulties she said she dealt with. I asked her why she had chosen Netzarim. She replied that it was all part of what it meant for Jews to settle in Israel; that she had the same right to settle in Netzarim as in Tel Aviv or in Haifa. For the message which the settlers were keenest to send was that Israel reached from the River Jordan to the Mediterranean. It was all the Jewish homeland. Anyone else who wanted to live there – even if, in the case of the Palestinians, their families had lived there for centuries – had to understand and accept that. I asked Mrs Silberschein if she ever saw the day when the Jews could share the homeland with the Palestinians.

'Being a Torah observant Jew we are taught that this is the Jewish homeland, we have to be sovereign here, and we have to settle all parts of it, but any non Jews who would like to join us peacefully and live with us certainly can, and they're welcome. That's part of the…that certainly can fit in with the ultimate plan.'

'Can you ever see that happening in reality?'

'I have a strong belief in the prophecies. And the prophecies talk about non-Jews coming to our temple, and bringing scarifices, and we're going to be one big family, and there's going to be peace, and absolutely I believe in peace. It's very hard to see it now, but if I didn't have a vision, then I wouldn't be able to live here.'

My permission to visit Netzarim had followed Ariel Sharon's announcement that the Gaza settlements were to be evacuated – something which Mrs Silberschein flatly refused to believe then. Yet in the summer of the year which followed, 2005, that is what happened. Then, in the late winter of 2004, the settlers were bitterly disappointed by Mr Sharon's announcement that he had ordered the preparation of plans for their withdrawal. They had always looked to him as their champion and their defender. In his autobiography, 'Warrior', he talked proudly of how he helped to choose the location of the Gaza settlements, when he was in charge of the Israeli Army's southern command in the 1970s. The settlers saw themselves as the front line in Israel's 'war on terror'. They believed that they were heroically drawing fire which might otherwise fall on Tel Aviv or Ashqelon. If they were to go, Israel would simply be taking away a line of its defence. The idea that the settlements were provocative, that they were the root of the anger which led to attacks, was dismissed. As Mr Sternberg put it, 'We don't agree with these claims. We say that Netzarim is a finger in the dyke. Netzarim is seeing a very high level of terror. The moment that Netzarim ceases to exist will be the moment that the terror aimed at Netzarim will be aimed at the kibbutzim near the Gaza Strip.'

There was a primary school in Netzarim, a little down the slope from the heavily guarded entrance to the settlement, and away from the neat rows of white houses. It was bright inside: the walls were decorated with colourful charts and pictures drawn by the pupils. There was no natural light. In a land where there was blindingly bright sunshine most of the year, security came first. The windows were covered with metal shutters to protect the glass, and the children behind it, from bullets. With the door closed, and the windows covered, you would never guess that you were in the middle of a combat zone. The mathematics lesson went on pretty much as it would have done anywhere. Perhaps the most remarkable thing about it was the children's enthusiasm, and their good behaviour. The teacher only had to ask them to be quiet because they were so keen to answer her questions, not because they were talking out of turn. One little girl, dressed in pink, and with her hair neatly tied back with a band, looked up from her lesson for a moment and peered at the visitor through spectacles. Then her gaze fell back into its routine path of book, blackboard, and teacher. Across the yard, recorded electronic music came from another classroom, perhaps part of a lesson, or relaxation for the younger pupils. 'There's no place like home,' the words leapt into my head as the first notes reached my ears. I reflected how far from my childhood home I was, and wondered how far these children would travel, and which way, before they reached their thirties. Would their children go to school here, as they did? Would the gate still be kept locked, and guarded by a thin man with long sidelocks, and a large sidearm? Would the building no longer be a school? Would it be a ruin, or perhaps home to a poor Palestinian family, or perhaps a classroom where Israelis and Palestinians studied together, agreeing that there was no place like home, and they could both share it? Then, the most likely picture was impossible to predict, but after more than three years of bloodshed, and one lame attempt to bring peace, the most probable future felt like one where the two enemies would continue to strike at each other, to punch clumsily like exhausted bar brawlers, each hoping that the other would finally get tired, and give in. These pupils were only a few kilometres from Palestinian children the same age as them. They would probably never meet until their late teens, a couple of hundred metres apart, and armed.

From the edge of Netzarim, the land was open until as far as the Beach Road. It was strange to see landmarks, like the golden dome and minarets of the mosque which overlooked the shore, from the other side. Cars, many of them the shared Mercedes taxis, painted bright yellow, which were Gaza's public transport, moved along. At this distance, I could only imagine from memory the poor surface of the road, the reckless overtaking, and the extra speed to which the taxi drivers treated themselves when they reached one of Gaza's few open stretches of road. Here, behind the fence of the settlement, Palestinian daily life was something only witnessed from far away, and without detail. It was like seeing a videotape of an event from a distance, where the pictures were out of focus, poorly composed, and there was something wrong with the sound. The stretch of road which the settlement overlooked was frequently closed, and without warning. It might not seem much to be stuck in a traffic jam when hundreds of people each year were dying violent deaths in the conflict, but the sense of powerlessness and humiliation which came with not even knowing whether you could travel ten kilometres made the people of Gaza realize how much stronger than they were the occupiers. It made them angry. Sometimes, the road would be closed for up to three or four days at a time, and then opened for an hour or two. The road would be blocked 'after some terror attacks unfortunately, or something like this,' as Eran Sternberg put it, or during Jewish holidays. During Passover in 2003, the closure was imposed for four days. News that the way would be open at midday was broadcast on tv and radio, and spread rapidly through the streets. The Israeli Army were due to lift the roadblock for an hour. By 10.30am, a huge queue had already built up, starting at the checkpoint the Israelis had set up near Netzarim, and reaching back to the edge of the city itself. The traffic jam on the other side, the southerly section of the road, must have been at least as long: five kilometres or more. The summer sun was late that year. It was the last week of April, but heavy black clouds hung over the city, along the shore, and out to sea. The Mediterranean was restless. It often was here at its eastern end, but that day the waves seemed unusually violent, as if even they felt constrained by what was happening on land. There was heavy rain in the morning, and only the large, lukewarm drops and the mild temperature of the wind which drove them, gave any sense that winter might be ending. It was chaos. Petrol tankers, taxis, donkey carts, trucks carrying furniture, vegetables, or people, all fought for position. There was no sense that waiting in an organised line might actually help more people to get through. It was more like a sort of all-comers, occupation rules, grand prix: everyone would go as fast as possible and do their best to barge everyone else out of the way. The closure had been complete: not just the road, but movement in general. Now, in the hour before the way was due to be opened, pedestrians chose to avoid the crush on the road, the shambles of car horns, cutting up, and petrol fumes. They took to the beach, leaving the blocked main road, and running down to the sea like rivulets from a torrent which had been dammed. Almost everything natural seemed to be a shade of grey: the waves, the sky, even the sand. There were a few patches of green still surviving on the winter rain, and taking a final watering now, in late April, before the sun would scorch them. The only other colours on the beach were the reds in the traditional garments of the older women. Their clothes flapped in the rain and wind. Back on the road, the drivers were growing more and more impatient. 'Which Israeli Prime minister was it who said 'We will be afraid of the Palestinians when they can stand in line for a bus'?' a young man next to me asked sadly. Others were less in the mood for wry observation. 21 year old Abdelwahab was on his way to Rafah, near the Egyptian border, with a truck load of furniture and other household goods: gifts for a friend who was getting married. The presents were late. Abdelwahab had been stuck in Gaza City for four days. 'They talk about a 'Road Map', but look at this!' he said angrily. 'Nothing will change. It's all about security for the Israelis.'

Midday drew nearer. A shot rang out, then another. An ambulance siren howled somewhere behind us, coming from Gaza City, trying to get through the mass of cars, carts, trucks, and people. The noise of the siren came from one direction, the rumours from the other, up ahead. One man, it seemed, had been a little too eager to continue his journey. One of the shots we had heard further back in the queue (we were about 500 metres from the front) had been the signal that the traffic was allowed to move, the story reaching us went. The other had been fired into one traveller's leg after he moved forward too quickly. All his waiting, all his effort to secure a good place in the queue and make it to wherever he was going, were in vain. The IDF directed traffic with their guns and armoured vehicles. Any breaking of the rules might incur an on-the-spot fine: a bullet.

The settlers in Netzarim also depended on the Israeli Army for permission to come and go, but their situation was different. The Army were there to protect them, not to control and restrict them. Shlomit Zvi had a smile which showed perfect white teeth. Her hair was covered with a hat, and she wore glasses. 33 years old, she had lived in Netzarim for 11 years. She had seven children, ranging in age from 12 to 2. Her slightly hesitant English, with its occasional minor mistakes, almost made her seem timid. She too clearly saw herself as a woman of the frontier. Her views of Israel's history almost echoed, perhaps consciously, American tales of how the 'west was won' by fearless pioneers heading into the unknown.

'When the first Jewish people came here a hundred years, it was not easier. They had swamps. Their children were dead from malaria, and diseases, and they stayed. And if they won't stay, I wouldn't have been here, because the State of Israel wouldn't have been founded. Their strength gives me strength to stay.'

As we spoke, the songs and shouts of the kindergarten pupils drifted across the sandy space which was their playground. Like Eran Sternberg and Tammy Silberschein, Mrs Zvi was keen to point out the dangers of living anywhere in Israel. The example that she chose, though, was that of another settlement. Gilo, on the edge of Jerusalem, was considered by Israelis as a district of the city, although it, like Netzarim, was built on land outside Israel's internationally accepted borders. For her, it made no difference. It was all Israel. She told a story of going to spend *shabat*, the sabbath, in Jerusalem with her parents. After the sabbath was finished (no religious Jew would have permitted themselves to travel between sundown on Friday, and sundown on Saturday) they had gone to visit Gilo which, at that time, was coming under fire from a nearby Palestinian village, Beit Jala. Part of the purpose of the visit seemed to have been to demonstrate to the children that life in Gilo was not so different from their own, in Netzarim: in other words, that the kind of existence they knew, occasionally traumatizing (Mrs Zvi also mentioned that her children sometimes needed a psychiatrist) was perfectly usual. In Gilo, as in Netzarim, a wall of concrete protected the school from rocket and rifle round. The similarities seemed to have made an impression. On the way home, the children talked about where was the harder place to live: Netzarim or Gilo? There was shooting in both places, but enough of Netzarim was sheltered by concrete to ride bicycles; not so in Gilo. Yet in Gilo they could take a bus to the doctor's; in Netzarim they needed an armed escort. Eventually, it seemed that the children's verdict, having taken into account the pros and cons of their existence, was that Netzarim was better. Mrs Zvi's point was made. 'We know why we're here. Arabs around us want to hit us. The people in Gilo, a lot of them came to live in a city. They never dreamed that they will be shot. We at least know why we're getting shot. That's why it's better to be here. So they are with us. They understand that Gilo and Netzarim is one land. The Arabs want all of it, including Tel Aviv, including Haifa, and they're smart. They're doing step by step. They're trying to say there will be peace if you move.'

Mrs Zvi's parents had come to Israel before they were married, in the 1950s. She said that they had come because they believed that the place of the Jewish people was in the land of Israel. Mrs Zvi's parents' Zionist convictions had made them staunch supporters of the settler movement. As part of the peace treaty with Egypt in 1979, Israel returned land it had occupied in the Sinai, including land on which it had built. The settlement of Yamit was dismantled. Its houses were demolished, its residents moved. As a teenager, Mrs Zvi had gone there with her parents to support the settlers who were being relocated. She remembered the evacuation as 'a big trauma, for all the Israeli people'. Then, in February 2004, she refused to believe that Netzarim would go the same way, pointing out that the Israeli government had discussed such a move more than once before, and yet it had never happened. Nor did she believe it would help the cause of peace were it to happen. 'Netzarim is here 30 years, and Gush Katif a bit more. But the struggle between the Jewish people and the Arabs didn't begin 30 years ago. It began more than 100 years ago. And evacuating, and making this place a *judenrein*[4] is not going to bring peace.'

Mrs Zvi could see a day when Israelis and Palestinians could live together in a single homeland – only once the Palestinians understood that the land was Israel's. She said that Bill Clinton himself, speaking at Camp David, had conceded that, 'The temple was up on the mountain in Jerusalem much before Jesus was born, before Mohammed was born.' There's no soft 'h' in Hebrew, so Mrs Zvi, like many Israelis, pronounced 'Mohammed' as 'Mokhammed', as if she were clearing her throat of something which was annoying her. 'So first understand that we are in our home. Then, you want to stay peacefully with us, you can stay. But first you have to say that this is our land. That's the first step in going ahead.'

Modern ideas of borders and nation state were insignificant to the settlers. Giving up their presence in Gaza would be just the beginning of the Arab plan to seize the land 'step by step'. The lines which existed on modern maps meant nothing in comparison to the ties to the land, the rights to the land, which came with descent from Biblical patriarchs. The distinction between 'Israel proper'; Gaza; and the West Bank was an artificial, worthless, one. 'If we were looking at the land from the borders point of view,' Mrs Zvi continued, 'more than 150 years ago there were no borders. We were not here at all. So where do you say that our home is? Our home is where our first parents lived, and our first parents are Avraham, Abraham, and when Shlomo – Solomon – and David lived here, that's our borders. The fact that Romans kicked us out of here, and ruined our holy temple, doesn't mean it's not ours.'

This evocation of ancient history, of rights given by ancestors, whether or not by law, gave the settlers a striking lack of self-doubt. No doubt they had prepared the lines they were going to share with me in advance. Mrs Silberschein's unforced departure from the established message seemed to betray something which had not been rehearsed, or learnt, quite as it should. All the same, they seemed, despite their admission of recourse to child psychiatrists, to accept their situation which could seem to an outsider so needlessly provocative and dangerous; a life made intolerably burdensome by security precautions. Mrs Zvi saw an end to those measures – armoured buses, concrete blast walls – only once the people on the other side of the fence accepted that

---

[4] A Nazi term for a place where no Jews live

they were conquered, 'When the Arabs understand that this is our land, and then they'll know that this is nothing to fight for. They can live here, near us, as neighbours, but they're not fighting against us. Then they won't be necessary.'

At the edge of the settlement, those neighbours could only be seen in the distance. The midday call to prayer drifted across the wasteland from the Nuseirat refugee camp, a reminder that whatever the settlers felt, Gaza was home to more than a million Muslim Arabs. Mr Sternberg was keen to point out the spot where, in October 2003, Palestinian fighters broke into Netzarim, and killed three soldiers. Two of the soldiers were women, and their deaths restarted the row over whether Netzarim should be there at all. Israeli soldiers began to join the debate: one unit wrote an open letter to a newspaper revealing that they had refused to do reserve duty in Netzarim. Another soldier told a human rights group that he had been suspended from duty after refusing to obey an order to shoot anyone seen near the settlement with binoculars. Mr Sternberg explained what he thought was really at stake. 'The terrorists don't call this war intifada Gush Katif, intifada of the settlements, they call it, obviously, intifada Al-Aqsa. They not hide their intentions for Jerusalem. Those people of Nuseirat came from the area of Tel Aviv and Petah Tikva. The problem is the problem of entire Israel, not a problem of the settlements. The ones who want to give them the Gaza Strip and the settlements actually want to make them logical reason to continue fight for the rest of Israel. I think that two States for two people, this is quite good logical and rational solution. The problem is that the conflict is not rational and not logical. When you give a logical solution to a spiritual problem, like Oslo did, the Oslo agreement, it cause a disaster. This is what happens here.'

'You're saying that the refugees came from homes which are now inside Israel, don't you understand their desire to return to those homes?' I asked.

'I can understand the desire to return to those homes, but I can understand that ones who attack us, again and again, since the State of Israel is established, have to solve this problem. The Arab states attack us, the Arab states encourage them to escape, the Arab States have to solve the problem exactly like the Jewish refugee that escaped from the Arab States in '48. Million of Jews from Morocco, from Iraq, from Algeria, from Egypt, have restored their life in Israel. Today there are no refugees.'

'Maybe these people don't want to. They want to go back to the land which is now inside Israel. Don't they have a right to do that?'

'Look. There is a clash. There is a clash here of the Jewish people that 2,000 years have been hunted, and have been massacred, between very specific time of those poor people that maybe they left their houses but I think when, Jabotinsky said in the previous century, when a big injustice encounter with a little injustice so we don't have a choice.'

Ze'ev Jabotinsky was a 20th century Zionist who said that Jewish settlement in what was then Palestine should develop behind an 'iron wall' which the people he called the 'natives', i.e. the Palestinians, would, in his words, be 'powerless to break down'. Mr Sternberg looked out from behind his 'iron wall' towards the settlement's nearest neighbours, more than a mile away. 'Look. I can live with them peaceful and quiet, like it was here 30 years, 'til Oslo agreement. We lived with them, we have celebrations with them, we went into their towns, we managed our life together, we learned to drive in Khan Younis[5], we fix our cars over there, I'm ready to return. I'm prepared to return to that form of life. The problem here is that they won't be ready. They won't agree to that form of life. They want entire Israel. In their journals, in the mosques, in the addresses, they said it obviously. The problem is not the settlements. The problem is Israel. And if the problem is Israel, Israel cannot accept such a solution.'

An armoured personnel carrier bumped along the sand and scrub on the other side of the fence. As the noise of its engine faded away, the sound of another engine drew closer. It was the armoured bus, and it was time to leave. I got on the bus, found a seat, and slouched into it, taking care that my head was behind the armoured part of the glass. Mr Sternberg agreed with the Palestinian Islamic militant groups that this conflict was about the Al-Aqsa mosque, about the site where it stood, about Jerusalem. For the settlers and many of the neighbours they never met, the issue was who had the right to call where 'home', who controlled the land between the River Jordan and the sea, and who would do so in the future. When the 'Road Map' was launched, the settlers of the West Bank and Gaza held a demonstration against it in Jerusalem. 'We already have a road map,' read one sign, written in English. 'It's called the Bible.' Many Palestinians in Gaza are able to quote at length from the Koran to support their case for ownership of the land. With religion so important to both sides, the plans of man, like the 'Road Map,' seemed to have little chance of success. Even if moderate Palestinians and Israelis were still a silent majority, as the optimists would have it, they would never love a diplomats' document as much as others loved the word of God, would never lay down their lives for the land with as much courage as a true believer. A couple of months later, a pregnant settler and her four daughters were shot dead as they travelled through Gaza. Palestinian gunmen fired on the memorial service which was held a week later. Teenage Palestinian fighters continued to attack Netzarim, and to be killed. Everybody knew why they were getting shot: for the land, and for God.

---

[5] The Gaza Strip's second largest town.

CHAPTER 7

'ONE KILLED MY RELATIVE, AND WE'VE KILLED HIM.'

The faces of the dead looked down from lamp posts, from places where, in another time and place, shining white teeth might have smiled out from toothpaste advertisements. The Nuseirat refugee camp's main street was busy, especially in the mornings. The market was colourful and noisy, as if traders were making up in sound what they lacked in commerce. Few people had much money to spend, but still the stalls were well stocked. There were piles of appealingly rounded potatoes, which had grown in sandy soil, where stones wouldn't misshape them. There were tomatoes, less perfectly round, but tastier than their drug enhanced cousins in the supermarkets of the western world. They were gems in the dust. Much of the fruit and vegetables which had been brought by the cartload from the fields and gardens at the camp's outskirts, just beyond Mr Sternberg's gaze as he looked out from Netzarim, was imperfect, bruised and rotting, and covered in flies. The produce which was too putrid to be sold even to these poorest of people lay squashed underfoot, where it mixed with manure and plastic bags. The traders remained energetic, except for when the summer heat melted even their enthusiasm: 'Tomatoes! 10 shekels a box!' 'Potatoes! Potatoes!' 'Apples! Apples!'. Donkeys, wearier even than the men and boys who drove them on, rested while they waited for their carts to be loaded with unsold goods and empty boxes. Fish – fresh a short time ago – curled up stiff on top of the cardboard boxes where they had been placed for sale. The smell grew so strong as the sun climbed higher overhead that it came through the closed windows of passing cars. Whole families passed on donkey carts, women and girls veiled, and often dressed all in black. Gaza's refugee camps were conservative places, where traditional values remembered from ancestral villages governed daily life. Shame and honour were not outdated words or concepts, but ideas which carried great weight. Arab hospitality was real too – any outsider who wandered through the market would be warmly welcomed, and pressed to accept a cup of tea.

In death, the 'martyrs' looked down from above, down on the streets they had wandered in boyhood. The dead hero was usually shown as an unsmiling young man in battledress. He stood in the foreground. The background usually depicted his deeds, or the Dome of the Rock in Jerusalem, or both. The most dramatic one in Nuseirat market then remembered a man killed by the Israelis after he broke into a settlement and opened fire. He stood and gazed calmly at his beholder. Behind, there he was again – crouching at a gate, shooting down settlers between their rows of white-walled, red-roofed houses. The blood which spilt from the settlers' wounds was painted as a simple streak of red. It looked like the blood in renaissance pictures of Medieval battles, flowing from a deadly spear wound, or spouting from a headless neck. In Nuseirat and Netzarim, battles of that sort were still being fought – wars to drive out the infidel from the holy sites, or perish in the attempt, and go to heaven as a martyr.

Not all the battles were fought against the Israelis. One afternoon in October 2002, Emad Aqal, a hotheaded young member of a powerful clan, arrived by car in Nuseirat's market place. He entered the mosque which overlooked the street and took the microphone of the public address system. The imams who would call people to prayer without the aid of amplification are no more. Loudspeakers broadcast Friday sermons. They were also used to convey urgent news: telling fighters to get their guns when the Israeli Army was on the warpath, and often naming the latest 'martyrs' shortly afterwards. Emad Aqal also wished to announce a death, that of Colonel Rajeh Abu Lehya, Gaza's chief of police. Emad Aqal was himself the killer, and he was proud of what he had done. Once he had told the camp of his deed, he set fire to the car he had arrived in. It had belonged to Colonel Abu Lehya. Fearing, correctly, that the police would be after him, Emad made this his last public appearance. He disappeared. For weeks afterwards, the police maintained a checkpoint at the junction of the Beach Road and the turning to Nuseirat, but Emad Aqal was never caught. If you came from the camps, they were easy places to disappear back into. The alleys, yards, and tumbledown houses closed over their own when they needed it, allowing them to disappear like a fish diving deep after being returned to the water.

Colonel Abu Lehya had not been the first to die, and he was not the last. The police fought gun battles with the Aqal clan and their supporters in Nuseirat refugee camp and even in the main streets of Gaza City. Police stations were attacked by mobs of youths throwing stones and petrol bombs. Patrol cars were torched. Four more people were killed in the days following, before the streets calmed down. The fight even took on political overtones. For the Aqal clan were prominent supporters of Hamas, and the Palestinian Authority – of which the police force were then a part – were loyal to Yasser Arafat's Fateh movement. The opening shots in this feud had been fired twelve months earlier. The United States and its allies had just sent troops into Afghanistan to destroy Al Qaeda and their Taliban hosts. The radical youth of the Gaza Strip were infuriated by an American attack on a Muslim country. There was a big demonstration outside the Islamic University in Gaza. Protesters yelled their anger. The police apparently feared that the rally might turn into a riot. The Palestinian security forces were not well schooled in crowd control. The usual method of dispersing a crowd was to fire live ammunition, initially overhead. This time, they hit and killed four of the demonstrators, among them Yusef Aqal, brother of Emad.

'The Palestinian police attacked this march and started firing against demonstrators there. My cousin was one of them, and he was simply killed in cold blood.' Another member of the Aqal clan, a cousin of both Emad and Yusef, gave me the family's account of what had happened. He did not want his own first name used, because he was afraid of how the police might react to what he had to say. Ibrahim Adwan, one of the BBC's producers in Gaza, had found him a couple of days after the death of Colonel Abu Lehya. Ibrahim and I had gone to Nuseirat to try to learn more about the cause of the recent deadly confrontations. The cousin invited us into his house in the back streets of the refugee camp. The roads here were just sand, although a few saplings grew at the side, giving the place some feeling of civic pride. Away from the heat of the afternoon, we sat inside on cushions on the floor of an otherwise bare room. The light came through a window above our heads. The working day was over, and there was time to talk. This was the tale of a blood feud, the story of a family denied justice falling back on the traditional way of getting it.

The Aqal family had at first tried to make the law work for them, the cousin explained. They had petitioned the Palestinian Parliament, known as the Legislative Council, and Human Rights organizations, seeking their assistance in getting justice for the young relative who had been shot at the demonstration in the autumn of 2001.

It didn't work. The family decided that they would have to pursue other means of getting justice for Yusef. The cousin said that representatives of Fateh, Yasser Arafat's political movement, in the 'Middle Area', as that part of Gaza which included Nuseirat was known, came to talk to Emad, the brother of the dead student protester. The cousin described Emad, his own relative, as a 'gunman, and well known for that'. He said that Emad told the Fateh delegation 'in a frank way' that if they did not bring to justice those who had killed his brother, he would take revenge. The family were passed between politicians and police officials – none of whom ultimately addressed their complaints. Emad's cousin said that Emad was a patient man, but his patience was not endless. As he reached the key point of his story, his voice quickened and slowed by turn. He seemed excited by what he had to relate; keen that nothing should be lost in the telling by his speaking too quickly.

'So that's it. It's his brother. He has got his dignity and honour. He always sees that man who is the killer of his brother, and he couldn't wait for that long time. He decided to take revenge. The moment he did this, in front of me, he phoned many Palestinian officials, and told them: 'I have given you a chance for one year, and I think this was enough, so I did it myself. Myself, and not anyone else. And I warn you to take it as it is: it is me, Emad Aqal who revenged the killing of his brother, the martyred brother. It's not Hamas, it's not anyone else. I'm not against the Palestinian National Authority, you should take it as it is. It's me who avenged the killing of my brother. It's my right to avenge my brother, and that is simply what has happened.'

In the aftermath of the shooting, the feud had escalated – taking on political overtones because of the conflicting factional loyalties of the combatants. Emad's cousin did not want to portray this as a conflict between Hamas and the Palestinian Authority. Looking back now, though, it is hard to avoid the conclusion that such feuds may have been factors in provoking the armed confrontation which led to Hamas taking full control of Gaza after their 2006 election victory. Then in 2002, at least, it was a story of adherence to family honour delivering justice where the law, and human rights organizations, did not.

'It's like this. One killed my relative, and we've killed him. That's it. If you want to take it as it is, ok, this is the situation, and this is what should happen. If they want to apply justice, they should come and investigate the situation right from the very beginning. Let them bring killers to justice. If Abu Lehya is not one of the killers, let them inform us, and we will do what is better. If they want to apply justice, let them not apply it on one side. Let them do it against all sides. This is what I think they should do. They killed our relative because he was marching against the injustice of America. He did nothing against the Palestinian Authority; he did nothing against Abu Lehya. He didn't get near to any of the police stations or policemen, and they killed him, in cold blood.'

He said that another relative had been detained by the police, but the family would not be cowed.

'Now they kidnapped my brother, they may attack us. Let them do whatever they want. It's our dignity, and we will sacrifice our blood for the sake of our dignity.'

He stressed again that this was not a fight between Hamas and the Authority, but that its cause was what he saw as the Authority's contempt for his family and the loss they had suffered. 'Nobody came just to discuss things in a calm way, and to say: 'Ok, you have got one man killed. We want to finish these things. Ok, we will bring those who killed your son to justice and we want you to help us investigate the situation. They did nothing. I think they are like a gang,' said the cousin. 'We killed the murderer, and that's all. They should have made it like this. We think it's all over. We are asking for the law. Where was the law for one year?'

The only law which would allow the family their revenge was in the barrel of Emad Aqal's gun. In the end, he could wait no longer to pull the trigger. Funerals in Gaza were usually held soon on the day of the death, in accordance with Islamic tradition. Those who wish to pay their respects or present their condolences, but who are unable to come to the funeral, will come instead to a mourning tent. As we left the house, Ibrahim pointed to a tent which had been set up nearby. It was the mourning tent for Yusef Aqal, erected not immediately following his death, but a year later, after his family had taken their revenge.

Hamas and the Palestinian Authority continued to trade insults, but the shooting died down. The PA mounted a show of force. There were more members of the Preventive Security – the branch of the Authority which was supposed to curb the activities of the militant groups like Hamas and Islamic Jihad – on the streets than ever before. The PA – pointing to the attacks on police stations which followed the shooting of Colonel Abu Lehya – accused Hamas of trying to escalate the situation. Dr. Ismail Abu Shenab, one of Hamas' leaders, blamed the Palestinian Authority for presiding over lawlessness.

'This is a traditional situation. It is tradition in our society. The Aqal family lost their son last year in clashes between Palestinians and the Palestinian Authority police. The Aqals accused one of the policemen of killing their son. They asked the Palestinian Authority to put him on trial. The Palestinian Authority refused. So the Aqal family, according to Palestinian tradition, had to get revenge,' he explained. 'According to Islamic teachings, it is justified. According to Palestinian tradition, it is justified. According to the law, it is not justified. But we do not have enforcement of the law here. Things are loose. And in this sense, you open the road to the family traditions to take place. It is not the first incident in the Palestinian community. Last year, the family of another Palestinian killed a policeman, and the Palestinian Authority did not do anything. Many situations like this happened and the Palestinian Authority could not control the whole situation. In this sense there is justification for what happened.'

Dr. Abu Shenab was speaking less than a year before his own death. His car was blown apart as he travelled through Gaza City one afternoon the following August, as the *hudna* came to an abrupt and bloody end. His bearded face took its place among the hundreds of pictures of 'martyrs', and the organization he had been a prominent member of sought its revenge. He did not live to see Hamas become the government of Gaza, putting their Fateh rivals out of power in the territory. While the *intifada* continued, divisions in Palestinian society between clan and movement smouldered away, bursting into flame from time to time. Emad Aqal's cousin said that the police had warned his clan that once the battle with Israel had reached an end, or a pause, scores would be settled.

'About two or three months ago, this man, Abu Lehya, and one of his officers, arrested one of our family. And they threatened that: 'The moment the *intifada* comes to an end, we are going to arrest you, Aqal family, all. Do you want to bring us to justice? You will see what we will do after the *intifada* comes to an end. They threatened us. So we are under threat. The moment the *intifada* comes to an end (it will be), "Come here. During the *intifada*, we were concerned about national unity. We are ready for you now."'

Emad Aqal remained at large. The alleys of the camp where he had grown up continued to resound with explosions and gunfire from time to time, becoming more and more dangerous. For many people who lived in Nuseirat, like the residents of all the camps in the Gaza Strip, it was simply impossible to avoid getting involved in the conflict. Their neighbours were the fighters the Israelis were determined to destroy, and sometimes it was very hard to stay out of the way. Take the story of a man who heard a hammering on his door in the middle of the night. He was already awake. An Israeli armoured column was advancing into the camp. The man opened the door. 'Move your family to the back of the house,' he was told by a Hamas fighter. 'We've put a bomb in the street. If an Israeli tank passes, we will detonate it. It's safer if you're not here.' A poor householder in a refugee camp, he faced death from all sides. If they had seen him trying to defuse the bomb, Hamas could have shot him as a collaborator. If the invading Israeli force had seen him acting suspiciously near the pile of sand which covered the explosives, they would have shot him as a Hamas bomb-maker. Trying his hand at amateur bomb disposal would also have been highly dangerous, but so was waiting for the mine to blow up the front of his house and kill his family. The refugees lived in the middle of the war. There was nowhere safe for them to go. Any night could be the night of an Israeli raid. The workshops making the bombs to stop them were hidden among the alleys of the camps. 'Work accidents' – as premature explosions were euphemistically called – were not uncommon. In Nuseirat in April 2003, 'work accident' took off one man's lower leg, and burnt a sheikh's beard from his chin, destroying his dignity, but sparing his life. Nuseirat was a miserable place of unredeemed poverty and despair. To see young children there was to realize the impossibility of their growing up unscathed, mentally at least. When there was money to buy presents on feast days, the boys of Gaza craved guns and other weapons. Instead of collecting cards of footballers, they gathered spent ammunition, always proud to show off their prize items to any visitor who might appear. In the immediate aftermath of a battle, they would race to the scene to seek whatever new trophies might have been left lying around. They stuck grubby fingers into fresh bullet holes in their search for souvenirs. Houses demolished as a punishment for family a member's involvement in attacks on Israeli targets became after school playgrounds. The battle zones were also the places where the refugees were born, schooled, played, where they went to work, married, gave birth, and died. The children who went out to collect shrapnel and spent shells were always keen to act as tour guides to any visitor who came along. They would lift up bloodied clothing on sticks so it might better be examined, and pull you towards pools of blood among the sand and dirt. A bloodstain on a tree – where a man had been shot in the neck on his way home from dawn prayers – became a props which enabled the kids to tell their story even more vividly.

In March 2003, just a couple of weeks before the start of the war in Iraq, the Israelis mounted a massive raid into the Al-Bureij refugee camp, like Nuseirat, in the central area of the Gaza Strip. Eight people were killed: some of them armed fighters who had taken to the streets to confront the incoming Israeli armoured column, one of them a mother who was nine months pregnant. Nuha Al-Maqadma was trapped under the ruins of her house and bled to death. Her flimsy dwelling had been brought down by the force of explosives set to destroy another house – that of an Islamic Jihad member who had been killed as he carried out a suicide car bombing at an Israeli military post the previous month. The Israeli Army usually gave warning that they were going to blow up a building. It was usually – but by no means always – sufficient for able-bodied people to escape. The disabled, those with learning difficulties, those slow or hard of hearing because of advanced age, were not always quick enough. 40-year-old Mrs Al-Maqadma was too heavy with child to move fast enough. The day after the raid, the camp's residents gathered to survey the damage and exchange accounts of what had happened. To make it harder for their quarry, a leader of Hamas in his sixties, to escape, the Israeli Army had apparently turned off the power supply to the camp. Mrs Al-Maqadma might have heard the warning to leave the house, but her attempt to escape, if she made one, if she was not already paralysed by fear, would have not been made any easier by the confusion which would have gripped her as she was surrounded by the noises of battle in the impenetrable darkness. Her body was found in the rubble of the house she had shared with her husband and ten other children. Around the corner, another pile of rubble was all that was left of the family home of 65-year-old Mohammed Taha, a founder member of Hamas, and the target of the previous night's raid. After an exchange of gunfire and grenades, he had been taken into custody along with three of his sons, and their house had been destroyed. It was only March, but it was hot and unpleasantly humid. Each breath was filled with the taste of the aftermath of a battle: dust – containing, certainly, small particles of explosives and concrete; perhaps blood. Kids clambered over the ruins. Each incursion brought a new place to play and explore, a new chance to find spent bullets and pieces of shrapnel. One boy held a doll's head on the end of a stick. Among the rubble, there were schoolbooks, scraps of clothing, slippers, pots and pans. Hassan Taha sat calmly nearby. His father and three of his brothers had been captured, but he remained free. 'First they blew open the door. My father was behind the door, so he was injured. Then they came into the house and started firing into the rooms,' he recounted.

His voice was slow, lazy-sounding, probably because he hadn't slept. It made him appear contemptuous of what had happened – as if he couldn't dignify the Israeli action by summoning the energy to talk about it. His family had suffered, but Hassan felt sure that would only increase their standing among their neighbours.

'They look at our family with respect, they respect us more and more. At the same time, there is a feeling that we would love to have revenge, to retaliate for these attacks from the Israelis.'

Among Hassan's drawl, there was defiance, a determination that the struggle must go on. This was only a minor setback.

'Thank God, I don't think that people are upset about what happened to their houses. It's a normal thing for them – that's my feeling – and anyone who built one house can build twenty houses.'

Hassan's father was released a little over a year later, and returned to the camp to a massive welcome. One of his brothers, Yasser, also won a place among the heroes of the Gaza refugee camps – but as a 'martyr'. A missile from an Israeli helicopter gunship blew his car apart three months later as he travelled through Gaza City. His baby daughter and 25-year-old wife, Islam, were unfortunate enough to be in the car too. Like him, they were killed. Like Mrs Al-Maqadma, Mrs Taha was pregnant when she died.

They took their places among the posters and paintings of 'martyrs', almost the only pictures in the refugee camp. Below them, life in the camp went on as normally as possible. Battered yellow taxis tooted their horns incessantly in the hope of cramming in just one more passenger. The market traders touted their wares. Tired donkeys dragged whatever they were forced to drag. As the *intifada* continued, the economy contracted, and unemployment remained steady at around 70 percent. Many goods actually fell in price – costs dropping to what the market would bear. Olive pickers – who bought the rights to harvest orchards in the autumn – complained that the fee they paid could not be covered in sales of the crop. Those who pressed the olives and sold the oil were themselves not selling enough. Few people had the money to buy the best quality product and so they made do with whatever they could get. Some commodities did go up in value: ammunition, for example, which became scarce whenever the Israelis discovered and stopped a smuggling route. A senior Israeli Army officer in the south of the Gaza Strip once explained to me that they knew when the Palestinians had received a new consignment of kalashnikov ammunition, because their informers told them that it had gone down in price. The only people – apart from arms smugglers – whose assets seemed to grow in value were horse and donkey dealers. Fewer and fewer people had jobs, so fewer and fewer of them could afford petrol for their cars. Donkeys were cheaper to run, and more versatile. They could go over rubble, or across country or along the beach when the roads were closed. I once paused on the shore to chat to Ibrahim Al-Daoudeh, a grandfather-fisherman casting his net from the water's edge with his sons and grandsons. It seemed a pleasant enough way to make a living, if you didn't stop to reflect that they were not at the beach under the Mediterranean sun for relaxation, but for backbreaking work casting and hauling a net for hours on end, in the hope of catching a few small fish. Ibrahim – his stubble silver, his face weathered by sun, saltwater and wind – pointed to the cart where his paltry catch was collected in a bucket. From the beach, it would be taken home, or, if the quantity was sufficient, or the need for cash particularly great, to the market for sale. There were two donkeys: one in harness, and a younger one tethered to the back of the cart. Perhaps the younger one would one day serve the next generation of fishermen as its mother now served

Ibrahim. 'To use the donkey it costs three shekels worth of beans to feed him,' he explained. 'To use the car, it costs ten shekels worth of petrol.' Saving the extra seven shekels – about a pound – was a major economy.

Money was counted just as cannily at Nuseirat's weekly livestock market. It took place on Mondays, on a piece of open ground at the end of the street which ran past the camp's main market. There were sheep, cows, goats, and donkeys – some tied to stakes in the ground, others standing unsteadily on the back of pick-up trucks. There was an incessant bleating, and only occasional lowing or braying. The sheep seemed to be the most vocal commodity. Donkeys almost doubled in price during the *intifada* because they were reliable and cheap to feed. You had to know what you were looking for, however, if you wanted to be sure to get your money's worth. Jihad Abu Umtihan was there buying and selling. He spoke through teeth brown from tea and tobacco. His eyes suggested both that he was shrewd at driving a hard bargain, and that the questions of a western reporter were not to be answered entirely seriously. 'Before the *intifada* you could get a donkey for $100. Now you'll need to spend $200. The price has doubled.' He explained the price range. 'This donkey's a weak donkey – it costs $50. It's a little bit of sugar, as we say, it has no energy. But that one costs $150, and that one costs between $200 and $300. How can you tell how much they're worth? Well you can tell just by looking, like a pretty woman. If it looks good and expensive, it's worth more.'

Jihad did concede that a value didn't lie in looks alone 'The real quality is in the strength of the donkey,' he said, pointing to a sturdy specimen. 'People who want to buy a donkey need it to carry a heavy weight, and some can't.'

But he also seemed determined to stress the importance of appearance.

'When you look at the donkey, it has to look strong and beautiful. And white donkeys are more expensive than other donkeys.'

'Why?'

'It's like a white house or a white woman. They're just more beautiful.'

The latter remark was largely aimed at my BBC colleague, Susannah Nicol, who was working with me that day – but the whole crowd of traders and street kids who had gathered to see the foreigner chat to one of the donkey merchants burst out laughing. There wasn't much fun to be had in Nuseirat, and seeing a foreigner being made a fool of in the donkey market was pretty high on the list of entertainments young boys might hope to find. Girls over the age of ten were rarely to be seen out playing in the camps. Their brothers enjoyed freedoms which were forbidden to them. The boys took advantage of being allowed out of the house by behaving as badly as possible. It was impossible to imagine how bored these young lads must be. There were few play facilities. They also grew up in a very closed society, with no experience of, and little knowledge of, what lay beyond the edge of the refugee camp. There were many people in the Gaza Strip who had never even been to Gaza City, never mind beyond the territory's claustrophobic confines. Their playthings were spent shell casings. Their heroes, their role models, were not footballers or film stars but 'martyrs'. Anything outside their narrow world was to be mocked, treated with suspicion and aggression. At the sight of any foreigner, they would gather around. First they would repeat, 'How are you?' or 'What's your name?' endlessly, rarely waiting for, or responding to, an answer if it came. Sometimes older boys, aged about 15, would arrive at the back of the crowd of younger urchins. There would be the occasional bookish one who was thrilled to get a chance to speak some of the English he had learned at school. There would be other, slightly menacing ones, who might hiss *'Yehud!'* (Jew!) through broken or cracked teeth. Outsiders who ventured into the camp were often Israeli soldiers who did so in tanks and armoured personnel carriers, so outsiders became something to be feared and hated. Once the kids were bored with chanting 'How are you?' they would kick the backs of your legs or throw stones. Women got their bottoms pinched by teenage hands whose owners were over excited by seeing uncovered female hair. This was a society in which everybody was expected to conform to conservative Muslim values. There was simply no concept of living any other way. Anyone who did so deserved, and received, the scorn reserved for Israelis. There was no way you could safely respond: any attempt to tell them off would make them laugh in your face; and sterner measures, like a push or a slap, might land you in real trouble with elder brothers or cousins who might arrive with stones and eventually guns.

As the *intifada* continued, people seemed to cling more closely to their faith. The teenage daughters of secular parents, those who had supported the left-leaning Palestinian nationalism of the 1970s, would argue when their mothers said they should not cover their heads. Wearing a headscarf became a sign of radicalism and rebellion, not repression, as westerners might see it. Mourning ceremonies were one ritual of traditional Palestinian, Islamic, life which was strictly and frequently performed. Some months in the Gaza Strip the death toll had to be measured in dozens. On Monday October 20th 2003, the Israeli Air Force carried out five strikes on targets in the Gaza Strip in the space of a little over twelve hours. The earlier ones were aimed at a Hamas weapons store, and two men who had left the area where it was located a short time before. The missile which killed them struck in the middle of a city street. The last attack of the evening was in the main street of Nuseirat. A car was hit by a missile fired from a helicopter. When a crowd gathered at the scene, the helicopter fired a second missile, eyewitnesses said. Eight people were killed, most of them civilians, according to Palestinian medical staff. Not so, said the Israeli military. The street had been empty when the missile hit. The Israeli Air force even released video showing the car exploding with nobody nearby. Whatever the truth, there were dead civilians: among them Zein al-Aabedeen Mohammed Shahin, a doctor who had run out from a nearby clinic where he was working. He was the cousin of Seif Shahin, a television journalist whom I had seen many times and chatted too, as far as my few words of Arabic, and his limited English, permitted. Like me, he worked from the building which housed the BBC office in Gaza. Thirty-six hours after the strike, a group of Palestinian journalists decided to go to Dr. Shahin's home in the Al-Mughazi refugee camp, which, together with Nuseirat and Al-Bureij, made up the 'Middle Camps' of the Gaza Strip, to offer their condolences. I went too.

The mourning tent took up most of a street. There were hundreds of chairs under the awning which stretched across the road. The black flags of Islamic Jihad, and the green ones of Hamas, hung beneath it. This was not a wealthy part of Gaza. Such places were few and far between in any case, and were not to be found in the back streets of Al-Mughazi refugee camp. The street was not surfaced, and the shops which opened on to it were poorly stocked with the cheapest goods: fizzy drinks, and small bags of snacks which sold for half a shekel each. 'Welcome!' one ancient shopkeeper called out from under a brilliant white skullcap when he saw me. His cap was about the only thing in the street which wasn't discoloured by dust. A long row of male relatives stood ready to receive the mourners. Women came to present their condolences separately, inside the house. Seif stood at the front of the line. When my turn came to talk to him, I kissed him 4 times on the cheeks, as I had seen the others do, and said '*Azzam Allahu azhraq*' ('May God reward you in heaven' – expressing the wish that God will compensate the bereaved for the loss they have suffered), a phrase which Rushdi had taught me as we drove down from Gaza City. Seif looked as if he had been crying. He looked as drained as only those whom grief has kept awake can. His light brown skin, kept healthy looking by year-round sunshine, seemed to have a greyish sheen. I don't know how old he was. He had greying hair, but that meant very little. Most people in Gaza looked about ten years older than they really were. Seif's cousin's age had variously been given in news reports as 29, 30, and 35 so perhaps they grew up together. They must have been close, or he would not have been at the head of the line receiving the mourners. We passed along the line, shaking hands with each man in turn. Some thanked me in English for coming. We took seats under the awning. We were served bitter coffee in tiny china cups, and dates. My Palestinian colleagues greeted friends and acquaintances. We stayed for ten or fifteen minutes, talking in soft voices and sipping our coffee. Then it was time to leave. The mourning tent would stay there for days, giving as many people as possible time to pay their respects. Unlike the Aqal family, the Shahin family's near neighbours in the Middle camps, the talk here was not openly of revenge. The doctor's death, though, was felt like another wound on the body of the homeland and its people: another blow, another death of the kind which made it harder for either Israeli or Palestinian to forgive.

There are two Commonwealth War graves cemeteries in the Gaza Strip. One of them is in Gaza City. The second is in the middle of the territory, and our route back to Gaza City from Al-Mughazi took us past it. I had been to the one in Gaza City before, but had never had the chance to visit this one. A few months later, in February, returning from the Rafah refugee camp near the Egyptian border, I stopped and went in. They were few lawns in Gaza. Water is so scarce that it is used almost exclusively for fruit and vegetables, not grass. The cemetery was an oasis. There was grass. There were flowers. It was quiet. A friend from Nuseirat told me once that he and his classmates used to go there to revise for exams. If you lived with your extended family in a crowded house in the noisy, cramped, refugee camp it was probably the only place you could find a quiet spot to think about your studies. The graves were placed in ordered columns and rows. The headstones stood in narrow flower beds whose borders were straight and neat. The headstones were the same ones which are found across Flanders and northern France. The palm trees which marked the graveyard's border showed that it was somewhere very different, but it was also very different from its surroundings. The noisy chaos of Gaza stopped at the cemetery gate.

The men buried here had died driving the Turks out of the Gaza Strip during the First World War. It was the end of the Ottoman Empire, an era when there was going to be a new Middle East. The French and British might almost have called their drawing of borders a 'Road Map' if such a phrase had been the diplomatic fashion of the time. Few people at that time could have foreseen the creation of the State of Israel, an event which would change the landscape and demography of what was then Palestine more than either World War did. Most of the graves bore names and serial numbers; some had the 'Known unto God' which often meant that only pieces of a person had been recovered. One headstone stood apart. It didn't break ranks; it stood in place among the columns and rows. It stood out because instead of a cross beneath the regimental crest, it had a Star of David. This was the grave of Private S. Rosenberg, who died on the 21st October 1918. Eighty five years later to the day, Seif's cousin was buried, a casualty in the war fought between the army of the Jewish state, and those who wanted a state of their own between the river and the sea. The Commonwealth War Graves Commission website gave few details of Private Solomon Rosenberg's life, or of the cause of his death. He was 'Son of Aaron Leybush Rosenberg and Malka Rosenberg, of Wloszcrowie, Kielecka, Polska, Poland; husband of E. Rosenberg, of 17-18, Carburton St., Great Portland St., London'. In the cemetery, 'E. Rosenberg' was given a more human face than the official record allowed. Beneath the Star of David, an inscription read, 'In fond memory from Esther, your loving wife'. Did Esther come here to visit her husband's grave? What had separated Solomon from his Polish parents, and brought him to Carburton Street, before his soldiering in Palestine? Did Aaron and Malka live long enough to fear the Holocaust, or were they already resting in peace by the genocidal evil swept across Europe? When Solomon breathed his last in the sandy scrub of Gaza, did he ever imagine that his fellow Jews would be fighting to defend their houses in nearby Netzarim? The cemetery was a quiet place, but nothing in Gaza could escape the rage of the second *intifada*. Private Rosenberg's gravestone, like those of some of his comrades in arms, had been chipped. Half way up one side, a bullet had broken the edge of the marble. In May 2004, following reports that British troops in Iraq were mistreating their captives, headstones in the cemetery in Gaza City were defaced and uprooted. Whatever Private Rosenberg and his fellow soldiers had thought they were doing in Gaza, theirs was not a war to end all wars.

In October 2002, when the second *intifada* was two years old, the British Consul General presided over a ceremony at a hotel on the Gaza seafront. Ibrahim Jarada was retiring after 44 years as the Commonwealth War Graves Commission's gardener in the Gaza Strip. His father and grandfather had held the post before him; his son was taking over. 'I remember everything is good. I don't have any accident. I was in a quiet, safe, place,' he said after the ceremony, speaking in the gentle, relaxed tones of one who has learnt to cope with troubles around him. He would continue to live near the cemetery, and planned to record his knowledge so that others could benefit of his experience of gardening in Gaza's salty, sandy, climate. 'Now I am writing my notes about my history. What I doing, what I plant, what plants is good for salt water. What trees is good. I'm writing it in a horticultural book now.' I saw Mr Jarada again a few months later, when I visited the cemetery. His optimism carried him through 44 years of work under Egyptian occupation, then Israeli invasion, then Israeli occupation. Hopefully it sustained him through retirement. In November 2003, the British consulate decided not to hold a Remembrance Day ceremony in the Gaza Strip – the highlight of Mr Jarada's professional year – because they felt it was unsafe. Six months later, the graves in Gaza City were desecrated, and the anger that spread across the Middle East after the occupation of Iraq spilled over into Mr Jarada's 'quiet, safe, place', violating its sanctity and tranquillity, like an angry tide sweeping away a sandcastle on the shore.

There were times when the cemetery in Deir el-Balah, and the area around it, enjoyed calm. In the summer of 2003, during the *hudna*, when the people flocked to the beach, the area was quiet. Palestinian security forces tentatively moved back to positions they had abandoned two years before, spending first the daylight hours there, and later feeling bold enough to man them round the clock. The Palestinian Naval police returned to a guard post along the Beach Road where it followed the coast next to the Middle Camps. The Palestinian flag flew in the strong warm summer breeze coming off the sea. A couple of hundred metres down the road, the Israeli flag flew above a concrete wall which marked the edge of Gush Katif, the block of Jewish settlements which took up the southern third of Gaza's Mediterranean coast. The Palestinian officer and his men were friendly enough, but they didn't want their names used, and they didn't want me to quote them. The officer feared for his men's safety. He just didn't want to say anything which might inflame the situation, and put them in danger. The *hudna* had been declared a couple of weeks earlier. 'It's too early to say anything, maybe in one month,' the officer said, apologetically. As we sat and drank tea under the shade they had put up, it became clear that he just didn't believe it would last. There was nothing he could say which might not seem controversial. If he gave his honest view, that in a month or so the fighting would start again, he would have been accused of incitement. If he said it was all fine, he would have been seen as giving in too easily, and saying what Israel wanted to hear, that the *intifada* was over. It felt, in that time after the launch of the 'Road Map', and the coming of the *hudna*, that everyone was playing a game. Everyone knew that it wouldn't last, but nobody wanted to be blamed for ending it. Nobody in an official position, even this police officer, even wanted to say that this new emperor, sent forth from Washington to bring peace to the Middle East, had no clothes. A car arrived at the checkpoint. Two of the police officers got up to stop it, search it, and check the driver's papers. The one thing which was not popular about the *hudna* was that the police felt able to take to the streets to go carry out their duties. As a result, many people who had blissfully been driving around without licences or insurance were stopped from doing so. Not that the system functioned perfectly. Around this time, I was travelling through Gaza City in a friend's car. Another motorist ran into the back of us. My friend got out to talk to him. As the two vehicles were in the middle of the road, the other driver suggested they pull over to discuss the matter. He got back into his car and, instead of pulling over, drove off. We managed to make out his number plate through the dust which swirled in his wake. We went to the police, who had just reopened a department to deal with traffic violations. My friend reported the incident. He was told that there was little the police could do, and, if he still wanted them to open an investigation, my friend would have to pay for it up front. He declined, and as we left the police station, he concluded, 'I will have to resolve this through unofficial channels.'

If they didn't have time, money, or inclination to go after minor offenders, then the police wouldn't be tackling the Palestinian militant groups. The Naval police I was visiting allowed us to take pictures of them stopping the car, but they also made it clear that they were not confiscating weapons. This was not what the 'Road Map' called 'dismantling the terrorist infrastructure'; what the majority of Gazans would have called 'collaboration'. It was routine police work, and nothing more. Anything more adventurous might have been dangerous. The Palestinian Authority knew from their experience with the Aqal clan and other similar incidents that it was not worth confronting Hamas and its supporters head-on. As speculation grew in the spring of 2004 that the Israeli government was preparing to withdraw some or all of its settlers from the Gaza Strip, anyone with any power in Gaza wanted to make sure that they would hold onto it after the withdrawal. Journalists who wrote the wrong thing were punished. Seif Shahin, less than three months after he had buried his cousin, was assaulted in broad daylight in one of Gaza City's main streets. Four masked men fired shots in the air and beat him until he was able to flee. He believed his crime had been in a report he had filed about a Fateh rally: he had reported that 'thousands' of people had attended. His assailants would apparently have preferred the phrase 'tens of thousands'. A couple of weeks later, Ghazi Al-Jabali, the Gaza police chief whom Emad Aqal's cousin said had done nothing to help the family over the death of Yusef, was the victim of what his spokesman described as an 'assassination attempt'. Nonsense, said a statement from another 'official security source', it was an argument which got out of hand. Whatever the truth, one of General Al-Jabali's bodyguards was shot dead, and the sound of the gun battle in the police compound was heard across the city. More and more family feuds were settled with kalashnikovs, in the street. The words which Emad Aqal's cousin attributed to Colonel Abu-Lehya, the man whose life they took in revenge, seemed to sum up what could happen if the Israelis did withdraw from Gaza: 'You will see what we will do after the *intifada* comes to an end. During the *intifada*, we were concerned about national unity. We are ready for you now.'

CHAPTER 8

'WE HAVE A MIRACLE HERE,
BECAUSE UNTIL TODAY, ONLY
ONE SOLDIER WAS KILLED'

Settlers spoke of a Jewish community living in Gaza for centuries before leaving after riots in the 1920s. After the 1967 Arab-Israeli war, when Israel took Gaza from Egyptian control, they returned in small numbers. At the beginning of 2004, there were about 7,500 Jewish settlers in the Gaza Strip. Netzarim was their most isolated and exposed outpost; Gush Katif, a bloc made up of several individual settlements, their largest. In his 2001 autobiography, *Warrior*, Ariel Sharon said it was he who had recommended where they should be located[6]. Gaza City then was a huge island of Palestinian population in a territory which was elsewhere gripped by these 'fingers', as Mr Sharon described them. In February 2004, as the Palestinians celebrated the Feast of the Sacrifice, Mr. Sharon announced that he was planning to withdraw the settlers. There was little initial sign of the 'fingers' loosening their grip. The cemetery where Private Solomon Rosenberg was buried was near the village and refugee camp of Deir-el-Balah. The village took its name from the tall date palms which soared above it, and which lined the road as it headed south to Khan Younis, the Gaza Strip's second largest city. To me, the most memorable thing about Deir-el-Balah was the impression it gave of what the Gaza Strip could have been were the situation there different. To an outsider, the palm trees were part of a vision of an Arab land, from childhood books and TV programmes, made real. This oasis would be such a pleasant place to break your journey under the trees whose fronds spread far above your head. In a place where so much had been destroyed and ripped up by war, the palm trees seemed to stand as a symbol of a gentler, calmer, time. When the medieval Moroccan traveller, Ibn Battutah, travelled through Gaza, he described it as 'a place of spacious dimensions, and large population, with fine bazaars. It contains numerous mosques, and there is no

---

[6] *Warrior*, New York, Touchstone (2001), p 258.

wall around it'[7]. In 2004, the population was still large, and growing. The mosques were still numerous. The bazaars were not as fine as they might be, though, the dimensions not spacious, and it was impossible to imagine it without a wall around it. What was used to keep enemies out in the Middle Ages served then to keep people in. Any 1001 Nights reveries which came with a look at the palm trees were torn away by the sign nearby pointing to the 'Al-Aqsa Martyrs' hospital,' reminding you, just in case for a split second you had forgotten, that you were in the middle of a war zone. The palm trees were soon gone, and the road arrived in the centre of Deir-el-Balah. No 'fine bazaar' here, but a grubby market, ill-stocked shops, and 'martyr posters'. Deir-el-Balah never used to be on the main road south, but, with the main road blocked near Netzarim, and the beach road from here southwards closed to Palestinians, it was now. In Gaza, there was never a direct way of getting from one place to another. You ceased to think of making a journey by the shortest, most logical, way. It was bound to be blocked somewhere. Here, all traffic was forced to swing inland, and pass through dusty Deir-el-Balah. From there, the road went further south, past more palm trees, towards the Israeli Army checkpoint at Abu Houli.

This was the place where the Israelis controlled movement between the north and the south of the territory. Sometimes, when they believed the security situation required it, they would split the territory into two, by closing Abu Houli. Sometimes, they would also close the Beach Road near Netzarim and cut Gaza into three parts, each almost completely sealed off from the other. The wait at Abu Houli could last for hours and hours, and, unless the closure had already been in place for a couple of days, it would come without warning. There was always, whatever the situation at the time you left, a risk that any trip to the south of the Gaza Strip, to Khan Younis or to Rafah, could end up lasting for days. Leaving Deir-el-Balah, you would sometimes run into the back of the queue even before the checkpoint came into view. The wait could begin in Deir-el-Balah itself, some 5 kilometres from the crossing point. Once, the traffic jam even began on the Beach Road out of Gaza City, 14 km to the north. At other times, the traffic moved slowly, and you felt encouraged, as you rounded the corner where the checkpoint first came into view, if it was moving at all. Because of the Israelis' fear of suicide car bombs, no vehicle with fewer than three occupants was allowed through. Ragged kids stood at the last bend before the Israeli Army's guard post, holding up three fingers. They offered themselves for hire as extra passengers, for a shekel a time. They would be dropped off on the far side of the checkpoint, and wait for someone to bring them back the way. With the exception of a brief period during the *hudna*, Abu Houli was not open around the clock. The result was that the passengers for hire might find themselves stuck on the wrong side of the checkpoint, and unable to get home for the night. Their families would pretend that nothing was amiss, that they

---

[7] *The travels of Ibn Battutah*, Tim Mackintosh-Smith (ed) London, Picador (2003) p26.

were staying with relatives and would be back the next day. They did not want to admit that their children were touting for money. The household welcomed the income that even a few shekels represented. When there were delays, but the area was still reasonably calm, impromptu market stalls sprang up alongside the traffic jam. There were falafel sandwiches, soft drinks, cigarettes, nuts, and fruit. Grubby boys too young to enter the rent-a-passenger trade served their apprenticeship selling chocolate or chewing gum from boxes they balanced on their shoulders as they walked along the line of cars. Money was so hard to come by that no opportunity, no captive market, could ever be ignored. Sometimes the anger and frustration here could be felt. The atmosphere it produced made waiting here in the heat even more unpleasant. Remarkably, there were rarely arguments. There were sometimes exchanges of angry words, perhaps when one motorist ran into another, but nothing too serious. The only time I ever saw a fistfight as a result of 'road rage' was in Gaza City in the middle of the afternoon. There was a collision between a taxi and a donkey cart. I happened on the scene only after the accident, so couldn't judge who might have been to blame. The donkey cart driver's shirt was in shreds across his back: not an acceptable way to be seen in public in Gaza. Perhaps such fights were fewer because they risked such a loss of modesty and dignity. That is not to say that any such slight would be allowed to go unpunished. In the spring of 2004, as what little law and order there was in Gaza crumbled, at least one minor traffic accident was avenged by one of the parties going home to collect his kalashnikov and shooting the man who had run into him.

There was a traffic light as you approached the beginning of the checkpoint. The Israeli soldiers rarely stood on the ground. They would have been too exposed. Instead, they peered out from a low concrete tower. A gun barrel pointing out of a letterbox-sized hole was all that was usually visible. I drove a Mercedes jeep with British licence plates. Combined with the white face behind the wheel, it ensured that I stood out. Sometimes the light would go red as I approached, perhaps so the soldiers could have a look at me, perhaps to delay me. Israeli soldiers I met face to face would often complain that the BBC was 'pro-Arab'. Foreign reporters in general were believed to have adopted an anti-Israeli bias. The traffic could only cross the checkpoint in one direction at a time. When the light went red, you waited while the cars coming in the other direction came across. The one way stretch was only a few hundred metres long, and, at the other side, there was another Israeli Army tower. Going south, the left hand side of the road was barricaded with concrete blocks designed to stop gunfire. The traffic was one way because the other carriageway was on the other side of the sniper screens. It was for the Jewish settlers who didn't want to drive within kalashnikov range of the Palestinians. About half way along the stretch of road between the two towers, there was a bridge. As you approached, there was a sign which said in Arabic, English, and Hebrew 'No stopping under the bridge!' The guard post had been attacked by gunfire, and at least once by a suicide car bomber. For a couple of weeks, the tangled, torched, remains of the vehicle lay by the side of the road. The bridge was part of a road which no Palestinian was allowed to take. It came into the Gaza Strip from outside – through an Israeli Army position – and led to Gush Katif, the Jewish settlement bloc which took up the southern third of Gaza's coastline, and which was the home of Eran Sternberg, the settlers' spokesman who accompanied me on my trip to Netzarim.

Before the bridge was completed, the Palestinian traffic had to wait whenever a convoy of settlers or soldiers wished to use the junction. The Gaza Strip is mostly flat, part of the plain below the hills of Jerusalem and the West Bank, but here, where the settlers' road came in from Israel, it came down a slope. Reflected sunlight bounced off the windows of their armoured buses, and off the windscreens of the Israeli Army jeeps which accompanied them. Then, as they approached the bridge, they disappeared behind the sniper screens which lined its parapet, like the armour plating of a concrete stegosaurus stretched across the road. There were two blocks of flats at the junction, and a low building which looked like it might have been a warehouse. That was now fortified with concrete, and usually had an Israeli Army vehicle parked outside it. The two blocks of flats were empty of their inhabitants, who had either fled or been driven out. The white walls of the empty homes which remained were so covered in bullet holes that it seemed that a monster sized strain of mould were spreading unstoppably across them. They looked diseased. The road which passed beneath them had lost its surface. There was no tarmac, and there were usually big holes. Any vehicle passing this way had no choice but to slow down as it passed the guard posts.

This was the point in the Gaza Strip where Palestinians and Israelis passed closest to each other: close enough to see facial expressions, to see each other as human beings with individual characteristics, instead of just 'them', or as outright enemies. The division remained complete, most of the time. Proximity was no reason for rapprochement. Even if they came close to each other, there were still barriers, concrete screens, and soldiers, to make sure that no Palestinian crossed a line he was supposed to remain behind. In the summer of 2003, during the *hudna*, it was different – for a while. I was invited to a briefing in Gush Katif, the main Israeli settlement bloc, with a senior Israeli Army officer. He wanted to outline the way that the army viewed the *hudna*, how Israeli forces saw the situation developing.

The situation had not yet improved so much that I was able to drive straight to the point where the briefing was to take place. It was less than twenty kilometres from the area of Gaza City where my flat and office were, and, even allowing for traffic, should only have taken half an hour at the most. Of course, the reality was not that simple. I had to leave two hours before the appointed time, cross the checkpoint at Erez, drive along one of the roads outside the Gaza Strip, then wait, at a car park next to an army post where the settlers' road entered Gaza, to be met by representatives from the Army press office. It was late July, and it was very, very, hot. The air conditioning in my jeep was not working well. The windows could not be opened anyway as a security precaution. Getting outside to wait in the car park brought little relief. The air was so hot that just breathing in dried up the moisture in your mouth. The Army press officers arrived. The IDF's arrangements for the trip suggested that they had little faith in the *hudna*. The press had to leave their vehicles behind and travel in a bus. We crossed over the 'stegosaurus' bridge, and I was able to look down at the Palestinian traffic below, reflecting that I was one of a very small number of people who would have passed through this junction both under the bridge and over it. We arrived in Gush Katif without incident. There was a table set out with cold water, coffee, cake and watermelon for us, then we were ushered into a lecture theatre. I knew that just a kilometre or so away, there were Palestinians living in tumbledown houses, small time farmers and shepherds, who were living the way people across the Middle East had for centuries. This modern, air-conditioned, auditorium was a world away, and was separated not only by technology, but also by guns and armour.

The officer who gave the briefing was very softly spoken. A woman in a large hat complained that she could not hear what he was saying. The officer looked at her as he might have done at an insolent private soldier and suggested that if she were to remove her hat she might hear better. His words about the situation were just as direct. His talk was of the need to defend Israelis living in the Gaza Strip and near its border; of 'containment' of the 'terrorist threat'; of plans for 'surgical arrests' (as opposed to raids which often caused civilian casualties, too); and, more bluntly, of 'offensive operations'. The fifth point the officer wished to make was that the army intended to try to facilitate Palestinians' economic activity. There were small signs of that. The number of work permits to get into Israel had increased (although it still stood at only a little over ten per cent of what it had been before the *intifada*). The number of people visiting the cafés on the beach was an indication that there was more money around. The officer was not optimistic, though. He said that shooting, mortar, and grenade attacks had continued since the *hudna* had been declared. Making life easier for the Palestinians would not, in the officer's view, mean that peace was more likely. On the contrary, he said, 'The threat of terror attacks may increase as restrictions on Palestinian movement are lifted.' The Palestinian fighters' real agenda, the officer believed, was to use the cease-fire to regroup and rearm; to organise and strengthen, and to test new versions of their homemade missile, the 'Qassam' rocket, named, like the military wing of Hamas, for Izzedin al-Qassam, a guerilla leader who fought the troops of the British Mandate. He said that more than 1,000 rockets and missiles were currently being manufactured in the Gaza Strip. This figure was impossible to confirm, and few reporters were willing to use it just because a senior Israeli military source had. *The Jerusalem Post* made the claim the subject of a huge front page headline the next day. Many of their readers would probably be willing to take at face value pretty much anything an IDF officer said. He shared their fears, and criticised the Palestinians for not tackling the armed groups head on. Instead, new, improved Qassam rockets were being developed in the yards, garages, and metal workshops of the Gaza Strip's refugee camps. 'The Qassam is a stupid rocket, not a 'Tomahawk',' the officer conceded. 'But it can cause a lot of damage, a lot of psychological pressure.' It would be almost a year before a Qassam rocket actually killed anyone, but for many Israelis they were a reason why the army should not ease its grip on Gaza.

We left the lecture room and got back into the bus. After a short journey we got out again, to chat with another Israeli officer. We were right next to the junction at Abu Houli, where the settlers' road – the one which had now been superseded by the stegosaurus bridge – crossed the Palestinian road. We walked right up to the edge of the Palestinian road. If my car had not been in the army base at the crossing where we had entered Gaza, I could have just taken a taxi back to my flat. The only problem, a major one, would have been that the next time I wanted to leave Gaza through Erez, it would have been noticed that I didn't have an entry stamp, and I would surely have been suspected of somehow having smuggled myself in. One Palestinian colleague told the story of a man he had talked to who found himself in that situation. He was living outside Gaza, and desperately wanted to go back to visit his family. The trouble was that he was wanted by the Israelis. He paid $5,000 to be brought into Gaza through one of the smugglers' tunnels. Once there, he could not leave again, even though he was not supposed to be there in the first place. If you were only visiting the IDF posts, or Jewish settlements, of Gaza – as I was that day – you did not get a stamp on the piece of paper which served as an Israeli visa. A group of soldiers stood around, listening to the officer talking. It all seemed so calm. Then a minibus taxi full of Palestinian workers heading south caught sight of the TV cameras. The minibus slowed down and the workers, young men mostly leaned out the windows making 'V for victory' signs. The soldiers became agitated, and waved their rifles in the air. The vehicle moved on. The officer who was talking to us watched what was happening, but said nothing. He did try to be optimistic, saying that both sides were making a conscious effort. 'But,' he warned, 'we know that violence could turn the wheel back.' There was no great confidence, or feeling of imminent cooperation. The two sides had not discussed the possibility of having joint patrols, as they had in the initial days of Palestinian autonomy in the mid 1990s. 'It usually causes more friction,' was the reason given. The Israelis said that they had struck an agreement with the Palestinians whereby nobody who had been involved in violence against Israel should be allowed to man a checkpoint. At a more senior level, there was some sort of contact. This officer said that he had daily contact with his opposite number on the Palestinian side, and that they met face to face every ten days. Like the Palestinian Naval captain I had spoken to a week before, the officer refused to be interviewed on the record, refused to allow his name to be written next to his words. Both seemed afraid of being quoted when they spoke frankly: they might say something which could later be held against them, something which would be seen as contributing to the collapse of the cease-fire which anyone living with the conflict knew must come. There were two more stops on the tour. The first was on the other side of the checkpoint. We were shown a sandy track which the IDF had reopened to Palestinian traffic. There was not much sign of life. A few curious villagers came out to stare at the reporters. A couple of television cameramen filmed them from a distance. It was as if they were making a wildlife documentary, and could not go too close to the wild beasts they could see in their viewfinders. Then our hosts showed us the fence that surrounds the Gaza Strip. The nearest Palestinian posts were 800 to 1000 metres inside it. 'At night, anyone attempting to infiltrate the fence is seen as a terrorist,' the officer explained, the implication being that soldiers would immediately shoot to kill. 'During the day, farmers can work.' They could, of course, but it was still dangerous. One man and his son were shot when soldiers had seen them working on something in the ground. 'Suspected of planting an explosive device,' was the IDF's explanation. If the soldiers had stopped to consider that a farmer might be digging for another purpose than laying a landmine, they had not given it much thought. When I got back into my car to begin my circuitous route home, I reflected that I had shaken hands with senior Israeli Army officers just a week after shaking hands with Abdel Aziz Rantissi, the Hamas leader. They had all seemed to think that, in all probability, in a few weeks they would once more be trying to kill each other. That was the way it turned out.

I was able to learn something else. For a couple of weeks, the Israeli Army had been working on an area of waste ground just next to where we had stopped by the Palestinian road that afternoon. They had flattened an area of a few hundred square metres, and were covering it with concrete. It could have been a car park under construction, or even perhaps a helicopter landing pad, or both. Work appeared to have stopped. Major Assaf Librati, who would later show me round the industrial zone at Erez, was with us that afternoon, so I asked him what was being built. My Palestinian colleagues and I had been wondering ever since we had first seen the work underway. 'An area for checking vehicles,' he replied, adding, 'but we won't need it now.'

Six months later, they did. Now the vehicle pen was completed. Concrete screens, like those which made up the armour plating of the stegosaurus bridge, surrounded it, keeping out prying eyes, bullets, and bombs. 'ГАЗА' – 'Gaza' in Cyrillic letters – was sprayed on the outside wall, no doubt by a roughneck who had preferred military service at Abu Houli to Alkhan Yurt in Chechnya with the remnants of the Red Army.

I was coming back in a minibus from a trip to the Rafah refugee camp with the United Nations. We had been travelling in a convoy with Peter Hansen, the head of the United Nations agency for Palestinian refugees, or UNRWA. Israeli soldiers had suddenly emerged from behind their concrete screen. Their jeeps blocked the road. They ordered everyone to turn off and wait in the vehicle pen. Had we been behind Mr. Hansen's car, his diplomatic status might have ensured our passage. But we had driven on ahead, not wishing to wait while he stopped to take a telephone call. Without him, we were just another group of people in a UN minibus with a Palestinian driver. I was with my Palestinian BBC colleagues Fayed Abushammala, and Ibrahim Adwan. We were stuck. The Israelis gave us no reason as to why all the cars had been stopped. They just stood staring, some with their weapons shouldered. We could not talk to them from where we sat, and getting out of the bus to speak to them could have been dangerous. They might have seen any approach towards them as potentially hostile, and opened fire. Soon the rest of the convoy arrived and was stopped on the road. Mr Hansen's car caught up with the other vehicles. His diplomatic statues meant that the Israelis were obliged to let him pass. He apparently insisted that all the vehicles be allowed to go with him. The soldiers came over to check our papers. The soldier nearest the window, who had a round, moon-like, dozy face of the type I had seen so very often when covering the war in Chechnya, had his gun pointing almost directly at me. Mr. Hansen's influence prevailed, and we were soon released. I don't know how long the other cars were kept for. In the 20 or so minutes that we were there, the soldiers didn't approach any cars of them, so who knows what they were looking for. Perhaps it was just harassment, or as Fayed put it, 'humiliation'. The Israelis wanted to give the Palestinians a gentle reminder of just how completely they were in charge; how unshakeable was their control over the road. The days of the *hudna*, with its comparatively easy movement, were long gone.

Beyond the bridge, where the road was cracked and rutted, where the bullet holes spread across the apartment blocks like monster-sized mould, the Israelis had built their largest series of settlements: Gush Katif. Neveh Dekalim ('Place of palm trees') is one of those settlements. Gush Katif stretched along the coast of the southern third of the Gaza Strip, cutting off Palestinians from the sea, and taking much of Gaza's scarce water for hothouses. The area was surrounded by a high, reinforced concrete wall. From watchtowers built into it, the Israeli Army overlooked the Palestinian refugee camp of Khan Younis on the other side. It was here that I first met Eran Sternberg. It was just before I moved permanently to base myself in Gaza City. I drove down from Jerusalem to visit the settlers one Friday morning. I knew that once I was in Gaza City, such a visit would be more difficult. For one thing, it would involve that lengthy, and potentially dangerous, roundabout journey. Mr Sternberg met me and Nofrat Porat, the production assistant from the BBC bureau in Jerusalem who had come with me as a Hebrew speaker, at the entrance to the settlement. He didn't appear to be armed, although it later turned out he had a handgun in the glove compartment of his car. We went in his vehicle. He told us to leave our armoured jeep in the car park. He objected to the Arabic letters on the outside (we had 'Press' written in English and Arabic characters in the hope that it would lessen the chance of our being shot at).

On the way to the settlement, we had driven a long a road which was lined on both sides by sand dunes. Here you could really appreciate how very dry the Gaza Strip was. Anywhere left untended was sand. Now, in August, not even a single weed grew. If there had been any scrub or bushes, they had long since been torn up so that they could not provide cover for would-be ambushers. Just before we arrived at Neveh Dekalim, we passed a Palestinian village, on the opposite side of the road to the settlement, between it and the sea. This was Al-Mawasi – trapped inside Gush Katif, and cut off from the rest of the Palestinian population. The dwellings there, at the edge of the village, were little more than tents, and other crude shelters which looked like they might have been made out of packing cases. There was litter all over the ground at the side of the road, as if scraps of paper and torn plastic bags had taken the place of the foliage which couldn't grow for lack of water. There were a few skinny goats looking for food. A few of the village's residents sat sullen in the shade. There was little sign of activity of any kind. When we passed this way again a short time afterwards in Mr Sternberg's car, he cautioned against my drawing any conclusions from, or making any comparisons with, they way the villagers of Al-Mawasi and the settlers lived. 'People show two photographs, and say 'look how poor the Palestinians are', but it's like taking a picture of New York, and one of Bangladesh. They are not poor because of us.' Al-Mawasi was hard to visit, and a source of terrible stories. Anyone wishing to enter or leave had to pass through the Israeli Army checkpoint next to the edge of the concrete wall which surrounded Gush Katif. The tale was told of a woman who was returning to Al-Mawasi with a bottle of hydrogen peroxide, apparently for cleaning her husband's fishing boat (although it can also be used as an ingredient for an explosive). The story went that the soldiers had demanded to know what was in the bottle. When the woman had told them, they had told her to drink some. This she did, and was seriously ill in consequence. I heard this story several times, but it was never clear why the woman had agreed to drink the chemical. Perhaps she was just too terrified to refuse.

Neveh Dekalim, like Netzarim, seemed a piece of American suburbia dropped into the desert. Spacious houses were surrounded by well-tended gardens with luxuriant lawns, even though the greenery was besieged by sand dunes. It was almost impossible to believe that we were just a few hundred metres from Khan Younis refugee camp, which clung to the dusty, drab, outskirts of the city, the second largest in the Gaza Strip, from which it took its name. To see it, its people, its streets, hear the call to prayer from its mosques and feel the scorching midday sun, would leave you in no doubt that you were in part of the Arab and Muslim world. Neveh Dekalim's shopping centre appeared to be modelled on the main street of a small town in the mid-West of the United States. Shops a single storey high stood in a neat line with car-parking spaces marked out in front of them. There was a grocer's, and even a shop selling greetings cards and wrapping paper. At the end of the line of shops, on the pavement in from of the parking area, there was a kiosk selling lottery tickets. Settlers with side-locks and assault rifles had taken the place of the 'soccer moms' you might have expected to see in such surroundings. A burly, brawny figure with long curls and a big beard climbed out of his car and strode towards the shops, an M16 rifle slung across his white-shirted back. Where the 'frontier' in the United States was no longer wild, in Gaza it was. For all the settlers had ostensibly come for ideological reasons, to settle what they saw as 'the entire land of Israel'; perhaps there was also an element among them who thrived on the danger and the challenge of living in such hostile surroundings. I don't think I had ever encountered a group of people who had such an unshakeable belief that what they were doing was right. If there was any self-doubt among the settlers of Gaza, it did not show. Neveh Dekalim's school was just a short distance away. The school bus stopped near the shops. There were sheets of corrugated iron stretched over the bus shelter to provide shade from the sun which could be uncomfortably hot, even in December. Below them, the front of the bus shelter, the part which almost anywhere in the world would be open to allow passengers to get on board, was blocked with concrete screens. Once the bus arrived, the children would emerge through gaps in the fortifications to board it. They had to be shielded from snipers while the waited. The 'school bus' was an armoured truck painted military green; its drivers, soldiers. Mr. Sternberg said had been married five years. He said he had two children, with a third due the next week. How did he feel about having children in such an obviously dangerous place? He answered that these days, Tel Aviv was dangerous too. A larger wall towered up a short distance behind the bus stop. Mr Sternberg drew my attention to it. 'We call it ironically Berlin wall. It separates between the edge of Khan Younis, and the industrial zone of Neveh Dekalim, which suffered a lot from attacks from Khan Younis, from the high buildings there. The Army built this wall because they wanted to let us work peacefully and quietly in our industrial zone. You can see the height. I think it's ten metres high, or something like that.'

The other side of the wall was steadily becoming a wasteland. Khan Younis was retreating as the Israeli Army demolished the buildings which were closest to the wall, saying that they were being used as firing positions to attack the settlement. Almost nobody dared to spend the night there. Some people, loath to abandon their homes completely, came back during the day to water plants or put plastic sheeting over windows, but they did not dare stay there once night had fallen. An old refugee who gave his name as Abu Mohammed owned one of the last houses left standing. He said that the Palestinians would never live in peace with the Jews, and then chastised me for the Balfour Declaration, which had prepared the ground for a Jewish homeland in Palestine. The fact that I was born sixty years after the Balfour declaration counted for nothing. It was my people who had made it. I must be prepared to justify it, or be criticized for it. Beyond Abu Mohammed's house, all was in ruins. The stronger buildings still stood, but no one could live in them. They were probably structurally unsafe after being pounded with shells. One such wreck stood defiantly close to the wall, in full view of the Israeli watchtower which stood at the corner, the northern limit of Gush Katif. The pillars which still supported it (the ground floor of Palestinian houses was frequently left without all its walls to make a sort of open air living room to escape the heat of summer nights inside) no longer looked too straight or sound, but they did seem almost to be drawing on final reserves of strength to mount a final attack on the nearby redoubt of the enemy. The house was like a soldier severely wounded but still willing to fight, knowing that in any case, death is not far away. Across the road from Abu Mohammed's front door there was a tent, home to the most recently homeless. There were bullet holes in some of the walls facing away from the settlement: either the aftermath of an Israeli raid into the camp itself, or the marks left by inaccurate outgoing fire, bullets loosed off randomly by trembling teenage trigger fingers. Despite the fact that the wall was so high, Mr. Sternberg still had an idea of what life was like on the other side. He was not particularly sympathetic to his neighbours.

'Maybe they really live in poorness and poverty, but it's their fault, not our fault.'

I asked him why.

'Because all the money that your country gave to them, and the European Union gave to them, go to private pockets, go to industry of gamble and drugs, and the money has not arrived to the real consumer. So it's their fault. This is the leadership they chose. What you see is what you get.'

Mr Sternberg might have correctly analysed the widespread corruption in the Palestinian Authority – the people of Gaza had few illusions themselves. Then, during the *intifada*, anger about officials' wealth, as much as I heard it, was confined to muttered jokes. Mr Sternberg perhaps did not understand that one consequence of the anger among ordinary Gazans would be the coming to power in the territory of Hamas, who were seen as less corrupt, and closer to the people, than their PLO counterparts.

We drove to Kfar Darom, an isolated settlement in the centre of the Gaza Strip, not far from Abu Houli. The roads were so much better than the ones in the areas of Gaza which the Palestinian Authority were supposed to maintain. Kfar Darom was originally founded in 1926, then vacated between 1948 and 1967, during the Egyptian occupation. It seemed pretty quiet. Many of the settlers' critics inside Israel suggested then that the settlers did not actually live in the settlements, but simply kept property there for ideological reasons. When you put this view to settlers during a visit, they always said that it was quiet because it was the middle of the working day. The settlers, though, often had large families – six or seven children was quite common, ten or more far from unknown – so you would have expected there to be more sign of mothers and young children at home, even during the working day. Besides, this was a Friday, and Mr Sternberg had specifically asked us to come early because everyone needed to get home to prepare for the sabbath with began in the late afternoon. For all this, there was not much sign of life. Mr Sternberg, though, was upbeat as he pointed to a row of portable cabins: 'Here you can see a new neighbourhood – ten families that came last week into these new houses.'

There was a museum in Kfar Darom which told the story of the Jews' wanderings between the destruction of the second temple, and the founding of the state of Israel. Maps 'proved' that Gaza was part of Israel. There was a film – *Perseverance above all* – of the history of the settlement. A veteran of the 1948 war which led to the creation of Israel sat around a camp fire and told children of his battles. Much was made of an elderly Arab who had kept the keys to the Jewish settlement during Egyptian occupation, and returned them to the settlers after the 1967 war. The last part of the film was a curious mixture of happy pictures of children playing in sand pits and footage of an attack in the early 1990s. Soldiers crawled towards positions from where they could fire on their Palestinian attackers while a helicopter landed to evacuate the wounded. When we drove on, Mr Sternberg pointed out the former homes of people in the film who were now dead. In one family, all three children had apparently lost their legs in a mortar attack. Still, as we came out, new houses were being built. Mr Sternberg was proud of those who were coming to join him in what he saw as an ideological struggle. He knew that the Gaza settlements would be one of the first issues to be discussed if the peace talks were to restart – and this was some 18 months before Ariel Sharon announced his 'disengagement' plan. To pre-empt this, Mr. Sternberg said, he was trying to persuade more people to move to Netzarim. Both Netzarim's supporters and its opponents knew it would be the first settlement slated for removal. It made sense to try to get as many people there as possible. 'Creating facts on the ground' had never failed Israel as a tactic for expanding Jewish settlements beyond the internationally recognised borders of Israel. In the settlers' view, the struggle which was now going on was part of the historical sufferings of the Jewish people. It followed on from the destruction of the second temple, two millennia in the Diaspora, and the Holocaust. Mr Sternberg had answers for anyone who sought to question his right to make his home in the Gaza Strip. He had a response to every question, and one particularly blunt one for people who demanded to know what gave him the right to be there: 'My grandfather escaped from Poland when his neighbours tried to kill him. One year ago there was a correspondent from Polish TV, a Polish journalist, come and ask me (why he lived in the Gaza Strip). So I ask him back: where do you want I will go? To the place that my grandfather escaped when your father or his neighbours tried to kill him? I don't have any other place in the world.'

Rivkah Goldschmidt's house was being cleaned in preparation for the sabbath. In South African accented English she explained how 'they' i.e. the Palestinians, were not to be trusted. The accent reinforced the impression of apartheid. Leave Israel alone, she said. There were plenty of Arab countries in the region. Why could the Jews not have one which was historically theirs by right? 'The parts that belong to Israel have come back to us,' she argued. 'It's not that we have taken anything from anyone. That's one reason why there's no place for two states, for two nations. They've got about 22 states, Arab states, Muslim states. When tiny little Israel, poor Israel started in 1948, in the 1950s the tiny community here helped thousands of refugees to come and settle, because this is homeland. I expect the Arabs to do the same.' Mrs Goldschmidt, it seemed, was wary of the Arabs having any more than the twenty-two states she mentioned. In any case, she continued, the Palestinians had never had a state, so why should they have one now? She even saw their influence behind the war in the Balkans. 'Two states: there's no such thing. Because anywhere you have an Arab minority, a big Arab minority, they want a state. Look what happened in Bosnia. Look what happened in other parts of the world. So you can't start a state wherever you've got a big Arab minority. They've never ruled here. Before were here the British, and before the British were here the Turks, there was never a Palestinian government, there was never a Palestinian police force, there was never a Palestinian state here. This place was only called Palestine, which doesn't give a good enough reason for us to give our homeland to another nation.'

The leaves in the spacious garden were being cleared up by sullen Thais. They had taken the jobs of the Palestinians, who were 'not to be trusted'. What did they make of the weird circumstances in which they now found themselves? Their presence was a small, but depressing, sign of how low relations between the Israelis and the Palestinians had sunk. Within a few hundred metres of the settlement's concrete wall, there were thousands of people being fed by the United Nations because they couldn't find work. Here were jobs they could do, and in some cases had previously done, now lost to them – probably for good. In the hothouses where the settlers grew flowers for the Israeli market and those beyond, the workers were almost all Thais or Chinese. They laboured hard, striving to make the blooms in their care as fine as possible. One of the settlers, apparently in a supervisory position in the hothouse, became annoyed when he saw me. I could not follow the exchange between him and Mr Sternberg in Hebrew, but its gist seemed clear. Why was he allowing a western journalist to visit here? The problem apparently stemmed from a recent report by another correspondent who had mentioned the well-watered greenhouses, lawns, and swimming pools which the settlers had built in a territory where much of the population was desperately short of water. The hothouse workers got on with their job.

As he drove us back to where we had parked our car, Mr. Sternberg pointed to the neat houses which lined the roadside. 'The houses around us, you see, with no damage, they're nice, but I can tell you that every house here was damaged from mortar bombs. Till today we count almost 1,400 mortar bombs that landed about us, that landed on us, and we have a miracle here, because till today, only one soldier was killed.'

Lack of skill in weapons-making and firing probably had more to do with the 'miracle' than divine intervention. This, though, was a sea of religious fervour which extended past the walls of the settlement, and into the mosques of Khan Younis refugee camp beyond. The settlers had come on a divine mission to their 'homeland'; the Palestinian refugees pray to God that he will return them to theirs.

Mr Sternberg was not hopeful that he would ever again enjoy anything like normal relations with the Palestinians who lived nearby. 'Our neighbour is not interested if they are shooting on mother, on children, and baby, not like every army in the world. You have a mistake, and after it, you apologize. They do it to kill children and mother and babies, and whatever they can.' Mothers and babies were dying on the other side of the wall too, sheltering, sometimes in vain, behind the thin walls of their poorly-built homes when the shooting started. Abu Mohammed and the others who tried to live in the ruins of the edge of the refugee camp said exactly the same of the Israeli Army, the army which Mr. Sternberg was ready to praise for its apparent willingness to apologize for its mistakes. The children who were growing up during this second *intifada* would never get the chance to know their contemporaries from the other side as anything but deadly enemies. Once, in the old city of Jerusalem, I stopped to chat to a Palestinian café owner, reduced to idleness by the fighting which had meant that the tourists only came in ones and twos instead of in the large groups which had once filled his tables. He reflected sadly that the generation in their late teens and early twenties had lived their childhood in the first *intifada*, and were now going through youth and adolescence in the second. People of his age (at a guess, he was in his mid-forties) at least had memories of some good times. Those younger than him had none, and there was no prospect of their acquiring any.

On the coast of Gush Katif there was a resort hotel, now closed. Menachem, a short, stocky, man with a deep tan and bright brown eyes, worked in a building which doubled as tourist information office and community centre. He sipped cool lemon juice next to a window which was open to the breeze from the Mediterranean. His shorts and sleeveless white shirt were not the traditional garb of the settler. He explained that he had come here to stay true to the founding ideals of Israel; true to the pioneering spirit. He lamented the lack of contact with the Palestinians who lived only a few hundred metres away. He also claimed that he had had 30,000 visitors that year, to what he himself described as a battlefield. That seemed unlikely if the hotel had had to close, and Mrs

Goldschmidt had expressed regret that the number of people opting to take a holiday at the settlement by the sea had dramatically declined in the last couple of years. Those who did come came for ideological reasons, or to study at the *yeshiva*, the college for study of the scriptures. On a later visit to Gush Katif, Mr. Sternberg introduced me to a man who worked at the *yeshiva*. I asked if we could film inside so that we could get some pictures of the man going about his daily business. The answer was no. I was not surprised. Religious institutions are often reluctant to allow cameras inside. I later found out the real reason. It appeared that inside there was a member of the United States Senate who did not want to be caught on camera. Four settler surfers walked along the road near the beach. They had long hair, bare feet, and boards tucked under their arms. If they had appeared a few kilometres to the north, on the part of the coast which the Palestinians were allowed to use, they would have been derided and then possibly pelted with stones. If the boys and youths who hung around the beach had realized they were Israelis, they would probably have been lynched. Here, they were just making the most of the best surf which the Mediterranean, at its often stormy eastern end, had to offer. They were also trying to make a point about who owned this part of the coastline. The next time the beach in Gush Katif did see a crowd was in May 2004. Thousands of settlers from the West Bank, and sympathisers from all over Israel, flocked here to hold their independence day barbecues. This was after Ariel Sharon's 'disengagement plan' had been made public, and they came to show their opposition, to show that they planned to have barbecues on the beach in Gaza, with the Star of David flying overhead, for many years to come.

Gush Katif stretched along the southern third of the Gaza Strip's coastline. The Palestinians could not approach the sea, nor were they allowed to take to the water from further north to go fishing off this part of the shore. Inland, Khan Younis was dusty and dull, very conservative, a town which saw few visitors. There was little reason to stay here. Most days when my work took me to the south, it was easy enough to return to Gaza City, which always seemed impossibly relaxed and even cosmopolitan by comparison. One night, the roads were closed while the Israeli Army moved into Rafah, the grim town and refugee camp on the Egyptian border. My colleagues and I passed one checkpoint, after being held there for three hours, and were reluctant, now after nightfall, to have the same experience again. We spent the night in a hotel on the top floor of a hospital. It was strange to feel so trapped: unable to move north or south, and never knowing when the road might be open again. This was just how most Palestinians lived in Gaza: the existence of a road did not mean that it could be used, that it could take you to a different place. At 4am, helicopter gunships clattered overhead. I went to the window to see if I could make out anything of what was happening in the darkness. I could see nothing, but the sounds which came to me on the top floor seemed to explain everything. The dawn call to prayer from the surrounding mosques could be heard when the helicopters' path took them far enough away. The imam's words broke through the din whenever they could: one side below, one side in the skies above – each battling to show the other they would not be beaten.

South of Khan Younis, the road led towards Rafah: the most dangerous, the poorest, the most benighted, in short, the worst place in the whole of the Palestinian territories. Just outside Rafah, a side road led to 'Gaza International airport', built in the early days of autonomy, its runway destroyed in the early days of the *intifada*. It had ceased to function, standing instead as a symbol of the Palestinians' dream of having a state, and the Israelis' ability to crush any such ideas. The terminal building was still intact. It had check-in and passport control, a luggage carousel, banks, shops, and a café. A Moroccan architect had designed it. He had decorated his creation with a frieze where the walls met the ceiling. Now it was completely empty, except for a few birds which had made nests in what they felt was a quiet, safe, place. A few guards, keeping an eye on the place for want of anything better to do, sat in a hut near the front gate. You were allowed to go in if you asked politely, even to drive out onto the runway. That had been completely destroyed at one end. The concrete looked like earth which had been broken up in preparation for planting. Just in case any smaller aircraft might have been bold enough to try to land, there were two or three other trenches torn in the surface. As we left the runway, I was driving. From habit, I stopped at a junction. The airport security man in the passenger seat was amused. 'Don't worry! You won't run into another car here, never mind a plane.' There was no way out of Gaza; not by land, by sea, or even by air. The very idea that there might be was laughable.

CHAPTER 9
'NOWHERE TO GO.'

That autumn just going to Rafah required a steeling of the nerves. There was always the unsettling thought that if you managed to get there, and stay in one piece, you might not be able to get out again. The southern edge of the refugee camp was the most dangerous place in the whole of the Palestinian territories. A European face or a vest with 'TV' written on it was no guarantee of protection. In the first few months of 2003, the Israeli Army killed three foreigners, two Britons and an American. Tom Hurndall, who was with the pro-Palestinian international solidarity movement, or ISM, and James Miller, who was a cameraman, were both shot. Tom lay in a coma for months before he finally died. Rachel Corrie, a young American woman also with the ISM, was crushed to death by an Israeli Army bulldozer during a protest against house demolitions. In Rafah, the rules did not apply. Students who had come to demonstrate against the activities of the Israeli Army perhaps thought that, as in western Europe or the United States, the worst that could happen to them would be a whack with a policeman's stick, a gutful of teargas, and a night in the cells. They were wrong. Rafah was the end of the road, the edge of the Gaza Strip, and, once you entered this frontier zone, you left behind all you could count on in the civilized world. Getting to Rafah was rarely easy, and it never felt safe. In October 2003, the queue to get there started more than 25 km away at the edge of Gaza City. The Israeli Army were carrying out a huge raid on the refugee camp. 'Operation Root Canal' was launched against the tunnels under the border area, tunnels which brought in ammunition, contraband, and even people, from Egypt. That day, the 25km journey took more than 5 hours.

South of Abu Houli checkpoint Palestinian traffic was at least allowed to use the main road again. It was one of only two parts of the Gaza Strip where a driver could enjoy a stretch of open road, and as a result, everybody drove too fast. Ibrahim Adwan, one of the BBC's local producers in Gaza, was from Rafah. His father had had a trucking company. Ibrahim once told me on a drive south that his father had once gone from Gaza City to Rafah in twelve minutes. I told him I did not believe it. 'He did,' he insisted, going on to explain that he had done it when Salah el-Din road was open all the way. I was forced to concede that then it might have been possible. I had only known the Gaza Strip when the road was blocked and barred and the only possible route was usually also the most circuitous. I could not imagine Ibrahim's father jumping in his truck and driving all the way to Rafah without having to take a detour or stop. That October, the warning signs could be read in the road which approached the town. Israeli tanks and bulldozers had torn up many of the trees which had stood in the sand at the roadside. The army controlled the main road completely, and would make no exceptions for who was allowed to pass. On one visit, we left Rafah after the time at which we had been told the road would close, imagining that we would be able to get permission to pass in any case. Our vehicle then had German plates, and we had Israeli government press accreditation. The Israelis always insisted that they had no intention of hampering journalists' work – any delay was usually down to 'security reasons'. That afternoon, we were stopped by a tank at 3 o'clock. I called time after time to Jerusalem to ask the Army press office to give us permission to move. Of course, foreign journalists were hardly a priority. The sun began to set. The outline of the tank, the gun barrel of which swung above the roof of our car, became sharper against the fading light. The details of its tracks and turret disappeared into the gloom. An armoured personnel carrier bumped over the sand to take up position for the night. A huge armoured bulldozer of the kind which the IDF used to demolish houses stood a couple of hundred metres away. It was an uneasy time. If any Palestinians were going to fire on the tank or the apc, we would be in the way. We discussed what to do if the shooting started. Eventually, we were allowed to leave, driving fast towards Khan Younis, the only vehicle on the only road north in a time of curfew and road closure. It felt very unsafe – either side could have opened fire at us. Arriving in Khan Younis was a joy, and even the noise of muezzin and machine gun fire before dawn was comforting in a strange way. At least we were among the population, where there was a feeling of safety in numbers, rather than alone on the dark road where we could see nothing beyond the beam of our own car's headlights.

There was never a happy reason to go to Rafah. A journey there always followed or preceded death. I had been once, when I first arrived in Gaza, just to have a look. The next time was following an Israeli attack in which several civilians were killed. I spent the afternoon on the road outside the hospital in Rafah, waiting for information, and then passing it on. The turn off the main road, leading towards the town itself, passed some pleasant houses. These were mostly the homes of wealthy families who had lived in this desert land before the great refugee influx which followed the war of 1948. It was hard to imagine what life must have been like then: hard, as always, making a living in the desert, but presumably quieter, simpler, and safer. It formed part of the picture of old Palestine which featured so vividly in the dreams of Mr Abdullah, the schoolteacher in Jabalya refugee camp. The Palestine where 'we were able to go to Jaffa, and to Jerusalem, on a donkey, on a camel, with no passport, and no one would stop you.' Now you couldn't even be sure of getting to the next town or village without being stopped, and going to Jaffa or Jerusalem was out of the question.

Any sense of happiness or well-being you had before entering Rafah soon evaporated. It was dirty and poor. Driving in one afternoon I saw on a street corner a group of children were torturing a puppy in the dust. The wretched creature was being dragged along by a rope around its neck. It had a large sore or cut in its side. The children were hitting it with sticks and kicking it. Perhaps they were going to hang it. Palestinians considered dogs dirty, so children were free to treat them as cruelly as they pleased. Dogs' lives were accorded no more importance than that of a fly or a slug might be in Britain. In any case, the power to mistreat animals was at least some form of power. Naturally, given the circumstances in which they lived, the human life which they saw around them, many children who got the chance to abuse power do so, even if it was only by sentencing a puppy to a long and slow death. I sometimes saw horses and donkeys violently beaten in the street, too. Perhaps the most striking thing about Rafah was that there was just nothing to do there except go to school, the mosque, or play in the street. There was one internet café, but that was beyond the pockets of most of the residents of town and camp. Even in Gaza City, there were a couple of little amusement arcades, with a pool table or two and some antiquated video games. Here, there was nothing. The people were poorer, and, perhaps in consequence, more pious. Hamas' view that it was not appropriate to have celebrations during the *intifada* was widely held in Rafah. In any case, hardly anyone could have afforded a party even if they wanted to. There was a market which took up part of the main street. For every item on sale, there seemed to be several flies. Broken boxes, donkey dung, and fruit too rotten even to be scavenged by the destitute lay underfoot. The town's only landmark was the central mosque, sitting next to a roundabout near the market. Countless posters of 'martyrs' were plastered across its walls. More children were killed in Rafah during the intifada than in any other part of the whole of Gaza and the West Bank. Their blank faces stared out from the garish copied pictures. The expressions, such as they were, sometimes seemed too knowing for ones so young. Their eyes seemed to betray the fact that, as their photograph was being taken, they knew already it might be the one used to commemorate their death. Death meant glory; an escape from the cage of misery and poverty. Sometimes funerals in Gaza were massive, noisy, defiant occasions. Other times, they had obviously set out to be so, and failed. As the *intifada* continued, it seemed that the crowds sometimes struggled to summon up sufficient energy and anger. The funerals for the civilians killed in the attack following which I spent the afternoon at the hospital took place the next day. Given that at least five of the dead had not been armed – three of them were females, aged 9, 30, and 70 – I had expected the funerals might be big. The processions were due to depart from the mosque following Friday prayers. We had a long wait for the funeral to start. The atmosphere was threatening. As we hung around, we were taunted by a crowd of teenage boys. One of them, with lank, greasy hair, parted in the middle of his head, and bad teeth, was convinced that I was Jewish. '*Yehud!*' he snarled. Eventually, seeing that his aggression was eliciting little reaction, he turned to jokes. 'These my friend,' he said, indicating three other unsavoury youths next to him. The sun was hot and high now, so we were sitting on steps in front of a shop, beneath an awning which protruded from the front of the building. 'Michael Jordan, George Bush, and Ariel Sharon,' he explained, to hoots of laughter from the crowd. Eventually, there was movement in the street before us. A group of figures wearing black hoods came around a corner, into the street which rang alongside one wall of the mosque, and formed up as if preparing to lead the procession. They were supposed to look frightening, but they were puny, and, from their physique, looked only about 14 or 15. Some carried kalashnikovs, and others rockets. When you looked closely, you could see that the rockets had been made out of plastic drainpipes, painted black. The noses and tails of the 'missiles' had been fashioned from papier maché, and painted red.

In this part of Rafah, near the mosque and the market, the intifada was played out mostly in pictures and processions, although the noise of gunfire and explosions would carry up to the shopping area from the battleground closer to the border. The wind would bring clouds of teargas to choke the shopkeepers as they sat in front of their open stores. From here, leaving this comparatively safe area, the wisest route was never obvious. Deserted streets were usually best avoided. There was non one there because it was dangerous. Residents sheltering behind protruding houses or in the doorways of their own homes would wave their hands to attract your attention, in order to warn you that there was an Israeli tank lurking just out of sight. Even at a bright, sunny, noon certain streets would be empty, silent, and still. No one went outside unless they absolutely had to. It was not worth the risk. The closer to the edge of the camp you went, the less safe it felt. Each time I went to Rafah during my time in the Gaza Strip, the landscape changed. More and more buildings were destroyed; more and more land left open, too dangerous to venture into. There was nowhere to take cover. As you approached the edge of the camp, there was an uneven dirt and sand road which ran parallel to the Israeli army positions a few hundred metres away. Crossing that took you into the most dangerous part of the most dangerous town in one of the most dangerous territories on earth.

The Yibna area of the refugee camp was named for the village in Mandate-era Palestine from which its residents, or their ancestors, had fled. The houses here were the usual refugee dwellings: poorly constructed from breeze-block and concrete. Even if they were big, they were still cramped because of the size of the families who squeezed into them. The sandy road itself was unsafe. There was often an Israeli tank at one end, where the road petered out into open ground. From here, you could see into the distance, into the Jewish settlement where Mr. Sternberg lived. Beyond that, the Mediterranean looked as blue and inviting as it might in any holiday brochure for Greece, Spain, or the French Riviera. How Rafah's residents must sometimes have wished to escape from the dust for an afternoon and head for the cool water. They could not because their enemy with his watchtowers, guardposts, and razor wire lay between them and the sea. Each time the Israeli Army demolished houses, there was more open space, more space where you might be hit by a bullet if you were not careful, or if you were unlucky. Perhaps the most discomforting thing about this place was its tense emptiness. Even though the houses were so overcrowded, and the street was the only place where one might breathe freely, the alleys around here were often deserted, even in the middle of a winter's day, a time when the temperature might rise to a pleasant 20 degrees Celsius. The road surface was uneven – potholes became puddles in the winter rain, and collected rubbish and dead rats all year round. There was once a huge grey rat lying in the street here: it had been squashed completely flat, as if by a steamroller, or a giant cartoon iron. Understandably, perhaps, no one had wanted to move it, and the municipal services, if there were any in the Rafah refugee camp, did not appear to have been that way recently.

The people who lived along that road had a stoicism which seemed quite incredible. As my time in Gaza went on, we came to know each other by sight and to say hello. Not everyone seemed to cope well with the hopeless situation in which they found themselves. Once Fayed and I were pursued by a gentleman with broken teeth and ill-fitting thick glasses, who leapt up from the broken chair he was sitting on to run after us. He wore a dirty *jelabiya*, the full-length shirt favoured by many Arab men, and was unshaven. He demanded to know why we had not made a note of his name. We had not even talked to him, but had been to visit a family who were living on the edge of the empty area between the camp and the Israeli Army positions. It seemed that he believed that if his name were published or broadcast, along with an account of the terrible situation in which he found himself, then he would surely receive compensation. He was worried that if the reporters left without recording his name, he would miss out.

Sami Al-Shams lived on the sandy road. The house's front door opened onto the street, just near where the squashed rat lay at one time. Mr Al-Shams had ten children. He was a pharmacist by trade, but hadn't worked since shortly after the *intifada* began. One reason for that was that it was hard to find work of any kind. Another was that his eldest son, Mohammed, was disabled and needed constant care. Mohammed had been hit in the head with a rubber bullet in the early days of the uprising, the autumn of 2000. That was when it seemed as if rubber bullets might be sufficient to bring the *intifada* to an end. Mohammed's injuries were not fatal, but they did cause brain damage which left him paralysed. He was about 17 when I met him: not particularly tall, and his body wasted from lack of use. He lay in bed just inside the house, a few metres from the street. In this part of Yibna, and everywhere south towards the Israeli Army posts, the people had to live with the constant fear that their house would be demolished. It was more likely to happen at night, when most IDF raids were executed, but it could happen at any time. Families had to be ready to run. This was not easy with a disabled, brain-damaged, teenaged boy in the house. Mr Al-Shams lived in a state of constant readiness to carry his son to safety. Everybody knew that when the Israelis had said they would demolish a house, they would carry out their threat. The deaf, the decrepit, the disabled, and the heavily pregnant had all paid for their lack of speed with their lives. Mr Al-Shams always managed to be cheerful whenever I saw him. He had a big bushy beard which came halfway down his chest, and bright eyes. I felt a certain affinity with him because we were the same age but our lives were similar only that we both lived in the Gaza Strip. I could not imagine life with a wife and ten children in a refugee house in Rafah. He probably never had the time nor the desire to imagine my life.

Across the road from Mr Al-Shams lived Fawzi Ali Yusef. I first met him in October 2003, the day when it took five hours to travel the 25 kilometres from Gaza City to Rafah. It was a hot afternoon. The air was still, and the sun bounced up so forcefully from the stones and sand underfoot that even standing in the shade didn't guarantee coolness. Mr Yusef was sifting through the rubble of his house which had been blown up by the Israeli Army some 48 hours before. More than 1,000 people were made homeless in that single IDF operation. The Israeli Army said that they had only destroyed buildings from which they had been fired on, or which they said concealed the tunnels used for smuggling weapons. The United Nations, who faced the task of rehousing those left without a roof, some families for the second or third time since 1948, said the scale of the destruction could not be justified. Of, course, every single person whose home had been demolished denied that fighters had been using their property. It seemed hard to believe that they could all be lying. Mr Yusef had six children. The whole family was going through the ruins, but they hadn't found much. 'The Jews destroyed everything,' Mr Yusef said, his voice cracking. 'I don't find money, I don't find gold, I don't find clothes for me, for my wife, for my baby, for my girls. We can't find schoolbags – everything is destroyed.' He invited me to sit down on a lump of shattered concrete as if we were about to take our ease in comfortable chairs. He apologized that he couldn't offer me tea. He told me the story of what had happened: the sound of fighting, the approach of heavy armoured vehicles, just enough time to escape, the loss of all he and his family owned. At least none of them had been killed, or even hurt, physically at least. When I next met Mr Yusef, it was a few months later. He and his family – his wife, and six children – had managed to rent a single room in the house next to the heap of rubble which had once been their home. His son sat quietly doing his homework in a space barely big enough to fit the table at which he sat. I asked Mr Yusef how things were. He had recognized me when I arrived, but seemed to have forgotten where we had met before. He began his reply by telling me what had happened the night the house was knocked down:

it was as if his life had simply stopped at that moment, and, like a ghost haunting the site of a decisive event in life, was condemned to relive forever in the moment which had so traumatized him.

Before the big Israeli raid began that October, the residents of the refugee camp were already convinced that it was coming. The *hudna* had collapsed a couple of months before and there was a feeling that with that failure, the fighting would resume with a new ferocity. Beyond the road where Sami Al-Shams and Fawzi Ali Yusef lived, the last few rows of houses marked the edge of the Rafah refugee camp. There was an area of open wasteland, an area which, until the start of the *intifada*, had been covered with more rows of houses, tightly packed together, divided only by alleys so narrow that an adult with outstretched arms could almost touch the buildings on both sides. As the conflict continued, the Israeli Army steadily destroyed the houses which lay closest to their positions. They swept them away as surely as incoming tide washed sandcastles into the waves, just as destructive, but less graceful, with more noise, more violence. Under the terms of its peace treaty with Egypt, Israel had control of a swathe of land some 100m wide between the end of the Gaza Strip, and the beginning of Egyptian territory. The IDF positions here were fired on almost nightly. The Army was consolidating its grip on this patch of sand and stony earth. A fence of dark metal, solid, and around 10 metres high, was being built across the line, giving Israeli troops protection to move around freely behind it, and, in watchtowers and observation posts built into it, a place from which to open fire on any actual or potential foes. I could never look at this fence without remembering Jabotinsky's words about 'an iron wall which…the natives…would be powerless to break down'. Some eighty years after he saw the 'iron wall' as a desirable tool for the conduct of Israeli-Arab relations, here it was taking shape. In the shadow of the iron wall, there was desolation. The area between it and the first houses grew wider and wider as more and more houses were demolished. When, one morning, a family suddenly found themselves in the front row, they knew that they would soon lose their home. Even before 'Operation Root Canal' which left 1500 or so refugees once more without a roof, there was a sense of weary resignation about the people who lived at the edge of the camp. Horse and donkey carts were driven down the narrow alleys to be loaded up with anything which could be moved. Even on quiet afternoons, where the bursts of gunfire were few and infrequent, the people here seemed to have the certain knowledge that they did not have long to save what they could. They packed up as if the sky were already growing dark with a hurricane on the way. Even horses – waiting while the loads they were to draw were prepared – hung their heads, as if even they shared the expectation of destruction to come.

The people of Rafah felt abandoned. The only help they ever got came from the United Nations. They often complained that the world as a whole had turned its back on them. Compared to other war zones around the world, the north Caucasus in particular, the Israeli-Palestinian conflict appears to receive a disproportionate amount of media attention. The numbers killed during the second *intifada*, whichever estimate one chooses to use, were tiny compared to the deaths in Chechnya, or Congo, or Darfur, a conflict which took months to attract any notice from the world's news media. Rafah, though, often seemed ignored while other places would get covered. It was too far from Jerusalem, where almost all the foreign press were based, and too hard to get to. The situation here did not get reported as much as it merited. Nevertheless, word of what was happening did filter through, and the town and its refugee camp became a magnet for activists from Europe and the United States who wished to help the Palestinian cause. The 'International Solidarity Movement', as they called themselves, were in the forefront of demonstrations against the house demolitions.

I first met the ISM activists in January 2003. They had called to ask journalists to come to Rafah to witness a demonstration they were planning to hold. I was collecting material for a story on house demolitions, so I decided to go. The weather in Rafah always seemed hotter than in Gaza City, even though it was only 25 km further south, but not even the humid air, warmed by the desert winds, could life the overcast gloom of this winter day. The sky had taken on the shade of dark grey which means that rain is inevitable. The ISM had gathered near the last row of houses, at the edge of the open ground which lay before the fence. There were perhaps twenty of them: all young, aged, I would guess, between 20 and 25. They were all from Western Europe: the UK, the Netherlands, Sweden, Italy, and France. They looked like students. At least one of the group, whom I met later, had abandoned his university course to come to Gaza as an activist. Some were dressed in combat trousers and heavy boots; others trainers, as if they were on their way to university lectures. Many wore the Palestinian *kefiyeh* as a scarf. One or two of the men had long, matted dreadlocks; some had their heads shaved. In short, they looked like a group of students at any European University might, but they were in a war zone, not a café on a campus. They looked determined. Whatever opinion you might have of their aims or means, it seemed difficult to question their dedication. Some had hi-visibility vests, like those worn by construction workers, over their jackets. At this time, the 'iron wall' was still being built. The ISM had come to protest against its construction, and the destruction of Palestinian buildings. The demonstrators were getting ready to move out from one of the alleys which opened on to the wasteland. The point up to which the iron wall had been built was just a short distance away. A small crowd of Palestinians – boys and youths – stood behind a pile of rubble and churned up earth. This seemed either to have been the work of an Israeli bulldozer, seeking to block of the end of the alley to motor vehicles, or, more likely perhaps, placed there by the people who lived in the alley in order to afford themselves some protection as they walked out their front door. The group of lads would climb up onto the top of the barricade to get a better view of what was happening. None seemed to want to go beyond, into the open, exposed, area. More children were killed in Rafah during the *intifada* than in any other part of the Palestinian territories. These onlookers were content, today, to remain spectators. They must all have seen people shot, and knew only too well the risks they were taking. The ISM activists perhaps did not.

I was with Ibrahim. Having grown up in Rafah, he knew the terrain and the people very well. We parked the jeep, having taken care to turn it round so that it was facing back the way we came in case we needed to leave quickly. This alley was never a safe place to be. I never liked to stay there long. Shooting could start at any moment – even when the day seemed calm and quiet. The demonstrators prepared to walk towards the iron wall, where an armoured bulldozer was working on preparing the foundations of the next section. They advanced slowly across the flattened earth. They held a banner which said 'Stop shooting us'. They took turns to address the Israeli troops through a loudhailer. 'We are unarmed internationals. Don't shoot,' they cried, the words distorted by the hand held megaphone. 'You are committing war crimes,' they continued, all the time waking slowly closer and closer to the wall, and continuing to pass the megaphone around, as at some kind of gathering where each person present is expected to make a speech or recite a poem. The Israelis fired long bursts to try to drive them back. Bullets whipped the dust and mud, sometimes close to the line of protesters. They did not flinch. I became convinced that the situation was more dangerous than they realized. The ground was broken and uneven, strewn with stones and fractured concrete. A bullet could easily have struck one of these and flown anywhere. I went back to the car and got my flak jacket, telling Ibrahim to do the same. When I returned, I spoke briefly to 'Ellie' – the ISM people usually only gave first names. They knew that if they were identified by the Israelis, they would almost certainly be banned from entering Israel for life. The only ways into Gaza or the West Bank, of course, were either through Israel, or in the case of the border between the Gaza Strip and Egypt, controlled by the Israeli Army. Ellie was short and slight, with dark hair. She spoke softly. I felt a fool standing there in body armour when she only wore a light jacket. Ellie conceded that the Israelis would continue to demolish houses; that the wall would be completed. She and her fellow activists seemed content to draw attention to what was happening, pleased if they could at the very least delay both the construction and the demolition to which they were so bitterly opposed. If they had any idea of the danger they were in, they did not show it. It was time to go back to the office in Gaza City to send the material. We drove back through Rafah. On the way, we saw one of Ibrahim's brothers on the street. We stopped to say hello. When we opened the car door, tear gas flooded in. The Army must have been using it down at the edge of the refugee camp to disperse the protesters. People on the streets covered their noses and mouths, shopkeepers clutched cloths over their faces as they carried out their trade. There were no serious incidents that day, but I remember it very clearly because

I left Rafah convinced that sooner or later one of the protesters would be killed by the Israeli Army. Within three months, two of them had been.

Tom Hurndall was shot in the head just near the mound of earth and rubble which stood at the end of the alley. There were bloodstains on the wall behind for weeks afterwards – a landmark which the street kids of the refugee camp vied with each other to point out to visitors. 'It seems that the IDF have just shot this guy and are not prepared to admit it,' I wrote in my diary that day. The Israeli Army sources I contacted said they were only aware of an incident in which one of their soldiers had fired on, and hit, 'an armed Palestinian in combat gear who had opened fire on one of their positions.' Rushdi had already heard this account on the Israeli media, and had anticipated my request for him to call the hospitals in the area to check the claim. No such incident was reported. It was too late in the day to go down to Rafah except in an emergency. The next morning, a group of ISM members, clearly traumatized, gathered, near the place where Mr Hurndall was shot, to give their account of what had happened. A group of kids brought out a jacket soaked in blood. It had been worn by one of the people who carried Tom Hurndall away after he had been shot. Tom Hurndall lay in an Israeli hospital in Be'er Sheva for months, before being taken back to the UK. He died in hospital in January 2004, never having come out of his coma. Eventually, the IDF reported that one of their men had shot him.

He was the second ISM activist to die. Rachel Corrie, 23, from Washington State in the USA, had been crushed to death by a bulldozer less than a month before. She and her fellow protesters had been trying to stop the bulldozer carrying out demolition work. Rachel's parents became frequent visitors to Gaza as they strove to find out more about their daughter's death, and draw attention to what had happened. Mr Corrie had been in the US Army in Vietnam. One of his responsibilities was looking after military bulldozers. Rachel Corrie's death, like that of Tom Hurndall afterwards, really seemed to shock Rafah. Even a place as used to death as this grim refugee camp was surprised that the IDF had killed two foreigners. Opinion of the ISM among the residents of Rafah seemed divided: some people appreciated their presence, others feared that if just provoked the Israeli Army into treating the Palestinians more harshly, still others didn't really understand why they had come there. 'Abu Mazen (then Palestinian Prime Minister) wouldn't let his son go to Rafah,' a Palestinian friend remarked. For some people in Rafah, the arrival of the ISM did serve as something of a morale booster. The fact that a young woman like Ms Corrie could come of her own accord (without being accompanied by a male relative) was something of a shock to begin with. The fact that she had come, from this outside world which seemed to care little about what happened in Rafah, the fact that she had come from the United States, the government of which was seen in Rafah as being totally anti-Arab, anti-Muslim, and pro-Israeli, was a revelation. The fact that she was killed, apparently with impunity, demonstrated once again how powerful the

Israelis were. Rachel Corrie was revered as a 'martyr'. Her picture appeared on the walls near where she had been killed, and on the side of the house in the town where the ISM had rented an apartment. Slogans in Arabic and English praised her courage. Eighteen year old Anees Mansour lived just a few doors along the sandy road from Sami Al-Shams and his disabled son. Anees had met Rachel Corrie when she was in Rafah. Now, some months after her death, he had collected pictures of her, and stuck them up on the wall inside his family home. Anees had had to move bedrooms, because an Israeli tank had damaged the part of the house where he used to sleep. Now it stood open to the street. There are countless young men all over the world with pictures of blonde young women on their bedroom wall. Usually though, they are singers or supermodels whom the boys like looking at, or dreaming about. Anees may of course have had some of these sort of feelings for Ms Corrie, but her picture had been placed on the wall not because of her blonde hair, but because she had been killed by the Israelis. In Rafah, simply to have a picture of a woman on the wall because you liked looking at her might not have been acceptable. To have a picture of a 'martyr' was noble.

Anees Mansour's house was already damaged. He lived a short way back from the open ground where Rachel Corrie had been crushed to death. The place where Tom Hurndall had been shot was just along the road. The wasteland, the demolition area, was coming closer and closer to the Mansour family house. The sandy street in front was where the people who lived in the houses closer to the edge would come to seek shelter and even to sleep at night, too afraid to lie in their own beds, or too scared that they would not be quick enough to flee should they need to. In September 2003, Abu Ali Radwan lived in the last line of houses. His brother, Ismail, lived across the narrow alley. Much of Mr Radwan's house was already in ruins. His home was made up of a series of rooms around an open area. The outer wall of his house was the edge of the whole camp: beyond it, there was open ground and then the Israeli Army's iron wall. The narrow alley which led to his house was a playground for grubby kids who emerged from the homes on either side of it. At the end of the alley, where there might have been an open space to let in a little light and air, Mr Radwan and his family had built a flimsy wall of brick and stone. It had no cement; the bricks and stones were just piled on top of one another. It blocked out the sun. It also acted as a sniper screen. It would not stop bullets, of course. It might mean that the Israeli soldiers opposite could not see what they were shooting at, and so might not bother. Mr Radwan was 70 years old. He was a refugee from Jaffa. Like all of the people of his generation, he had believed for many years that the return to the homeland wasn't far away. Now, he knew he would never see it. This was his home: a miserable hovel which in Europe would have been demolished because it was not fit for habitation. Here it was likely to be demolished because of where it was; because there were people living in it. Every scrap of land was being fought over: even if the Israelis did not want this land to live on themselves, they felt threatened by the fact that the refugees did. Mr Radwan brought tea and we sat and talked. 'We don't know when the Jews will destroy our house,' he said. 'But it will be soon. Each night, when the shooting starts, we have to run out and sleep in the street.' His sons and daughters were all married. Some of his sons remained in the family home. While we drank tea, one of them returned. He had been looking for a room to rent. The family were so sure that the house where we now sat would be destroyed that they were already planning to move. Mr Radwan's son, in his forties perhaps, though it was always hard to tell in Gaza, looked worn out. His search had been fruitless. The best offer he had had was to rent a room for $100 a month – impossible riches for an unemployed Rafah refugee. So, for the foreseeable future, this would be home. The rooms on the side of the house nearest to the iron wall were no longer inhabitable. There was a huge hole in the wall of one. I risked a quick look through it, but Mr Radwan and his grandson told me to keep my head down. One corner of the house was falling down. A huge palm tree grew above it. Mr Radwan's TV set lay in pieces in the middle of the yard. It looked beyond repair, but there was no way he could afford another one, so perhaps he had plans to try to put it back together. Ismail, Mr Radwan's brother, joined us for tea. It tasted smoky because the water had been boiled on a fire at our feet. The brothers had a few words of English: they cursed the 'Jews' and said the Middle East would never know peace while they remained. It was getting late. It would be dark soon, and I always wanted to cross Abu Houli before nightfall. Ismail insisted on taking us into his house before we left. His kitchen wall was full of large holes which looked as if they had been made with a sledgehammer. They must have been made by heavy machine gun bullets: not the kind that would put a hole in your head, the kind that could take it clean off. The Radwan brothers were of the generation who were the original refugees. Each year, their number grew smaller. They were living their old age as they had their boyhood: in the midst of conflict, and on the verge of losing their home, now for the second time. If they were resigned to their fate, they did not accept it willingly. They seemed destined to die with a dream of Jaffa in their heads, and hatred in their hearts. Thus had they lived, and such was the legacy they would leave to the children and grandchildren they shared their hovels with.

The next time I came to Rafah, Mr Radwan's house was gone. That day, it was too dangerous to go all the way down to where it had stood. Although it was a warm sunny afternoon, and the Mediterranean looked blue and calm in the distance, there was a lot of shooting, and there were Israeli tanks moving around and to walk around any corner might bring you face to face with them. It was the wise neighbours who had been packing up on my previous visit. Now the wave of demolition had pushed further north, and more people, who had probably once imagined themselves to be far enough from the high tide mark of destruction, were getting ready to go. From the end of the alley which had led to Mr. Radwan's house, you could see a cart being loaded. The sun had moved just enough from its height at midday for the weary horse which was to pull it to cast a shadow. The sun shone where before it had not. Most of this alley had been in shade most of the day: Mr. Radwan's makeshift wall had limited the light which penetrated even at midday. Now the wall was gone, and with it his house. The Israel Army's iron wall rose up in the near distance: the newest construction in the area, but now the only one which had an air of permanence. The houses which still stood in the alley were empty. It seemed that no one dared to live south of the sandy road anymore. Even the ones that looked as if they had only suffered superficial damage had been abandoned. There was no sign of Mr Radwan. I suspect that he had fled with the rest of the people from this area of the camp to Rafah's football stadium, where they had set up makeshift shelters while they waited for the United Nations to bail them out. For those who were still stuck making the best of it in the ruins, the UN had sent a small tanker of clean water. There was a frantic crush of children and plastic bowls and buckets around the tap at the back.

Some of the houses on the sandy road itself had been demolished too. The newly homeless here were going through the rubble. Their neighbours, who seemed to have found somewhere to go, were packing up. A father and his teenage sons were lifting a refrigerator onto a cart which looked barely strong enough to hold it. The horse looked barely big enough to pull it. Fighters from the refugee camp were still trading shots with the Israeli Army across the open ground near where Mr Radwan's house had formerly stood. The gunfire sounded close, but the people here were so involved in their pressing task that they did not react. Emad Abu Matr and his family had lost everything, everything except the few odds and ends they were uncovering under the lumps of concrete that had once been their home. 'More than four families were living in this house, now some of them live in the mosque, some of them in our relatives, some with friends, some rent house, more than 20 children were living here, and you see everything is gone. That's it.' Mr Abu Matr's family had at least got away before the house came down. 'Just before they come, about 20 minutes, all of us escaped from the house, and we couldn't take anything. Even the money is under the destruction.'

Mr Abu Matr was in his mid thirties, and seemed to be in good health. His strength had clearly been sapped by sleeplessness, and the exertion of going though the ruins of his home. There was just the hint of a stammer in his speech. While we talked, one of his brothers found a large glass jar of pickled cucumbers, miraculously intact. There was an ironic cheer. The rest of the remains of family life lay invisible under the wreckage, and strewn on top of it: odd flip flops; schoolbooks; pots and pans crushed and battered out of shape; fragments of clothing; broken toys. For some reason, there were often dolls' heads in the ruins of homes demolished by the Israeli Army. Perhaps they were treasured playthings, held close and tight at night when the fighting started, then left behind in the panic and terror when father, mother, or elder brother came to tell you to get up, get dressed, and run for your life. Mr Abu Matr, despite his weariness, was determined not to let his circumstances get the better of him. 'We have to manage because this is our land', he declared. 'We have to live in our land, we cannot leave this land. This is our home. Even after what happened, what will happen – this is our home.'

I asked him if the Israelis had singled out his house because people had been shooting from it. He said not, then continued in words which echoed those of Mr Sternberg when he spoke of the dangers faced by the settlers in Gush Katif. The two men had never met, and almost certainly never would, yet their lives were defined by the presence of the other, and by the mistrust, fear, and hatred which that presence generated.

'Our neighbour is not interested if they are shooting on mother, on children, and baby,' Mr Sternberg had said of the Palestinian refugees who lived on the other side of the concrete wall. 'They do it to kill children and mother and babies, and whatever they can.'

Now, among the ruins of his home, Mr Abu Matr's fatigue seemed to fall away. He became animated as he cursed his enemy: 'This is the peace of the Israeli Army. They destroy the houses. They kill the people. They kill the children. Kill the woman. Kill the babies.' The reason, he felt, was clear: the Israelis wanted the land, and they wanted to drive those who lived there away.

'This is the policy of the army to make the people leave the land and leave the houses, especially by the border near Egypt.'

It was hard to imagine Mr Sternberg and Mr Abu Matr ever agreeing on anything. Although they were both relatively young, it was hard to imagine that in their lifetimes the day would ever come when they could sit down and talk to each other. If it ever did, they might well recognize each other's phrases in their descriptions of their own lives, and of each other. This would not be a starting point for finding common ground, so much as a confirmation that they agreed that there seemed little prospect of a solution to the conflict until one side or the other was vanquished.

On a wet winter day, Yibna was more joyless than ever. It is impossible to imagine how much more gloomy the Gaza Strip would seem were it not for almost year-round sunshine. In February, when the rain fell and even the scorching desert sun of southern Gaza could not find the strength to shine, the only colour came from graffiti on the drab walls. The slogans praised the militant groups and prophesied victory over Israel. Only the lines of washing hanging in the damp air, and the ubiquitous rubbish, showed that some people still lived there. There was a severed hoof – presumably left over from the recent *Eid al-Adha*, or 'Feast of the sacrifice' – lying next to a pool of water. Grimy children, barefoot even in this coldest month of winter, played in the puddles. Beyond the street, south, towards the Israelis' iron wall, life had been driven into open air among the ruins. In the late morning, under the rain-laden grey sky, a thin soup bubbled above the crackling of a wood fire, fuel dragged from the wreckage of homes. It spat when rain drops fell into the flames. The matriarch of the three generations squatting, sitting, and standing around, trying to get warm, stretched a jumper across the stump of a nearby palm tree, hosed it down with cold water, then beat it clean. Somewhere nearby, a bird was a thin and joyless song. The remains of the Abu Hashem family house were still strewn around, but a small vegetable patch, along with this makeshift cooking and washing area, were cleared of rubble. 'They say there was some tunnels here. They didn't found any tunnels,' Naji Abu Hashem said as he stirred the soup. 'This, look, it was my house!' he continued, looking at the empty land around. Mr Abu Hashem was in his forties, with a round face and a moustache. He wore an old black anorak, which looked too thin to keep out the damp and cold. He was hoping for some help from the UN. He had managed to rent a room, but it was so cramped that even on a day like this, it was easier to spend as much time as possible outside. The determination to stay was real. Some of the refugees, although they had been offered brand new UN houses near Khan Younis, had been angry that their homes had not been rebuilt where they stood, in the shadow of the concrete wall which surrounded Gush Katif. The UN argued that it was too unsafe to build there and, in any case, the new houses might just be knocked down as the original ones had. The refugees countered that by leaving the land empty, it was simply being given up forever. They were probably right. Mr Abu Hashem, left with little more than a rented room and the blackened pot which bubbled at his feet, drew strength from Islam. I asked him why he didn't just try to leave. 'This is my religion tell me to stay here. This is my Palestinian land. This is our land.' In any case, he said, all of the people here were refugees: some from 1948, some from 1967, then asked 'Where we go a third time?'

I asked him if he would ever go back to Yibna, not the Yibna which stood in ruins around him, but the Yibna which was his family's home before 1948.

'This is in the future,' he laughed, 'The future, future. The future of the future.'

'Do you think it will be possible one day?'

'Yes. We are sure, because this is our religion. If I think another thing, this means I am not Muslim.'

I wondered what had happened to Emad Abu Matr, five months after we had talked as he worked in the scorching heat to salvage his family's belongings. The house looked much as it had that October afternoon – the ruins may have been searched thoroughly for anything which could be saved, but the rubble had not been cleared away. It had changed colour: no longer bleached by the sun of the late summer, it was now grey with streaks of winter rain. Mr Abu Matr was not there any more. He was in the office from which he tried to run a building business. Potentially, there was plenty of work, but in practice moving materials from one place to another, and finding someone who could pay for them once they got there, was a nightmare. Mr Abu Matr's premises were in Rafah town itself, a little way north of the war zone that was the refugee camp, where his house still lay in ruins. Mr Abu Matr said that he was sharing a flat nearby with his brother. His mother was living close to the office too. The extended family which had lived in the house in Yibna had been broken up. The road outside was paved, and the rain bounced off the surface. Cars and taxis splashed by; a horse trotted past pulling a cart.

Mr Abu Matr seemed pretty relaxed. After the usual polite greetings, we talked of politics, and of the future. Like Mrs Silberschein, the settler in Netzarim, he said that the Israelis and the Palestinians could live together. Like Mrs Silberschein, he believed that this could only happen if his people had sovereignty.

'We don't want to get the Israeli people out of Israel or out of Palestine. We can live with each other, but under the Palestinian State, not under the Israeli State.'

'Well that's the thing, because the Israelis say that theirs is a Jewish state, and that's why they want to keep the Jewish majority, surely that means it will be impossible for you to go back,' I said.

'No, no, the Jewish is not the majority. If you count the Palestinian population, there is about 2 millions in Jordan, there is half million in America, half million in Kuwait. We are the majority, and we are the owners of the land. You cannot measure that they are the majority they have to take the land. No, no, no, no. We are the owners of the land. We are the majority by our rights in the land.'

Mr Abu Matr was becoming more agitated. Perhaps he was feeling again the hot sun on his head, and his finger nails breaking as they clawed at rubble. 'For the time being they are the stronger,' he conceded. 'They can make what they want. But the future is coming.'

Like Mr Sternberg and Mrs Silberschein, like Mr Abu Hashem, Mr Abu Matr drew finally on his faith to support his argument. 'In Qu'ran it says the Israeli state will finish. We have to believe that the Israeli state will finish one day and we will go back to our homeland. The time is not known. But we believe this.'

Mr Abu Matr, having started out by saying that the Israelis were free to stay provided that the Palestinians had sovereignty, now seemed to harden his attitude. His view of Judaism, like the settlers' view of Islam, was of a faith which drove its adherents to want to seize land. As Eran Sternberg said of the people of Khan Younis, 'they don't hide their desire for Jerusalem'. Mr Abu Matr believed that the Jews simply wanted to control the entire Middle East: 'It is also something relating to their religion: 'Arab people must go out of Palestine.' Their land is from the Euphrates to the Nile. They build their thinking starting from this point.'

Starting from the point where Egypt, the Gaza Strip, and Israel all met, the Israeli Army were now building the iron wall. One afternoon I was invited there to talk to one of the commanders, and to accompany him on a patrol along the Philadelphi route, the stretch of sand and stone which Israel controlled between

Gaza and the Egyptian border. From my flat in Gaza City, it should have taken me about 45 minutes to get there or – if I had been with Ibrahim's father in the good old days of open roads – even less. Of course I could not go that way. In theory, I could have driven down to the edge of Yibna and walked across the open waste ground, the area which the then head of the UNRWA, Peter Hansen, once described as a 'free fire zone'. In practice, that would have meant certain danger and possible death. So I drove from my flat in Gaza to Erez, and then round on the roads outside the Gaza Strip, getting lost as I got close to the Egyptian border. This was where my Russian came in handy: the more God forsaken or perilous the IDF position, the more likelihood there was that the soldiers might be Russian. The Druze and the Bedouin also seemed disproportionately represented in dangerous places. Eventually, I found the car park where I was supposed to meet Major Librati, who had arranged the trip. I followed in my car as he drove along the desert road towards the Israeli Army post at the edge of Rafah. The base was pretty small, and well concealed, and it seemed well fortified. I met the officer who was to brief me: a career soldier, probably in his late 40s or early 50s, heavily built, but mobile enough to climb into an armoured personnel carrier. One of the other officers, a captain, I think, was briefly introduced to me as being British. He seemed a little shy, but said hello in an unmistakeably English accent. There was a quick safety briefing, and we got into the apc. It was the same kind as the one I would spend the night in during the raid on the Jabalya refugee camp. This time, though, I was able to stand up, and look out through the glass in the turret on top to see where we were going. The crew were all Russian speakers – the same age as the lads I had met when I was covering the Chechen war. These troops, though, were better fed, better shod, and cleaner. We set out along the road. It was not a safe place to be. The sand was an ideal surface under which to bury a bomb. About a year after I took this trip, Palestinian fighters blew up an Israeli apc travelling along this route – apparently with an anti-tank rocket. An officer and four soldiers were killed. It did not feel too unsafe that afternoon, but the crew of the apc were taking no chances. The heavy machine gun in the turret was loaded and made ready to fire.

It was a warm afternoon, hot, if you were wearing a flak jacket and helmet. There were a few white clouds in the sky, their presence betraying the fact that it was winter, and not summer when the sky would be unbroken blue. The sand stretched out away to our right as we left the army base. The shabby houses at the edge of the refugee camp were the first structures rising above the wasteland. The officer pointed to the buildings that still stood. 'We only destroy buildings which have been used for terrorist activity,' he said. It was February 2003, and the war was about to begin in Iraq. There was huge opposition to it in Gaza, but there was also an acceptance that it would certainly go ahead. The Palestinians were more worried that the Israelis would completely re-occupy the Gaza Strip when the United States and its allies attacked Iraq. The officer indicated the opposite. The Israeli Army seemed to see and treat the Gaza Strip as a whole as they did a Palestinian city on the West Bank. They would sit in strong positions at the edge, move into certain areas when they felt it necessary, and stay as long as they felt it was necessary. After a short journey in the apc, we arrived behind the metal fence, and got out. The Russian soldiers had brought some food with them and had a good natured argument over who was due what as his share. Near where we stopped, there was a deep hole in the ground. It was the remains of one of the tunnels which had been uncovered and destroyed. The tunnel entrance was filled in, but you could still make out its shape because of the wooden frame which had once supported it. The hole which remained had become a soldiers' toilet, and a rubbish bin for their food cartons. 'I am ashamed as an officer to show you this,' said the officer, apparently unpleasantly surprised by what we saw before us. The shine had been taken off this Israeli victory in part of the 'war on terror' by the fact that the triumphant soldiers had shat in their trophy. Some of the soldiers continued to squabble over their rations. The officer invited me up to the look out post which stood on top of the iron wall. Civilian contractors were putting the finishing touches to the interior. We climbed up a metal staircase. The heavily built officer seemed to struggle a little as we ascended. From the top, we had a clear view of the last few rows of the Rafah refugee camp and beyond. It was winter so the light was not as flat and harsh as it was between May and September. Beyond the open ground, the buildings of the refugee camp, and the town beyond, stretched out northwards. From up here you could appreciate detail as you never could on the ground: the precarious upper floors of the refugees' houses, evidence of amateur construction work, washing lines, bullet holes. The winter sunshine was gentle, illuminating detail that summer's blinding glare blotted out. There must be few places in the world from where you can see so many shades of brown, beige, and grey. You could also see a lot of what was going on, outside at least, presumably why the lookout position had been placed where it had. The officer seemed convinced that a military situation was the only one which could bring an end to the conflict: he talked in terms of hitting back harder at those who tried to hit at Israel. He said he had been saddened by the way the last few years had gone. 'When Oslo came, I thought, that's it, I'm going to have to retire!' That wasn't the way things turned out. 'Now I am going to have to stay here for longer, or teach my children to swim.' The Mediterranean lay blue and calm away to the west; the sea which both Israel and its deadliest foes had to accept was the border here. Other frontiers could be argued and fought over forever. This was the one which had been drawn by nature. The Zionists' enemies dreamed of throwing them into it, they dreaded one day having to 'learn to swim'. We climbed back down. The officer stopped to talk to the Russian crew, who had by now stopped rowing over the rations. The previous month, when I had seen the bullets from these positions hitting the ground just a few metres from the ISM protesters, the soldiers here had been Arabic speakers, probably

Druze. I knew this because as the ISM shouted 'You are committing war crimes!' through their loud hailers, Ibrahim had translated for me the soldier's reply 'Fuck your God!' Perhaps not capable of trading insults in English with a group of western politics students, they had decided to stick with a more traditional Middle Eastern version. I chatted to Major Librati. He caught me off guard by asking me if I had met any of the 'resistance fighters' in Rafah. The choice of language was such an important part of getting one's view of the conflict across, that he confused me by using the Palestinian description of the militant groups rather than the phrase 'terrorist' which the Israelis always preferred. We climbed back into the apc and set off on our return journey to the base. It was February. Before the end of May, soldiers in the positions I had just visited would kill three unarmed foreigners: Rachel Corrie, Tom Hurndall, and James Miller.

Getting the chance to see Rafah from above was rare. I never felt safe climbing onto the top of the refugee houses which stood across the wasteland from the iron wall. There was too much danger of being shot. During 'Operation Root Canal', we did find one vantage point, further back from the front line. The day I first met Mr Abu Matr was the day when the Israeli Army held us for three hours at their checkpoint. The material I had gathered that day was out of date for broadcast. After spending the night in Khan Younis, and being woken before dawn by the call to prayer and the attack helicopters, I decided to go back to Rafah. The main road was closed. Even if in theory the Israeli Army would allow journalists to pass, in practice the troops had rarely received orders to that effect, and they wouldn't allow Palestinians through under any circumstances. The only way back in was along a sandy track which wound through the scrubland, bypassing the tanks, and eventually joining the road into Rafah. There was a perfectly good road which went there, of course. For the moment, its edges were covered in places by fallen trees and piles of sand, its surface scarred by tank tracks, but there was a road. It was closed. People could still make their journeys to work, to university, even, in the case of particularly determined truck drivers, to transport goods. That was not the way things always were in Gaza. Every so often, there would be no roads open except the sandy back tracks, and as much of life as could make the move simply went that way. We made it into Rafah and tried to find a place to set up our equipment, somewhere we could broadcast from, and somewhere safe enough that we would be unlikely to have to leave in a hurry. We knew that one of the Arab channels had set up a satellite dish on a house on the main street, near the mosque, the day before. Ibrahim approached the owner, who rudely told Ibrahim to get lost. Apparently there had been some misunderstanding or dispute over payment. The owner said he would shoot us if we tried to get on the roof of the house. The landlord next door was more helpful. Once we were on the roof, we saw the first man looking at us. He had a huge black beard like a cartoon pirate. He was peering across from behind a line of washing drying in the warm wind. He didn't have a gun, thankfully.

A kilometre or two away, 'Operation Root Canal' continued. Tanks and armoured personnel carriers threw up clouds of dust as they raced along the Philadelphi route where the officer had taken me that afternoon some months earlier. I pictured him, sweating and swearing in the heat, yelling orders to his Russian-speaking troops, who, when they were allowed a break, would shit in the hole. There were occasional explosions, and frequent gunfire: the rifle bursts of the Palestinians often answered by the heavier machine guns of the Israelis. In the street below us, life went on pretty much as normally as possible. If the people of Rafah stopped what they were doing because there was fighting at the edge of the refugee camp, then they would almost never do anything at all. At around 5pm, as night began to fall, the traffic built up, accompanied by the inevitable honking of rush hour horns. The sound which reached us competed with the noise of war. To an outsider, even one who had lived in Gaza for more than a year, it still seemed incongruous. For the people of Rafah, that was just what rush hour often sounded like. A brilliant orange ball of sun sank rapidly into the sea to the west. It was dark, and no longer a good time to stand on a roof in Rafah. Soon it was completely dark: there was a power cut. Ian Druce, the cameraman, and I wandered along in the gloom trying to find a place to buy a torch. We soon picked up a following of young boys keen to show us the bullet casings they had collected. There was no hotel in Rafah so we rented a flat for the night. It was not too difficult. Even though living space was in desperately short supply, there were empty apartments, if you were willing to pay what seemed to us reasonable, what was by local standards extortionately expensive. The power was off at the apartment block, so we went to have dinner. The meal, for 8 of us – we joined a group of colleagues, some Palestinian, some westerners based in Jerusalem – was 80 shekels (then about £11.50). Our colleagues from Jerusalem thought it must be 80 shekels each. We went back to the flat. The power was on, but we were glad of our cheap Chinese torches, for we could have no idea how long it would stay that way. We had been this house before, the day after Tom Hurndall was shot. It was the house where the ISM had lived when they were in Rafah. By now, they had left. The Israelis had made it almost impossible for anyone without special, written, permission to enter Gaza, and the ISM were never going to get any such documents. Two of the younger, male, members of the Qeshta family, who owned the block, now sat on plastic chairs in the flat which had been the ISM's, smoking a water pipe. The arrival of young foreigners had been something of a draw for the young men of Rafah. They were not allowed to talk to Palestinian girls their own age, and they had almost no contact with the outside world. A first encounter with the west could not have been more fascinating. Now that contact was gone, and the two lads sat smoking the *shisha* as they probably once had with the students from Scotland and Seattle who had come to demonstrate on their behalf. Falling asleep in this almost empty house, decorated on the outside with 'martyr' posters of Rachel Corrie, it was hard not to reflect that his was where she and Tom Hurndall had both spent their last nights alive.

In the morning, the first sound was assembly at the school across the road. The Palestinian national anthem blared out, distorted by the poor sound system. There must have been a microphone left open. The sound of heavy machine gun fire coming from the direction of the Philadelphi route was picked up and amplified too. In Rafah all daily activities, whether it were the start of school, or the journey home from work, had shooting as their background soundtrack.

The wasteland between the iron wall and the edge of the refugee camp grew wider and wider. The Qeshta family, one branch of which owned the house where the ISM had stayed, were a big clan in Rafah – remarkable for the fact that they had lived in Rafah for generations, and were not, like most of the population, refugees. More than fifty years after the first Palestinians fled here, the distinction was reinforced, not forgotten. Town and camp were not always happy neighbours. The fact that relations with the larger neighbours, the Israelis, were murderous tended to disguise this. The refugees saw themselves only as temporary residents, even after more than half a century. People often only married within their clan – and it was estimated then that some 25 per cent of Gazans married their first cousins. If they married outside their clan, they would often marry within their 'village', that is, to someone whose family came from the same village in 1948, and not someone whose family was from the town they had arrived in.

While some of the Qeshta clan lived in the town centre, others lived at the edge of the town, in the shadow of the iron wall. This part of town was east of Yibna, closer to the border crossing with Egypt, closer to the Israeli Army base in the corner where Israel, Egypt, and the Gaza Strip all came together. The street, especially in February, was mostly mud. Puddles were playgrounds: puddles with odd flip flops floating in them, and empty tins rusting at the sides. One of them had contained 'corned mutton – donated by Islamic relief'. The Israeli Army's wall rose up about a hundred metres away. 27-year-old Hamid Qeshta had just returned to Rafah to marry, after ten years studying in Canada. He spoke English with a strong North American accent, and used terms he had picked up there. 'I can see no future, can never see no peace. Nine people from my ghetto already got shot,' he said to me. We had met by chance one afternoon when I was collecting material for a story about the refugees. Did he know, when he used the word 'ghetto', its origin? The accent of his drawl suggested he sought identification with run-down African-American neighbourhoods of big cities in the United States, yet he had borrowed a word invented for the area of 16th century Venice to which the co-religionists of his enemies had once been confined. Hamid went on to tell me that his father, and his father before him, had been born there. Never, not in 1948, nor 1967, had the family moved. Now he gestured towards the wall, and said he feared the Israelis moving further north. Some of his family's property had already been destroyed.

'The first house gone. And the second one, now half of it, it's gone. And there is no furniture inside,' he said. 'Bullets bullets bullets, you know holes from the bullets.' Hamid had been away for a long time, missing more than three and a half years of the second *intifada*. He had probably been excited about coming home, but he was clearly shocked by what he had found in his 'ghetto'. 'I don't think we're gonna live here even more than one year. Everybody's warning us to move, but nowhere to go.'

I asked him about the 'Road Map'. What did he make of its aim of giving the Palestinians a state by 2005? Did he think the Palestinians would have a homeland by then?

Hamid sighed. 'At this area I don't think so. Because if it get destroyed how we gonna come back and build it? To come back here, I don't think so. Because those people they got moved I don't think they're ever gonna come back. Maybe the action gonna start again like ten years, fifteen years after. They gonna put themselves at risk again? I don't think.'

Hamid's family had survived the conflicts of the last century more or less intact. They had held onto their homes and their land when thousands had lost theirs. Now he feared that his generation would be made homeless. Perhaps the bleakest part of his outlook was in his thoughts, peppered with his own version of American street idiom. Even if there were to be peace, maybe the action was 'gonna start again'.

A short distance from where we were standing, the Gaza Strip came to an end. Beyond lay Egypt. The border crossing was the only way in and out of Gaza for most Palestinians: only VIP's, urgent medical cases, and the day labourers were allowed to leave through Erez. That is not to say that getting in and out through Rafah was easy. It was frequently closed completely, even more frequently to males aged between 16 and 35, the group seen by the IDF as the most likely to carry out attacks on Israelis. Palestinian friends, those who had the financial means to travel abroad on the sort of family holiday many Europeans take for granted, would often set off in the middle of the night, only to return in the afternoon having been unable to cross. If they got past the Israelis, their problems might begin with the Egyptians. The stories of the way the Egyptians treated the Palestinians suggested that, for them then at least, Arab brotherhood was just a myth. One of the reasons that young Palestinians like Hamid Qeshta, who got the chance to study overseas, stayed away so long was because they feared a trip home might result in their being trapped and missing a semester. Many Palestinians grew up never leaving the territory, or not doing so for ten years or more. Trapped between Erez, Rafah, the security fence, and the sea, they bounced around like fish in a barrel, meeting obstacles whichever way they turned.

A few weeks after my conversation with Hamid, I left Gaza for the last time. Days before I did, a failed attack on Israeli troops at the Erez crossing point resulted in the destruction of the Palestinian police there – and in the closure of the crossing to vehicles. I had to leave through the tunnel which had been the day labourers' way to casual work. Having said goodbye to my Palestinian colleagues at the entrance to the tunnel, I made the crossing on foot. The tunnel was empty. The workers' permits had all been suspended in the aftermath of the attack, too. I had to leave most of my possessions behind and hope that, one day, they would follow me. What luggage I did have with me would have to squeeze through a two-metre high turnstile topped with barbed wire. As I entered the final stretch of the tunnel, I caught sight of two figures, dark against the sunlight. A woman with a child was pleading through the steel bars with a soldier who stared back at them: his face at once severe, and unsure.

Index

Lightning Source UK Ltd.
Milton Keynes UK
UKHW02f0950230818
327686UK00004B/141/P